The Quran With
Tafsir Ibn Kathir
Part 19 of 30:
Al Furqan 021 To
An Naml 055

The Quran With Tafsir Ibn Kathir
Part 19 of 30:
Al Furqan 021 To An Naml 055

With
Arabic Script, Transliteration of Arabic, Meaning in English
and Ibn Kathir's Abridged Tafsir (Explanation)

Muhammad Saed Abdul-Rahman

BSc, DipHE

© Muhammad Saed Abdul-Rahman, 2012
ISBN 978-1-86179-882-4

All Rights reserved

British Library Cataloguing in Publication Data. A Catalogue record for this book is available from the British Library

Designed, Typeset and produced by:
MSA Publication Limited, 4 Bello Close, Herne Hill,
London SE24 9BW
United Kingdom

Cover design: Houriyah Abdul-Rahman

TABLE OF CONTENTS

TABLE OF CONTENTS V

PRELUDE XI

    OPENING SERMAN XI

    OUR MISSION XII

    BIOGRAPHY OF HAFIZ IBN KATHIR (701 H - 774 H) XII

        Ibn Kathir's Teachers xii

        Ibn Kathir's Students xiii

        Ibn Kathir's Books xiii

        Ibn Kathir's Death xiv

PREFACE XV

    ABOUT THIS BOOK XV

    PERFORMING PROSTRATION WHILE READING THE QUR'AN XV

PART 19 FULL ARABIC TEXT 1

CHAPTER (SURAH) 25: AL-FURQAN (THE CRITERION, THE STANDARD), VERSES 021 – 077 ... 13

    Surah: 25 Ayah: 21, Ayah: 22, Ayah: 23 & Ayah: 24 13

        Tafsir Ibn Kathir 14

            The Stubbornness of the Disbelievers 14

            The Abode of the People of Paradise 16

    Surah: 25 Ayah: 25, Ayah: 26, Ayah: 27, Ayah: 28 & Ayah: 29 17

        Tafsir Ibn Kathir 18

            The Terrors of the Day of Resurrection, and how the Wrongdoers will wish that They had taken a Path with the Messenger 18

    Surah: 25 Ayah: 30 & Ayah: 31 19

        Tafsir Ibn Kathir 20

            The Messenger will complain against His Opponents 20

    Surah: 25 Ayah: 32, Ayah: 33 & Ayah: 34 20

        Tafsir Ibn Kathir 21

            The Reason why the Qur'an was revealed in Stages, the Refutation of the Disbelievers, and their Evil End 21

    Surah: 25 Ayah: 35, Ayah: 36, Ayah: 37, Ayah: 38, Ayah: 39 & Ayah: 40 22

        Tafsir Ibn Kathir 23

            Frightening the Idolators of Quraysh 23

    Surah: 25 Ayah: 41, Ayah: 42, Ayah: 43 & Ayah: 44 25

        Tafsir Ibn Kathir 26

            How the Disbelievers mocked the Messenger 26

            They took Their Desires as their gods and were more astray than Cattle 26

    Surah: 25 Ayah: 45, Ayah: 46 & Ayah: 47 26

        Tafsir Ibn Kathir 27

            Evidence of the existence of the Creator and the extent of His Power 27

Surah: 25 Ayah: 48, Ayah: 48 & Ayah: 50 28
   Tafsir Ibn Kathir 29
      This is also part of His complete power and supreme authority: 29
Surah: 25 Ayah: 51, Ayah: 52, Ayah: 53 & Ayah: 54 30
   Tafsir Ibn Kathir 31
      The universality of the Prophet's Message, how He was supported in His Mission and Allah's Blessings to Mankind 31
Surah: 25 Ayah: 55, Ayah: 56, Ayah: 57, Ayah: 58, Ayah: 59 & Ayah: 60 33
   Tafsir Ibn Kathir 34
      The Ignorance of the Idolators 34
      The Messenger brings Glad Tidings and Warnings 35
      The Command to the Messenger to put his Trust in Allah, and some of His Qualities 35
      Condemnation of the Idolators 36
Surah: 25 Ayah: 61 & Ayah: 62 37
   Tafsir Ibn Kathir 37
      Mentioning the Might and Power of Allah 37
Surah: 25 Ayah: 63, Ayah: 64, Ayah: 65, Ayah: 66 & Ayah: 67 38
   Tafsir Ibn Kathir 39
      Attributes of the Servants of the Most Gracious 39
Surah: 25 Ayah: 68, Ayah: 69, Ayah: 70 & Ayah: 71 40
   Tafsir Ibn Kathir 41
      The Attributes of the Servants of the Most Gracious include avoiding Shirk, Murder and Zina 41
Surah: 25 Ayah: 72, Ayah: 73 & Ayah: 74 44
   Tafsir Ibn Kathir 45
      More Attributes of the Servants of the Most Gracious 45
Surah: 25 Ayah: 75, Ayah: 76 & Ayah: 77 47
   Tafsir Ibn Kathir 47
      The Reward of the Servants of the Most Gracious, and a Warning to the People of Makkah 47

CHAPTER (SURAH) 26: ASH-SHU'ARAA (THE POETS), VERSES 001 – 227 48

Surah: 26 Ayah: 1, Ayah: 2, Ayah: 3, Ayah: 4, Ayah: 5, Ayah: 6, Ayah: 7, Ayah: 8 & Ayah: 9 48
   Tafsir Ibn Kathir 50
      The Qur'an and the Disbelievers turning away; 50
Surah: 26 Ayah: 10, Ayah: 11, Ayah: 12, Ayah: 13, Ayah: 14, Ayah: 15, Ayah: 16, Ayah: 17, Ayah: 18, Ayah: 19, Ayah: 20, Ayah: 21 & Ayah: 22 51
   Tafsir Ibn Kathir 53
      Between Musa and Fir`awn 53
Surah: 26 Ayah: 23, Ayah: 24, Ayah: 25, Ayah: 26, Ayah: 27 & Ayah: 28 54
   Tafsir Ibn Kathir 55
      Allah tells us about the disbelief, rebellion, oppression and denial of Fir`awn, as He says: 55

Surah: 26 Ayah: 29, Ayah: 30, Ayah: 31, Ayah: 32, Ayah: 33, Ayah: 34, Ayah: 35, Ayah: 36 & Ayah: 37 57
    Tafsir Ibn Kathir 58
    After the Rational Proof, Fir`awn resorts to Force 58
Surah: 26 Ayah: 38, Ayah: 39, Ayah: 40, Ayah: 41, Ayah: 42, Ayah: 43, Ayah: 44, Ayah: 45, Ayah: 46, Ayah: 47 & Ayah: 48 59
    Tafsir Ibn Kathir 60
    Between Musa, peace be upon him, and the Sorcerers Allah describes the actual encounter between Musa, peace be upon him, and the Egyptians in Surat Al-A`raf, Surah Ta Ha, and in this Surah. 60
Surah: 26 Ayah: 49, Ayah: 50 & Ayah: 51 61
    Tafsir Ibn Kathir 62
    Between Fir`awn and the Sorcerers 62
Surah: 26 Ayah: 52, Ayah: 53, Ayah: 54, Ayah: 55, Ayah: 56, Ayah: 57, Ayah: 58 & Ayah: 59 63
    Tafsir Ibn Kathir 64
    The Exodus of the Children of Israel from Egypt 64
Surah: 26 Ayah: 60, Ayah: 61, Ayah: 62, Ayah: 63, Ayah: 64, Ayah: 65, Ayah: 66, Ayah: 67 & Ayah: 68 65
    Tafsir Ibn Kathir 66
    Fir`awn's Pursuit and Expulsion of the Children of Israel, and how He and His People were drowned 66
Surah: 26 Ayah: 69, Ayah: 70, Ayah: 71, Ayah: 72, Ayah: 73, Ayah: 74, Ayah: 75, Ayah: 76 & Ayah: 77 67
    Tafsir Ibn Kathir 68
    How the Close Friend of Allah, Ibrahim spoke out against Shirk 68
Surah: 26 Ayah: 78, Ayah: 79, Ayah: 80, Ayah: 81 & Ayah: 82 69
    Tafsir Ibn Kathir 70
    Ibrahim mentions Allah's Kindness towards Him 70
Surah: 26 Ayah: 83, Ayah: 84, Ayah: 85, Ayah: 86, Ayah: 87, Ayah: 88 & Ayah: 89 70
    Tafsir Ibn Kathir 71
    The Prayer of Ibrahim for Himself and for His Father 71
Surah: 26 Ayah: 90, Ayah: 91, Ayah: 92, Ayah: 93, Ayah: 94, Ayah: 95, Ayah: 96, Ayah: 97, Ayah: 98, Ayah: 99, Ayah: 100, Ayah: 101, Ayah: 102, Ayah: 103 & Ayah: 104 73
    Tafsir Ibn Kathir 75
    Those Who have Taqwa and the Astray on the Day of Resurrection, and the Arguments and Sorrow of the Erring 75
Surah: 26 Ayah: 105, Ayah: 106, Ayah: 107, Ayah: 108, Ayah: 109 & Ayah: 110 76
    Tafsir Ibn Kathir 77
    Nuh's preaching to His People, and Their Response 77
Surah: 26 Ayah: 111, Ayah: 112, Ayah: 113, Ayah: 114 & Ayah: 115 78
    Tafsir Ibn Kathir 78
    The Demand of the People of Nuh and His Response 78

Surah: 26 Ayah: 116, Ayah: 117, Ayah: 118, Ayah: 119, Ayah: 120, Ayah: 121 & Ayah: 122 79
    Tafsir Ibn Kathir 80
    His People's Threat, Nuh's Prayer against Them, and Their Destruction 80
Surah: 26 Ayah: 123, Ayah: 124, Ayah: 125, Ayah: 126, Ayah: 127, Ayah: 128, Ayah: 129, Ayah: 130, Ayah: 131, Ayah: 132, Ayah: 133, Ayah: 134 & Ayah: 135 80
    Tafsir Ibn Kathir 82
    Hud's preaching to His People `Ad 82
Surah: 26 Ayah: 136, Ayah: 137, Ayah: 138, Ayah: 139 & Ayah: 140 83
    Tafsir Ibn Kathir 83
    The Response of the People of Hud, and Their Punishment 83
Surah: 26 Ayah: 141, Ayah: 142, Ayah: 143, Ayah: 144 & Ayah: 145 85
    Tafsir Ibn Kathir 86
    Salih and the People of Thamud 86
Surah: 26 Ayah: 146, Ayah: 147, Ayah: 148, Ayah: 149, Ayah: 150, Ayah: 151 & Ayah: 152 86
    Tafsir Ibn Kathir 87
    A Reminder to Them of their Circumstances and the Blessings 87
Surah: 26 Ayah: 153, Ayah: 154, Ayah: 155, Ayah: 156, Ayah: 157, Ayah: 158 & Ayah: 159 88
    Tafsir Ibn Kathir 88
    The Response of Thamud, Their Demand for a Sign, and Their Punishment 88
Surah: 26 Ayah: 160, Ayah: 161, Ayah: 162, Ayah: 163 & Ayah: 164 89
    Tafsir Ibn Kathir 90
    Lut and His Call 90
Surah: 26 Ayah: 165, Ayah: 166, Ayah: 167, Ayah: 168, Ayah: 169, Ayah: 170, Ayah: 171, Ayah: 172, Ayah: 173, Ayah: 174 & Ayah: 175 90
    Tafsir Ibn Kathir 92
    Lut's Denunciation of His People's Deeds, Their Response and Their Punishment 92
Surah: 26 Ayah: 176, Ayah: 177, Ayah: 178, Ayah: 179 & Ayah: 180 92
    Tafsir Ibn Kathir 93
    Shu`ayb and His Preaching to the Dwellers of Al-Aykah 93
Surah: 26 Ayah: 181, Ayah: 182, Ayah: 183 & Ayah: 184 94
    Tafsir Ibn Kathir 94
    The Command to give Full Measure 94
Surah: 26 Ayah: 185, Ayah: 186, Ayah: 187, Ayah: 188, Ayah: 189, Ayah: 190 & Ayah: 191 95
    Tafsir Ibn Kathir 96
    The Response of Shu`ayb's People, Their Disbelief in Him and the coming of the Punishment upon Them 96
Surah: 26 Ayah: 192, Ayah: 193, Ayah: 194 & Ayah: 195 97
    Tafsir Ibn Kathir 98
    The Qur'an was revealed by Allah 98
Surah: 26 Ayah: 196, Ayah: 197, Ayah: 198 & Ayah: 199 98

Table of Contents

Tafsir Ibn Kathir 99
 The Qur'an was mentioned in the Previous Scriptures 99
 The Intense Disbelief of Quraysh 100
Surah: 26 Ayah: 200, Ayah: 201, Ayah: 202, Ayah: 203, Ayah: 204, Ayah: 205, Ayah: 206, Ayah: 207, Ayah: 208 & Ayah: 209 100
 Tafsir Ibn Kathir 101
  The Deniers will never believe until They see the Torment 101
Surah: 26 Ayah: 210, Ayah: 211 & Ayah: 212 103
 Tafsir Ibn Kathir 103
  The Qur'an was brought down by Jibril, not Shaytan 103
Surah: 26 Ayah: 213, Ayah: 214, Ayah: 215, Ayah: 216, Ayah: 217, Ayah: 218, Ayah: 219 & Ayah: 220 104
 Tafsir Ibn Kathir 105
  The Command to warn His Tribe of near Kindred 105
Surah: 26 Ayah: 221, Ayah: 222, Ayah: 223, Ayah: 224, Ayah: 225, Ayah: 226 & Ayah: 227 108
 Tafsir Ibn Kathir 109
  Refutation of the Fabrications of the Idolators 109
  Refutation of the Claim that the Prophet was a Poet 111
  The Exception of the Poets of Islam 112

CHAPTER (SURAH) 27: AN-NAML (THE ANT, THE ANTS), VERSES 001–055 113

Surah: 27 Ayah: 1, Ayah: 2, Ayah: 3, Ayah: 4, Ayah: 5 & Ayah: 6 114
 Tafsir Ibn Kathir 115
  The Qur'an is Guidance and Glad Tidings for the Believers, a Warning to the Disbelievers, and it is from Allah 115
Surah: 27 Ayah: 7, Ayah: 8, Ayah: 9, Ayah: 10, Ayah: 11, Ayah: 12, Ayah: 13 & Ayah: 14 116
 Tafsir Ibn Kathir 117
  The Story of Musa and the End of Fir`awn 117
Surah: 27 Ayah: 15, Ayah: 16, Ayah: 17, Ayah: 18 & Ayah: 19 119
 Tafsir Ibn Kathir 121
  Dawud and Sulayman (peace be upon them), the organization of Sulayman's Troops and His passage through the Valley of the Ants 121
Surah: 27 Ayah: 20 & Ayah: 21 122
 Tafsir Ibn Kathir 122
  The Absence of the Hoopoe 122
Surah: 27 Ayah: 22, Ayah: 23, Ayah: 24, Ayah: 25 & Ayah: 26 123
 Tafsir Ibn Kathir 124
  How the Hoopoe came before Sulayman and told Him about Saba' 124
Surah: 27 Ayah: 27, Ayah: 28, Ayah: 29, Ayah: 30 & Ayah: 31 126
 Tafsir Ibn Kathir 126
  Sulayman's Letter to Bilqis 126
Surah: 27 Ayah: 32, Ayah: 33, Ayah: 34 & Ayah: 35 127

Tafsir Ibn Kathir 128
    Bilqis consults with Her Chiefs 128
Surah: 27 Ayah: 36 & Ayah: 37 .... *129*
    Tafsir Ibn Kathir 129
    The Gift and the Response of Sulayman 129
Surah: 27 Ayah: 38, Ayah: 39 & Ayah: 40 .... *130*
    Tafsir Ibn Kathir 131
    How the Throne of Bilqis was brought in an Instant 131
Surah: 27 Ayah: 41, Ayah: 42, Ayah: 43 & Ayah: 44 .... *133*
    Tafsir Ibn Kathir 134
    The Test of Bilqis 134
    Verily, it is a Sarh Mumarrad of Qawarir Sarh means a palace or any lofty construction. 135
Surah: 27 Ayah: 45, Ayah: 46 & Ayah: 47 .... *135*
    Tafsir Ibn Kathir 136
    Salih and Thamud 136
Surah: 27 Ayah: 48, Ayah: 49, Ayah: 50, Ayah: 51, Ayah: 52 & Ayah: 53 ..... *137*
    Tafsir Ibn Kathir 138
    The Plot of the Mischief-Makers and the End of the People of Thamud 138
Surah: 27 Ayah: 54, Ayah: 55 (end of Part 19), Ayah: 56, Ayah: 57 & Ayah: 58 (start of Part 20; used here to give the fullness the following tafsir) *139*
    Tafsir Ibn Kathir 140
    Lut and His People 140

PRELUDE

Opening Serman

Indeed, all praise is due to Allah. We praise Him and seek His help and forgiveness. We seek refuge with Allah from our soul's evil and our wrong doings. He whom Allah guides, no one can misguide; and he whom He misguides, no one can guide

I bear witness that there is no (true) god except Allah – alone without a partner, and I bear witness that Muhammad (peace and blessings of Allah be upon him) is His 'abd (servant) and messenger.

يَٰٓأَيُّهَا ٱلَّذِينَ ءَامَنُوا۟ ٱتَّقُوا۟ ٱللَّهَ حَقَّ تُقَاتِهِۦ وَلَا تَمُوتُنَّ إِلَّا وَأَنتُم مُّسْلِمُونَ ﴿١٠٢﴾

O you who believe! Fear Allâh (by doing all that He has ordered and by abstaining from all that He has forbidden) as He should be feared. (Obey Him, be thankful to Him, and remember Him always), and die not except in a state of Islâm (as Muslims (with complete submission to Allâh)).

يَٰٓأَيُّهَا ٱلنَّاسُ ٱتَّقُوا۟ رَبَّكُمُ ٱلَّذِى خَلَقَكُم مِّن نَّفْسٍ وَٰحِدَةٍ وَخَلَقَ مِنْهَا زَوْجَهَا وَبَثَّ مِنْهُمَا رِجَالًا كَثِيرًا وَنِسَآءً ۚ وَٱتَّقُوا۟ ٱللَّهَ ٱلَّذِى تَسَآءَلُونَ بِهِۦ وَٱلْأَرْحَامَ ۚ إِنَّ ٱللَّهَ كَانَ عَلَيْكُمْ رَقِيبًا ﴿١﴾

O mankind! Be dutiful to your Lord, Who created you from a single person (Adam), and from him (Adam) He created his wife (Hawwâ (Eve)) and from them both He created many men and women; and fear Allâh through Whom you demand (your mutual rights), and (do not cut the relations of) the wombs (kinship). Surely, Allâh is Ever an All-Watcher over you.

يُصْلِحْ لَكُمْ أَعْمَٰلَكُمْ وَيَغْفِرْ لَكُمْ ذُنُوبَكُمْ ۗ وَمَن يُطِعِ ٱللَّهَ وَرَسُولَهُۥ فَقَدْ فَازَ فَوْزًا عَظِيمًا ﴿٧١﴾

He will direct you to do righteous good deeds and will forgive you your sins. And whosoever obeys Allâh and His Messenger (peace be upon him), he has indeed achieved a great achievement (i.e. he will be saved from the Hell-fire and will be admitted to Paradise).

Indeed, the best speech is Allah's Book and the best guidance is Muhammad's () guidance. The worst affairs (of religion) are those innovated (by people), for every such innovation is an act of misguidance leading to the Fire

Our Mission

Our mission is to gather in one place, for the English-speaking public, all relevant information needed to make the Qur'an more understandable and easier to study. This book tries to do this by providing the following:

1. The Arabic Text for those who are able to read Arabic
2. Transliteration of the Arabic text for those who are unable to read the Arabic script. This will give them a sample of the sound of the Qur'an, which they could not otherwise comprehend from reading the English meaning.
3. The meaning of the qur'an (translated by Dr. Muhammad Taqi-ud-Din Al-Hilali, Ph.D. and Dr. Muhammad Muhsin Khan)
4. Explanation (abridged Tafsir) by Ibn Kathir (translated by Safi-ur-Rahman al-Mubarakpuri)

We hope that by doing this an ordinary English-speaker will be able to pick up a copy of this book and study and comprehend The Glorious Qur'an in a way that is acceptable to the understanding of the Rightly-guided Muslim Ummah (Community).

Biography of Hafiz Ibn Kathir (701 H - 774 H)

By the Honored Shaykh `Abdul-Qadir Al-Arna'ut, may Allah protect him.

He is the respected Imam, Abu Al-Fida', `Imad Ad-Din Isma il bin 'Umar bin Kathir Al-Qurashi Al-Busrawi - Busraian in origin; Dimashqi in training, learning and residence.

Ibn Kathir was born in the city of Busra in 701 H. His father was the Friday speaker of the village, but he died while Ibn Kathir was only four years old. Ibn Kathir's brother, Shaykh Abdul-Wahhab, reared him and taught him until he moved to Damascus in 706 H., when he was five years old.

Ibn Kathir's Teachers

Ibn Kathir studied Fiqh - Islamic jurisprudence - with Burhan Ad-Din, Ibrahim bin `Abdur-Rahman Al-Fizari, known as Ibn Al-Firkah (who died in 729 H). Ibn Kathir heard Hadiths from `Isa bin Al-Mutim, Ahmad bin Abi Talib, (Ibn Ash-Shahnah) (who died in 730 H), Ibn Al-Hajjar, (who died in 730 H), and the Hadith narrator of Ash-Sham (modern day Syria and surrounding areas); Baha Ad-Din Al-Qasim bin Muzaffar bin `Asakir (who died in 723 H), and Ibn Ash-Shirdzi, Ishaq bin Yahya Al-Ammuddi, also known as `Afif Ad-Din, the Zahiriyyah Shaykh who died in 725 H, and Muhammad bin Zarrad. He remained with Jamal Ad-Din, Yusuf bin Az-Zaki AlMizzi who died in 724 H, he benefited from his knowledge and also married his daughter. He also read with Shaykh Al-Islam, Taqi Ad-Din Ahmad bin `Abdul-Halim bin `Abdus-Salam bin Taymiyyah who died in 728 H. He also read with the Imam Hafiz and historian Shams Ad-Din, Muhammad bin Ahmad bin Uthman bin Qaymaz Adh-Dhahabi, who died in 748 H. Also, Abu Musa Al-Qarafai, Abu Al-Fath Ad-Dabbusi and

'Ali bin `Umar As-Suwani and others who gave him permission to transmit the knowledge he learned with them in Egypt.

In his book, Al-Mu jam Al-Mukhtas, Al-Hafiz Adh-Dhaliabi wrote that Ibn Kathir was, "The Imam, scholar of jurisprudence, skillful scholar of Hadith, renowned Faqih and scholar of Tafsir who wrote several beneficial books."

Further, in Ad-Durar Al-Kdminah, Al-Hafiz Ibn Hajar AlAsqalani said, "Ibn Kathir worked on the subject of the Hadith in the areas of texts and chains of narrators. He had a good memory, his books became popular during his lifetime, and people benefited from them after his death."

Also, the renowned historian Abu Al-Mahasin, Jamal Ad-Din Yusuf bin Sayf Ad-Din (Ibn Taghri Bardi), said in his book, AlManhal As-Safi, "He is the Shaykh, the Imam, the great scholar `Imad Ad-Din Abu Al-Fida'. He learned extensively and was very active in collecting knowledge and writing. He was excellent in the areas of Fiqh, Tafsfr and Hadith. He collected knowledge, authored (books), taught, narrated Hadith and wrote. He had immense knowledge in the fields of Hadith, Tafsir, Fiqh, the Arabic language, and so forth. He gave Fatawa (religious verdicts) and taught until he died, may Allah grant him mercy. He was known for his precision and vast knowledge, and as a scholar of history, Hadith and Tafsir."

Ibn Kathir's Students

Ibn Hajji was one of Ibn Kathir's students, and he described Ibn Kathir: "He had the best memory of the Hadith texts. He also had the most knowledge concerning the narrators and authenticity, his contemporaries and teachers admitted to these qualities. Every time I met him I gained some benefit from him."

Also, Ibn Al-`Imad Al-Hanbali said in his book, Shadhardt Adh-Dhahab, "He is the renowned Hafiz `Imad Ad-Din, whose memory was excellent, whose forgetfulness was miniscule, whose understanding was adequate, and who had good knowledge in the Arabic language." Also, Ibn Habib said about Ibn Kathir, "He heard knowledge and collected it and wrote various books. He brought comfort to the ears with his Fatwas and narrated Hadith and brought benefit to other people. The papers that contained his Fatwas were transmitted to the various (Islamic) provinces. Further, he was known for his precision and encompassing knowledge."

Ibn Kathir's Books

1 - One of the greatest books that Ibn Kathir wrote was his Tafsir of the Noble Qur'an, which is one of the best Tafsir that rely on narrations [of Ahadith, the Tafsir of the Companions, etc.]. The Tafsir by Ibn Kathir was printed many times and several scholars have summarized it.

2- The History Collection known as Al-Biddyah, which was printed in 14 volumes under the name Al-Bidayah wanNihdyah, and contained the stories of the Prophets and previous nations, the Prophet's Seerah (life story) and Islamic history until his time. He also added a book Al-Fitan, about the Signs of the Last Hour.

3- At-Takmil ft Ma`rifat Ath-Thiqat wa Ad-Du'afa wal Majdhil which Ibn Kathir collected from the books of his two Shaykhs Al-Mizzi and Adh-Dhahabi; Al-Kdmal and Mizan Al-Ftiddl. He added several benefits regarding the subject of Al-Jarh and AtT'adil.

4- Al-Hadi was-Sunan ft Ahadith Al-Masdnfd was-Sunan which is also known by, Jami` Al-Masdnfd. In this book, Ibn Kathir collected the narrations of Imams Ahmad bin Hanbal, Al-Bazzar, Abu Ya`la Al-Mawsili, Ibn Abi Shaybah and from the six collections of Hadith: the Two Sahihs [Al-Bukhari and Muslim] and the Four Sunan [Abu Dawud, At-Tirmidhi, AnNasa and Ibn Majah]. Ibn Kathir divided this book according to areas of Fiqh.

5-Tabaqat Ash-Shaf iyah which also contains the virtues of Imam Ash-Shafi.

6- Ibn Kathir wrote references for the Ahadith of Adillat AtTanbfh, from the Shafi school of Fiqh.

7- Ibn Kathir began an explanation of Sahih Al-Bukhari, but he did not finish it.

8- He started writing a large volume on the Ahkam (Laws), but finished only up to the Hajj rituals.

9- He summarized Al-Bayhaqi's 'Al-Madkhal. Many of these books were not printed.

10- He summarized `Ulum Al-Hadith, by Abu `Amr bin AsSalah and called it Mukhtasar `Ulum Al-Hadith. Shaykh Ahmad Shakir, the Egyptian Muhaddith, printed this book along with his commentary on it and called it Al-Ba'th Al-Hathfth fi Sharh Mukhtasar `Ulum Al-Hadith.

11- As-Sfrah An-Nabawiyyah, which is contained in his book Al-Biddyah, and both of these books are in print.

12- A research on Jihad called Al-Ijtihad ft Talabi Al-Jihad, which was printed several times.

Ibn Kathir's Death

Al-Hafiz Ibn Hajar Al-Asgalani said, "Ibn Kathir lost his sight just before his life ended. He died in Damascus in 774 H." May Allah grant mercy upon Ibn Kathir and make him among the residents of His Paradise.

PREFACE

In the name of Allah, Most Gracious, Most Merciful.

About this book

The previous publication of this book included some background information to the chapters of the Qur'an by an Islamic scholar known as Abul Ala Maududi. This information was used to shed more light on the chapters by giving a summery of why each chapter was given its name, It's period of revelation and the circumstances surrounding its revelatiom. However, some Muslims objected to the inclusion of the contributions of Maududi.

In this new publication of Tafsir Ibn Kathir, we have removed all traces of the contribution of Abul Ala Maududi. Personally, I do not know the reasons for the objections to Maududi, but this work concerns only the tafsir of Ibn Kathir, so we have not included anything from Maududi in it. We have also corrected all the typing and formatting errors found in the previous publication. We have not alter the structure of the book. The reader is still able to read the full Arabic Text of the thirty Parts of the Qur'an and follow its meanings in the English language. The transliteration of the Arabic text should also give the reader a taste of the sound of the original Arabic.

May Almighty Allah accept this effort from us, and make it a source of blessings for us in this world and in the next. I bear witness that there is none worthy of worship but Allah and I bear witness that Muhammad (may the peace and blessings of Allah be upon him) is the slave and messenger of Allah.

Performing Prostration While Reading the Qur'an

Question:

Could you please give a list of the Qur'anic verses when a prostration is recommended? What happens if we read these verses and not perform a prostration?

A. Jalil

Answer:

There are 15 verses in the Qur'an that mention prostration before God Almighty as a good action by God-fearing believers. Therefore, it is strongly recommended to perform such a prostration when we read or listen to any of these verses, whether during prayer or in any situation.

Some scholars are of the view that even if one has not performed ablution, one should prostrate oneself. These verses are given here, starting with the Arabic title of the surah which is followed by two numbers, the first indicating the surah, and the second indicating the verse,: Al-Araf 7: 206; Al-Raad 13: 15; Al-Nahl 16: 50; Al-Isra 17: 109; Maryam 19: 58; Al-Hajj 22: 18 & 22: 77; Al-Furqan 25: 60; Al-Naml 27: 26;

Al-Sajdah 32: 15; Saad 38: 25; Fussilat 41: 38; Al-Najm 53: 62; Al-Inshiqaq 84: 21 and Al-Alaq 96: 19.

If you do not perform a prostration when you read or listen to any of these verses, you have done badly because you miss out on the reward of performing a prostration for God. You incur no sin and violate no divine order.

Reference:
http://archive.arabnews.com/?page=5&section=0&article=97811&d=1&m=7&y=2007

The Glorious Qur'an Juz' 19 (Part 19): Chapter (Surah) 25: Al-Furqan (The Criterion) 021 To Chapter (Surah) 27: An-Nanl (The Ant, The Ants) 055

PART 19 FULL ARABIC TEXT

Chapter (Surah) 25: Al-Furqan 021-077

۞ وَقَالَ ٱلَّذِينَ لَا يَرْجُونَ لِقَآءَنَا لَوْلَآ أُنزِلَ عَلَيْنَا ٱلْمَلَٰٓئِكَةُ أَوْ نَرَىٰ رَبَّنَا ۗ لَقَدِ ٱسْتَكْبَرُوا۟ فِىٓ أَنفُسِهِمْ وَعَتَوْ عُتُوًّا كَبِيرًا ۝ يَوْمَ يَرَوْنَ ٱلْمَلَٰٓئِكَةَ لَا بُشْرَىٰ يَوْمَئِذٍ لِّلْمُجْرِمِينَ وَيَقُولُونَ حِجْرًا مَّحْجُورًا ۝ وَقَدِمْنَآ إِلَىٰ مَا عَمِلُوا۟ مِنْ عَمَلٍ فَجَعَلْنَٰهُ هَبَآءً مَّنثُورًا ۝ أَصْحَٰبُ ٱلْجَنَّةِ يَوْمَئِذٍ خَيْرٌ مُّسْتَقَرًّا وَأَحْسَنُ مَقِيلًا ۝ وَيَوْمَ تَشَقَّقُ ٱلسَّمَآءُ بِٱلْغَمَٰمِ وَنُزِّلَ ٱلْمَلَٰٓئِكَةُ تَنزِيلًا ۝ ٱلْمُلْكُ يَوْمَئِذٍ ٱلْحَقُّ لِلرَّحْمَٰنِ ۚ وَكَانَ يَوْمًا عَلَى ٱلْكَٰفِرِينَ عَسِيرًا ۝ وَيَوْمَ يَعَضُّ ٱلظَّالِمُ عَلَىٰ يَدَيْهِ يَقُولُ يَٰلَيْتَنِى ٱتَّخَذْتُ مَعَ ٱلرَّسُولِ سَبِيلًا ۝ يَٰوَيْلَتَىٰ لَيْتَنِى لَمْ أَتَّخِذْ فُلَانًا خَلِيلًا ۝ لَّقَدْ أَضَلَّنِى عَنِ ٱلذِّكْرِ بَعْدَ إِذْ جَآءَنِى ۗ وَكَانَ ٱلشَّيْطَٰنُ لِلْإِنسَٰنِ خَذُولًا ۝ وَقَالَ ٱلرَّسُولُ يَٰرَبِّ إِنَّ قَوْمِى ٱتَّخَذُوا۟ هَٰذَا ٱلْقُرْءَانَ مَهْجُورًا ۝ وَكَذَٰلِكَ جَعَلْنَا لِكُلِّ نَبِىٍّ عَدُوًّا مِّنَ ٱلْمُجْرِمِينَ ۗ وَكَفَىٰ بِرَبِّكَ هَادِيًا وَنَصِيرًا ۝ وَقَالَ ٱلَّذِينَ كَفَرُوا۟ لَوْلَا نُزِّلَ عَلَيْهِ ٱلْقُرْءَانُ جُمْلَةً وَٰحِدَةً ۚ كَذَٰلِكَ لِنُثَبِّتَ بِهِۦ فُؤَادَكَ ۖ وَرَتَّلْنَٰهُ تَرْتِيلًا ۝ وَلَا يَأْتُونَكَ بِمَثَلٍ إِلَّا جِئْنَٰكَ بِٱلْحَقِّ وَأَحْسَنَ تَفْسِيرًا ۝ ٱلَّذِينَ يُحْشَرُونَ عَلَىٰ وُجُوهِهِمْ إِلَىٰ جَهَنَّمَ أُو۟لَٰٓئِكَ شَرٌّ مَّكَانًا وَأَضَلُّ سَبِيلًا ۝ وَلَقَدْ ءَاتَيْنَا مُوسَى ٱلْكِتَٰبَ وَجَعَلْنَا مَعَهُۥٓ أَخَاهُ هَٰرُونَ وَزِيرًا ۝ فَقُلْنَا ٱذْهَبَآ إِلَى ٱلْقَوْمِ ٱلَّذِينَ كَذَّبُوا۟ بِـَٔايَٰتِنَا فَدَمَّرْنَٰهُمْ تَدْمِيرًا ۝ وَقَوْمَ نُوحٍ لَّمَّا

كَذَّبُوا۟ ٱلرُّسُلَ أَغْرَقْنَـٰهُمْ وَجَعَلْنَـٰهُمْ لِلنَّاسِ ءَايَةً ۖ وَأَعْتَدْنَا لِلظَّـٰلِمِينَ عَذَابًا أَلِيمًا ۞ وَعَادًا وَثَمُودَا۟ وَأَصْحَـٰبَ ٱلرَّسِّ وَقُرُونًۢا بَيْنَ ذَٰلِكَ كَثِيرًا ۞ وَكُلًّا ضَرَبْنَا لَهُ ٱلْأَمْثَـٰلَ ۖ وَكُلًّا تَبَّرْنَا تَتْبِيرًا ۞ وَلَقَدْ أَتَوْا۟ عَلَى ٱلْقَرْيَةِ ٱلَّتِىٓ أُمْطِرَتْ مَطَرَ ٱلسَّوْءِ ۚ أَفَلَمْ يَكُونُوا۟ يَرَوْنَهَا ۚ بَلْ كَانُوا۟ لَا يَرْجُونَ نُشُورًا ۞ وَإِذَا رَأَوْكَ إِن يَتَّخِذُونَكَ إِلَّا هُزُوًا أَهَـٰذَا ٱلَّذِى بَعَثَ ٱللَّهُ رَسُولًا ۞ إِن كَادَ لَيُضِلُّنَا عَنْ ءَالِهَتِنَا لَوْلَآ أَن صَبَرْنَا عَلَيْهَا ۚ وَسَوْفَ يَعْلَمُونَ حِينَ يَرَوْنَ ٱلْعَذَابَ مَنْ أَضَلُّ سَبِيلًا ۞ أَرَءَيْتَ مَنِ ٱتَّخَذَ إِلَـٰهَهُۥ هَوَىٰهُ أَفَأَنتَ تَكُونُ عَلَيْهِ وَكِيلًا ۞ أَمْ تَحْسَبُ أَنَّ أَكْثَرَهُمْ يَسْمَعُونَ أَوْ يَعْقِلُونَ ۚ إِنْ هُمْ إِلَّا كَٱلْأَنْعَـٰمِ ۖ بَلْ هُمْ أَضَلُّ سَبِيلًا ۞ أَلَمْ تَرَ إِلَىٰ رَبِّكَ كَيْفَ مَدَّ ٱلظِّلَّ وَلَوْ شَآءَ لَجَعَلَهُۥ سَاكِنًا ثُمَّ جَعَلْنَا ٱلشَّمْسَ عَلَيْهِ دَلِيلًا ۞ ثُمَّ قَبَضْنَـٰهُ إِلَيْنَا قَبْضًا يَسِيرًا ۞ وَهُوَ ٱلَّذِى جَعَلَ لَكُمُ ٱلَّيْلَ لِبَاسًا وَٱلنَّوْمَ سُبَاتًا وَجَعَلَ ٱلنَّهَارَ نُشُورًا ۞ وَهُوَ ٱلَّذِىٓ أَرْسَلَ ٱلرِّيَـٰحَ بُشْرًۢا بَيْنَ يَدَىْ رَحْمَتِهِۦ ۚ وَأَنزَلْنَا مِنَ ٱلسَّمَآءِ مَآءً طَهُورًا ۞ لِّنُحْىِۦَ بِهِۦ بَلْدَةً مَّيْتًا وَنُسْقِيَهُۥ مِمَّا خَلَقْنَآ أَنْعَـٰمًا وَأَنَاسِىَّ كَثِيرًا ۞ وَلَقَدْ صَرَّفْنَـٰهُ بَيْنَهُمْ لِيَذَّكَّرُوا۟ فَأَبَىٰٓ أَكْثَرُ ٱلنَّاسِ إِلَّا كُفُورًا ۞ وَلَوْ شِئْنَا لَبَعَثْنَا فِى كُلِّ قَرْيَةٍ نَّذِيرًا ۞ فَلَا تُطِعِ ٱلْكَـٰفِرِينَ وَجَـٰهِدْهُم بِهِۦ جِهَادًا كَبِيرًا ۞ وَهُوَ ٱلَّذِى مَرَجَ ٱلْبَحْرَيْنِ هَـٰذَا عَذْبٌ فُرَاتٌ وَهَـٰذَا مِلْحٌ أُجَاجٌ وَجَعَلَ بَيْنَهُمَا بَرْزَخًا وَحِجْرًا مَّحْجُورًا ۞ وَهُوَ ٱلَّذِى خَلَقَ مِنَ ٱلْمَآءِ بَشَرًا فَجَعَلَهُۥ نَسَبًا وَصِهْرًا ۗ وَكَانَ رَبُّكَ قَدِيرًا ۞ وَيَعْبُدُونَ مِن دُونِ ٱللَّهِ مَا لَا يَنفَعُهُمْ وَلَا يَضُرُّهُمْ ۗ وَكَانَ ٱلْكَافِرُ عَلَىٰ رَبِّهِۦ ظَهِيرًا ۞ وَمَآ أَرْسَلْنَـٰكَ إِلَّا مُبَشِّرًا وَنَذِيرًا ۞ قُلْ مَآ أَسْـَٔلُكُمْ عَلَيْهِ مِنْ أَجْرٍ إِلَّا مَن شَآءَ أَن يَتَّخِذَ إِلَىٰ رَبِّهِۦ سَبِيلًا ۞

۵۷ وَتَوَكَّلْ عَلَى ٱلْحَيِّ ٱلَّذِى لَا يَمُوتُ وَسَبِّحْ بِحَمْدِهِۦ ۚ وَكَفَىٰ بِهِۦ بِذُنُوبِ عِبَادِهِۦ خَبِيرًا ۵۸ ٱلَّذِى خَلَقَ ٱلسَّمَٰوَٰتِ وَٱلْأَرْضَ وَمَا بَيْنَهُمَا فِى سِتَّةِ أَيَّامٍ ثُمَّ ٱسْتَوَىٰ عَلَى ٱلْعَرْشِ ۚ ٱلرَّحْمَٰنُ فَسْـَٔلْ بِهِۦ خَبِيرًا ۵۹ وَإِذَا قِيلَ لَهُمُ ٱسْجُدُوا۟ لِلرَّحْمَٰنِ قَالُوا۟ وَمَا ٱلرَّحْمَٰنُ أَنَسْجُدُ لِمَا تَأْمُرُنَا وَزَادَهُمْ نُفُورًا ۶۰ ۩ تَبَارَكَ ٱلَّذِى جَعَلَ فِى ٱلسَّمَآءِ بُرُوجًا وَجَعَلَ فِيهَا سِرَٰجًا وَقَمَرًا مُّنِيرًا ۶۱ وَهُوَ ٱلَّذِى جَعَلَ ٱلَّيْلَ وَٱلنَّهَارَ خِلْفَةً لِّمَنْ أَرَادَ أَن يَذَّكَّرَ أَوْ أَرَادَ شُكُورًا ۶۲ وَعِبَادُ ٱلرَّحْمَٰنِ ٱلَّذِينَ يَمْشُونَ عَلَى ٱلْأَرْضِ هَوْنًا وَإِذَا خَاطَبَهُمُ ٱلْجَٰهِلُونَ قَالُوا۟ سَلَٰمًا ۶۳ وَٱلَّذِينَ يَبِيتُونَ لِرَبِّهِمْ سُجَّدًا وَقِيَٰمًا ۶۴ وَٱلَّذِينَ يَقُولُونَ رَبَّنَا ٱصْرِفْ عَنَّا عَذَابَ جَهَنَّمَ ۖ إِنَّ عَذَابَهَا كَانَ غَرَامًا ۶۵ إِنَّهَا سَآءَتْ مُسْتَقَرًّا وَمُقَامًا ۶۶ وَٱلَّذِينَ إِذَآ أَنفَقُوا۟ لَمْ يُسْرِفُوا۟ وَلَمْ يَقْتُرُوا۟ وَكَانَ بَيْنَ ذَٰلِكَ قَوَامًا ۶۷ وَٱلَّذِينَ لَا يَدْعُونَ مَعَ ٱللَّهِ إِلَٰهًا ءَاخَرَ وَلَا يَقْتُلُونَ ٱلنَّفْسَ ٱلَّتِى حَرَّمَ ٱللَّهُ إِلَّا بِٱلْحَقِّ وَلَا يَزْنُونَ ۚ وَمَن يَفْعَلْ ذَٰلِكَ يَلْقَ أَثَامًا ۶۸ يُضَٰعَفْ لَهُ ٱلْعَذَابُ يَوْمَ ٱلْقِيَٰمَةِ وَيَخْلُدْ فِيهِۦ مُهَانًا ۶۹ إِلَّا مَن تَابَ وَءَامَنَ وَعَمِلَ عَمَلًا صَٰلِحًا فَأُو۟لَٰٓئِكَ يُبَدِّلُ ٱللَّهُ سَيِّـَٔاتِهِمْ حَسَنَٰتٍ ۗ وَكَانَ ٱللَّهُ غَفُورًا رَّحِيمًا ۷۰ وَمَن تَابَ وَعَمِلَ صَٰلِحًا فَإِنَّهُۥ يَتُوبُ إِلَى ٱللَّهِ مَتَابًا ۷۱ وَٱلَّذِينَ لَا يَشْهَدُونَ ٱلزُّورَ وَإِذَا مَرُّوا۟ بِٱللَّغْوِ مَرُّوا۟ كِرَامًا ۷۲ وَٱلَّذِينَ إِذَا ذُكِّرُوا۟ بِـَٔايَٰتِ رَبِّهِمْ لَمْ يَخِرُّوا۟ عَلَيْهَا صُمًّا وَعُمْيَانًا ۷۳ وَٱلَّذِينَ يَقُولُونَ رَبَّنَا هَبْ لَنَا مِنْ أَزْوَٰجِنَا وَذُرِّيَّٰتِنَا قُرَّةَ أَعْيُنٍ وَٱجْعَلْنَا لِلْمُتَّقِينَ إِمَامًا ۷۴ أُو۟لَٰٓئِكَ يُجْزَوْنَ ٱلْغُرْفَةَ بِمَا صَبَرُوا۟ وَيُلَقَّوْنَ فِيهَا تَحِيَّةً وَسَلَٰمًا ۷۵ خَٰلِدِينَ فِيهَا

حَسُنَتْ مُسْتَقَرًّا وَمُقَامًا ۝ قُلْ مَا يَعْبَؤُا بِكُمْ رَبِّى لَوْلَا دُعَاؤُكُمْ ۖ فَقَدْ كَذَّبْتُمْ فَسَوْفَ يَكُونُ لِزَامًا ۝

(Al-Furqan 021-077)

Chapter (Surah) 26: Ash-Shu'araa 001-227

بِسْمِ اللَّهِ الرَّحْمَٰنِ الرَّحِيمِ

﴿ طسم ۝ تِلْكَ ءَايَـٰتُ ٱلْكِتَـٰبِ ٱلْمُبِينِ ۝ لَعَلَّكَ بَـٰخِعٌ نَّفْسَكَ أَلَّا يَكُونُوا۟ مُؤْمِنِينَ ۝ إِن نَّشَأْ نُنَزِّلْ عَلَيْهِم مِّنَ ٱلسَّمَآءِ ءَايَةً فَظَلَّتْ أَعْنَـٰقُهُمْ لَهَا خَـٰضِعِينَ ۝ وَمَا يَأْتِيهِم مِّن ذِكْرٍ مِّنَ ٱلرَّحْمَـٰنِ مُحْدَثٍ إِلَّا كَانُوا۟ عَنْهُ مُعْرِضِينَ ۝ فَقَدْ كَذَّبُوا۟ فَسَيَأْتِيهِمْ أَنۢبَـٰٓؤُا۟ مَا كَانُوا۟ بِهِۦ يَسْتَهْزِءُونَ ۝ أَوَلَمْ يَرَوْا۟ إِلَى ٱلْأَرْضِ كَمْ أَنۢبَتْنَا فِيهَا مِن كُلِّ زَوْجٍ كَرِيمٍ ۝ إِنَّ فِى ذَٰلِكَ لَـَٔايَةً ۖ وَمَا كَانَ أَكْثَرُهُم مُّؤْمِنِينَ ۝ وَإِنَّ رَبَّكَ لَهُوَ ٱلْعَزِيزُ ٱلرَّحِيمُ ۝ وَإِذْ نَادَىٰ رَبُّكَ مُوسَىٰٓ أَنِ ٱئْتِ ٱلْقَوْمَ ٱلظَّـٰلِمِينَ ۝ قَوْمَ فِرْعَوْنَ ۚ أَلَا يَتَّقُونَ ۝ قَالَ رَبِّ إِنِّىٓ أَخَافُ أَن يُكَذِّبُونِ ۝ وَيَضِيقُ صَدْرِى وَلَا يَنطَلِقُ لِسَانِى فَأَرْسِلْ إِلَىٰ هَـٰرُونَ ۝ وَلَهُمْ عَلَىَّ ذَنۢبٌ فَأَخَافُ أَن يَقْتُلُونِ ۝ قَالَ كَلَّا ۖ فَٱذْهَبَا بِـَٔايَـٰتِنَآ ۖ إِنَّا مَعَكُم مُّسْتَمِعُونَ ۝ فَأْتِيَا فِرْعَوْنَ فَقُولَآ إِنَّا رَسُولُ رَبِّ ٱلْعَـٰلَمِينَ ۝ أَنْ أَرْسِلْ مَعَنَا بَنِىٓ إِسْرَٰٓءِيلَ ۝ قَالَ أَلَمْ نُرَبِّكَ فِينَا وَلِيدًا وَلَبِثْتَ فِينَا مِنْ عُمُرِكَ سِنِينَ ۝ وَفَعَلْتَ فَعْلَتَكَ ٱلَّتِى فَعَلْتَ وَأَنتَ مِنَ ٱلْكَـٰفِرِينَ ۝ قَالَ فَعَلْتُهَآ إِذًا وَأَنَا۠ مِنَ ٱلضَّآلِّينَ ۝ فَفَرَرْتُ مِنكُمْ لَمَّا خِفْتُكُمْ فَوَهَبَ لِى رَبِّى حُكْمًا وَجَعَلَنِى مِنَ ٱلْمُرْسَلِينَ ۝ وَتِلْكَ نِعْمَةٌ تَمُنُّهَا عَلَىَّ أَنْ عَبَّدتَّ بَنِىٓ إِسْرَٰٓءِيلَ ۝ قَالَ فِرْعَوْنُ وَمَا رَبُّ ٱلْعَـٰلَمِينَ ۝ قَالَ رَبُّ ٱلسَّمَـٰوَٰتِ وَٱلْأَرْضِ وَمَا بَيْنَهُمَآ ۖ إِن كُنتُم مُّوقِنِينَ ۝ قَالَ لِمَنْ حَوْلَهُۥٓ أَلَا تَسْتَمِعُونَ ۝ قَالَ رَبُّكُمْ وَرَبُّ ءَابَآئِكُمُ ٱلْأَوَّلِينَ ۝ قَالَ إِنَّ رَسُولَكُمُ ٱلَّذِىٓ أُرْسِلَ إِلَيْكُمْ لَمَجْنُونٌ ۝ قَالَ رَبُّ

ٱلْمَشْرِقِ وَٱلْمَغْرِبِ وَمَا بَيْنَهُمَآ ۖ إِن كُنتُمْ تَعْقِلُونَ ۝ قَالَ لَئِنِ ٱتَّخَذْتَ إِلَٰهًا غَيْرِى لَأَجْعَلَنَّكَ مِنَ ٱلْمَسْجُونِينَ ۝ قَالَ أَوَلَوْ جِئْتُكَ بِشَىْءٍ مُّبِينٍ ۝ قَالَ فَأْتِ بِهِۦٓ إِن كُنتَ مِنَ ٱلصَّٰدِقِينَ ۝ فَأَلْقَىٰ عَصَاهُ فَإِذَا هِىَ ثُعْبَانٌ مُّبِينٌ ۝ وَنَزَعَ يَدَهُۥ فَإِذَا هِىَ بَيْضَآءُ لِلنَّٰظِرِينَ ۝ قَالَ لِلْمَلَإِ حَوْلَهُۥٓ إِنَّ هَٰذَا لَسَٰحِرٌ عَلِيمٌ ۝ يُرِيدُ أَن يُخْرِجَكُم مِّنْ أَرْضِكُم بِسِحْرِهِۦ فَمَاذَا تَأْمُرُونَ ۝ قَالُوٓا۟ أَرْجِهْ وَأَخَاهُ وَٱبْعَثْ فِى ٱلْمَدَآئِنِ حَٰشِرِينَ ۝ يَأْتُوكَ بِكُلِّ سَحَّارٍ عَلِيمٍ ۝ فَجُمِعَ ٱلسَّحَرَةُ لِمِيقَٰتِ يَوْمٍ مَّعْلُومٍ ۝ وَقِيلَ لِلنَّاسِ هَلْ أَنتُم مُّجْتَمِعُونَ ۝ لَعَلَّنَا نَتَّبِعُ ٱلسَّحَرَةَ إِن كَانُوا۟ هُمُ ٱلْغَٰلِبِينَ ۝ فَلَمَّا جَآءَ ٱلسَّحَرَةُ قَالُوا۟ لِفِرْعَوْنَ أَئِنَّ لَنَا لَأَجْرًا إِن كُنَّا نَحْنُ ٱلْغَٰلِبِينَ ۝ قَالَ نَعَمْ وَإِنَّكُمْ إِذًا لَّمِنَ ٱلْمُقَرَّبِينَ ۝ قَالَ لَهُم مُّوسَىٰٓ أَلْقُوا۟ مَآ أَنتُم مُّلْقُونَ ۝ فَأَلْقَوْا۟ حِبَالَهُمْ وَعِصِيَّهُمْ وَقَالُوا۟ بِعِزَّةِ فِرْعَوْنَ إِنَّا لَنَحْنُ ٱلْغَٰلِبُونَ ۝ فَأَلْقَىٰ مُوسَىٰ عَصَاهُ فَإِذَا هِىَ تَلْقَفُ مَا يَأْفِكُونَ ۝ فَأُلْقِىَ ٱلسَّحَرَةُ سَٰجِدِينَ ۝ قَالُوٓا۟ ءَامَنَّا بِرَبِّ ٱلْعَٰلَمِينَ ۝ رَبِّ مُوسَىٰ وَهَٰرُونَ ۝ قَالَ ءَامَنتُمْ لَهُۥ قَبْلَ أَنْ ءَاذَنَ لَكُمْ ۖ إِنَّهُۥ لَكَبِيرُكُمُ ٱلَّذِى عَلَّمَكُمُ ٱلسِّحْرَ فَلَسَوْفَ تَعْلَمُونَ ۚ لَأُقَطِّعَنَّ أَيْدِيَكُمْ وَأَرْجُلَكُم مِّنْ خِلَٰفٍ وَلَأُصَلِّبَنَّكُمْ أَجْمَعِينَ ۝ قَالُوا۟ لَا ضَيْرَ ۖ إِنَّآ إِلَىٰ رَبِّنَا مُنقَلِبُونَ ۝ إِنَّا نَطْمَعُ أَن يَغْفِرَ لَنَا رَبُّنَا خَطَٰيَٰنَآ أَن كُنَّآ أَوَّلَ ٱلْمُؤْمِنِينَ ۝ ۞ وَأَوْحَيْنَآ إِلَىٰ مُوسَىٰٓ أَنْ أَسْرِ بِعِبَادِىٓ إِنَّكُم مُّتَّبَعُونَ ۝ فَأَرْسَلَ فِرْعَوْنُ فِى ٱلْمَدَآئِنِ حَٰشِرِينَ ۝ إِنَّ هَٰٓؤُلَآءِ لَشِرْذِمَةٌ قَلِيلُونَ ۝ وَإِنَّهُمْ لَنَا لَغَآئِظُونَ ۝ وَإِنَّا لَجَمِيعٌ حَٰذِرُونَ ۝ فَأَخْرَجْنَٰهُم مِّن جَنَّٰتٍ وَعُيُونٍ ۝ وَكُنُوزٍ وَمَقَامٍ كَرِيمٍ ۝ كَذَٰلِكَ وَأَوْرَثْنَٰهَا بَنِىٓ إِسْرَٰٓءِيلَ ۝ فَأَتْبَعُوهُم مُّشْرِقِينَ ۝ فَلَمَّا تَرَٰٓءَا ٱلْجَمْعَانِ قَالَ أَصْحَٰبُ مُوسَىٰٓ إِنَّا لَمُدْرَكُونَ ۝ قَالَ كَلَّآ ۖ إِنَّ

مَعِىَ رَبِّى سَيَهْدِينِ ۝ فَأَوْحَيْنَآ إِلَىٰ مُوسَىٰٓ أَنِ ٱضْرِب بِّعَصَاكَ ٱلْبَحْرَ ۖ فَٱنفَلَقَ فَكَانَ كُلُّ فِرْقٍ كَٱلطَّوْدِ ٱلْعَظِيمِ ۝ وَأَزْلَفْنَا ثَمَّ ٱلْءَاخَرِينَ ۝ وَأَنجَيْنَا مُوسَىٰ وَمَن مَّعَهُۥٓ أَجْمَعِينَ ۝ ثُمَّ أَغْرَقْنَا ٱلْءَاخَرِينَ ۝ إِنَّ فِى ذَٰلِكَ لَءَايَةً ۖ وَمَا كَانَ أَكْثَرُهُم مُّؤْمِنِينَ ۝ وَإِنَّ رَبَّكَ لَهُوَ ٱلْعَزِيزُ ٱلرَّحِيمُ ۝ وَٱتْلُ عَلَيْهِمْ نَبَأَ إِبْرَٰهِيمَ ۝ إِذْ قَالَ لِأَبِيهِ وَقَوْمِهِۦ مَا تَعْبُدُونَ ۝ قَالُوا۟ نَعْبُدُ أَصْنَامًا فَنَظَلُّ لَهَا عَٰكِفِينَ ۝ قَالَ هَلْ يَسْمَعُونَكُمْ إِذْ تَدْعُونَ ۝ أَوْ يَنفَعُونَكُمْ أَوْ يَضُرُّونَ ۝ قَالُوا۟ بَلْ وَجَدْنَآ ءَابَآءَنَا كَذَٰلِكَ يَفْعَلُونَ ۝ قَالَ أَفَرَءَيْتُم مَّا كُنتُمْ تَعْبُدُونَ ۝ أَنتُمْ وَءَابَآؤُكُمُ ٱلْأَقْدَمُونَ ۝ فَإِنَّهُمْ عَدُوٌّ لِّىٓ إِلَّا رَبَّ ٱلْعَٰلَمِينَ ۝ ٱلَّذِى خَلَقَنِى فَهُوَ يَهْدِينِ ۝ وَٱلَّذِى هُوَ يُطْعِمُنِى وَيَسْقِينِ ۝ وَإِذَا مَرِضْتُ فَهُوَ يَشْفِينِ ۝ وَٱلَّذِى يُمِيتُنِى ثُمَّ يُحْيِينِ ۝ وَٱلَّذِىٓ أَطْمَعُ أَن يَغْفِرَ لِى خَطِيٓـَٔتِى يَوْمَ ٱلدِّينِ ۝ رَبِّ هَبْ لِى حُكْمًا وَأَلْحِقْنِى بِٱلصَّٰلِحِينَ ۝ وَٱجْعَل لِّى لِسَانَ صِدْقٍ فِى ٱلْءَاخِرِينَ ۝ وَٱجْعَلْنِى مِن وَرَثَةِ جَنَّةِ ٱلنَّعِيمِ ۝ وَٱغْفِرْ لِأَبِىٓ إِنَّهُۥ كَانَ مِنَ ٱلضَّآلِّينَ ۝ وَلَا تُخْزِنِى يَوْمَ يُبْعَثُونَ ۝ يَوْمَ لَا يَنفَعُ مَالٌ وَلَا بَنُونَ ۝ إِلَّا مَنْ أَتَى ٱللَّهَ بِقَلْبٍ سَلِيمٍ ۝ وَأُزْلِفَتِ ٱلْجَنَّةُ لِلْمُتَّقِينَ ۝ وَبُرِّزَتِ ٱلْجَحِيمُ لِلْغَاوِينَ ۝ وَقِيلَ لَهُمْ أَيْنَ مَا كُنتُمْ تَعْبُدُونَ ۝ مِن دُونِ ٱللَّهِ هَلْ يَنصُرُونَكُمْ أَوْ يَنتَصِرُونَ ۝ فَكُبْكِبُوا۟ فِيهَا هُمْ وَٱلْغَاوُۥنَ ۝ وَجُنُودُ إِبْلِيسَ أَجْمَعُونَ ۝ قَالُوا۟ وَهُمْ فِيهَا يَخْتَصِمُونَ ۝ تَٱللَّهِ إِن كُنَّا لَفِى ضَلَٰلٍ مُّبِينٍ ۝ إِذْ نُسَوِّيكُم بِرَبِّ ٱلْعَٰلَمِينَ ۝ وَمَآ أَضَلَّنَآ إِلَّا ٱلْمُجْرِمُونَ ۝ فَمَا لَنَا مِن شَٰفِعِينَ ۝ وَلَا صَدِيقٍ حَمِيمٍ ۝ فَلَوْ أَنَّ لَنَا كَرَّةً فَنَكُونَ مِنَ ٱلْمُؤْمِنِينَ ۝ إِنَّ فِى ذَٰلِكَ لَءَايَةً ۖ وَمَا كَانَ أَكْثَرُهُم مُّؤْمِنِينَ ۝ وَإِنَّ رَبَّكَ لَهُوَ ٱلْعَزِيزُ ٱلرَّحِيمُ ۝ كَذَّبَتْ قَوْمُ نُوحٍ ٱلْمُرْسَلِينَ ۝ إِذْ قَالَ لَهُمْ أَخُوهُمْ نُوحٌ

أَلَا تَتَّقُونَ ۝ إِنِّى لَكُمْ رَسُولٌ أَمِينٌ ۝ فَاتَّقُوا۟ ٱللَّهَ وَأَطِيعُونِ ۝ وَمَآ أَسْـَٔلُكُمْ عَلَيْهِ مِنْ أَجْرٍ ۖ إِنْ أَجْرِىَ إِلَّا عَلَىٰ رَبِّ ٱلْعَٰلَمِينَ ۝ فَاتَّقُوا۟ ٱللَّهَ وَأَطِيعُونِ ۝ ۞ قَالُوٓا۟ أَنُؤْمِنُ لَكَ وَٱتَّبَعَكَ ٱلْأَرْذَلُونَ ۝ قَالَ وَمَا عِلْمِى بِمَا كَانُوا۟ يَعْمَلُونَ ۝ إِنْ حِسَابُهُمْ إِلَّا عَلَىٰ رَبِّى ۖ لَوْ تَشْعُرُونَ ۝ وَمَآ أَنَا۠ بِطَارِدِ ٱلْمُؤْمِنِينَ ۝ إِنْ أَنَا۠ إِلَّا نَذِيرٌ مُّبِينٌ ۝ قَالُوا۟ لَئِن لَّمْ تَنتَهِ يَٰنُوحُ لَتَكُونَنَّ مِنَ ٱلْمَرْجُومِينَ ۝ قَالَ رَبِّ إِنَّ قَوْمِى كَذَّبُونِ ۝ فَٱفْتَحْ بَيْنِى وَبَيْنَهُمْ فَتْحًا وَنَجِّنِى وَمَن مَّعِىَ مِنَ ٱلْمُؤْمِنِينَ ۝ فَأَنجَيْنَٰهُ وَمَن مَّعَهُۥ فِى ٱلْفُلْكِ ٱلْمَشْحُونِ ۝ ثُمَّ أَغْرَقْنَا بَعْدُ ٱلْبَاقِينَ ۝ إِنَّ فِى ذَٰلِكَ لَـَٔايَةً ۖ وَمَا كَانَ أَكْثَرُهُم مُّؤْمِنِينَ ۝ وَإِنَّ رَبَّكَ لَهُوَ ٱلْعَزِيزُ ٱلرَّحِيمُ ۝ كَذَّبَتْ عَادٌ ٱلْمُرْسَلِينَ ۝ إِذْ قَالَ لَهُمْ أَخُوهُمْ هُودٌ أَلَا تَتَّقُونَ ۝ إِنِّى لَكُمْ رَسُولٌ أَمِينٌ ۝ فَاتَّقُوا۟ ٱللَّهَ وَأَطِيعُونِ ۝ وَمَآ أَسْـَٔلُكُمْ عَلَيْهِ مِنْ أَجْرٍ ۖ إِنْ أَجْرِىَ إِلَّا عَلَىٰ رَبِّ ٱلْعَٰلَمِينَ ۝ أَتَبْنُونَ بِكُلِّ رِيعٍ ءَايَةً تَعْبَثُونَ ۝ وَتَتَّخِذُونَ مَصَانِعَ لَعَلَّكُمْ تَخْلُدُونَ ۝ وَإِذَا بَطَشْتُم بَطَشْتُمْ جَبَّارِينَ ۝ فَاتَّقُوا۟ ٱللَّهَ وَأَطِيعُونِ ۝ وَٱتَّقُوا۟ ٱلَّذِىٓ أَمَدَّكُم بِمَا تَعْلَمُونَ ۝ أَمَدَّكُم بِأَنْعَٰمٍ وَبَنِينَ ۝ وَجَنَّٰتٍ وَعُيُونٍ ۝ إِنِّىٓ أَخَافُ عَلَيْكُمْ عَذَابَ يَوْمٍ عَظِيمٍ ۝ قَالُوا۟ سَوَآءٌ عَلَيْنَآ أَوَعَظْتَ أَمْ لَمْ تَكُن مِّنَ ٱلْوَٰعِظِينَ ۝ إِنْ هَٰذَآ إِلَّا خُلُقُ ٱلْأَوَّلِينَ ۝ وَمَا نَحْنُ بِمُعَذَّبِينَ ۝ فَكَذَّبُوهُ فَأَهْلَكْنَٰهُمْ ۗ إِنَّ فِى ذَٰلِكَ لَـَٔايَةً ۖ وَمَا كَانَ أَكْثَرُهُم مُّؤْمِنِينَ ۝ وَإِنَّ رَبَّكَ لَهُوَ ٱلْعَزِيزُ ٱلرَّحِيمُ ۝ كَذَّبَتْ ثَمُودُ ٱلْمُرْسَلِينَ ۝ إِذْ قَالَ لَهُمْ أَخُوهُمْ صَٰلِحٌ أَلَا تَتَّقُونَ ۝ إِنِّى لَكُمْ رَسُولٌ أَمِينٌ ۝ فَاتَّقُوا۟ ٱللَّهَ وَأَطِيعُونِ ۝ وَمَآ أَسْـَٔلُكُمْ عَلَيْهِ مِنْ أَجْرٍ ۖ إِنْ أَجْرِىَ إِلَّا عَلَىٰ رَبِّ ٱلْعَٰلَمِينَ ۝ أَتُتْرَكُونَ فِى مَا هَٰهُنَآ ءَامِنِينَ ۝ فِى جَنَّٰتٍ وَعُيُونٍ ۝ وَزُرُوعٍ وَنَخْلٍ طَلْعُهَا هَضِيمٌ ۝

وَتَنْحِتُونَ مِنَ ٱلْجِبَالِ بُيُوتًا فَٰرِهِينَ ﴿١٤٩﴾ فَٱتَّقُوا۟ ٱللَّهَ وَأَطِيعُونِ ﴿١٥٠﴾ وَلَا تُطِيعُوٓا۟ أَمْرَ ٱلْمُسْرِفِينَ ﴿١٥١﴾ ٱلَّذِينَ يُفْسِدُونَ فِى ٱلْأَرْضِ وَلَا يُصْلِحُونَ ﴿١٥٢﴾ قَالُوٓا۟ إِنَّمَآ أَنتَ مِنَ ٱلْمُسَحَّرِينَ ﴿١٥٣﴾ مَآ أَنتَ إِلَّا بَشَرٌ مِّثْلُنَا فَأْتِ بِـَٔايَةٍ إِن كُنتَ مِنَ ٱلصَّٰدِقِينَ ﴿١٥٤﴾ قَالَ هَٰذِهِۦ نَاقَةٌ لَّهَا شِرْبٌ وَلَكُمْ شِرْبُ يَوْمٍ مَّعْلُومٍ ﴿١٥٥﴾ وَلَا تَمَسُّوهَا بِسُوٓءٍ فَيَأْخُذَكُمْ عَذَابُ يَوْمٍ عَظِيمٍ ﴿١٥٦﴾ فَعَقَرُوهَا فَأَصْبَحُوا۟ نَٰدِمِينَ ﴿١٥٧﴾ فَأَخَذَهُمُ ٱلْعَذَابُ ۗ إِنَّ فِى ذَٰلِكَ لَءَايَةً ۖ وَمَا كَانَ أَكْثَرُهُم مُّؤْمِنِينَ ﴿١٥٨﴾ وَإِنَّ رَبَّكَ لَهُوَ ٱلْعَزِيزُ ٱلرَّحِيمُ ﴿١٥٩﴾ كَذَّبَتْ قَوْمُ لُوطٍ ٱلْمُرْسَلِينَ ﴿١٦٠﴾ إِذْ قَالَ لَهُمْ أَخُوهُمْ لُوطٌ أَلَا تَتَّقُونَ ﴿١٦١﴾ إِنِّى لَكُمْ رَسُولٌ أَمِينٌ ﴿١٦٢﴾ فَٱتَّقُوا۟ ٱللَّهَ وَأَطِيعُونِ ﴿١٦٣﴾ وَمَآ أَسْـَٔلُكُمْ عَلَيْهِ مِنْ أَجْرٍ ۖ إِنْ أَجْرِىَ إِلَّا عَلَىٰ رَبِّ ٱلْعَٰلَمِينَ ﴿١٦٤﴾ أَتَأْتُونَ ٱلذُّكْرَانَ مِنَ ٱلْعَٰلَمِينَ ﴿١٦٥﴾ وَتَذَرُونَ مَا خَلَقَ لَكُمْ رَبُّكُم مِّنْ أَزْوَٰجِكُم ۚ بَلْ أَنتُمْ قَوْمٌ عَادُونَ ﴿١٦٦﴾ قَالُوا۟ لَئِن لَّمْ تَنتَهِ يَٰلُوطُ لَتَكُونَنَّ مِنَ ٱلْمُخْرَجِينَ ﴿١٦٧﴾ قَالَ إِنِّى لِعَمَلِكُم مِّنَ ٱلْقَالِينَ ﴿١٦٨﴾ رَبِّ نَجِّنِى وَأَهْلِى مِمَّا يَعْمَلُونَ ﴿١٦٩﴾ فَنَجَّيْنَٰهُ وَأَهْلَهُۥٓ أَجْمَعِينَ ﴿١٧٠﴾ إِلَّا عَجُوزًا فِى ٱلْغَٰبِرِينَ ﴿١٧١﴾ ثُمَّ دَمَّرْنَا ٱلْءَاخَرِينَ ﴿١٧٢﴾ وَأَمْطَرْنَا عَلَيْهِم مَّطَرًا ۖ فَسَآءَ مَطَرُ ٱلْمُنذَرِينَ ﴿١٧٣﴾ إِنَّ فِى ذَٰلِكَ لَءَايَةً ۖ وَمَا كَانَ أَكْثَرُهُم مُّؤْمِنِينَ ﴿١٧٤﴾ وَإِنَّ رَبَّكَ لَهُوَ ٱلْعَزِيزُ ٱلرَّحِيمُ ﴿١٧٥﴾ كَذَّبَ أَصْحَٰبُ لْـَٔيْكَةِ ٱلْمُرْسَلِينَ ﴿١٧٦﴾ إِذْ قَالَ لَهُمْ شُعَيْبٌ أَلَا تَتَّقُونَ ﴿١٧٧﴾ إِنِّى لَكُمْ رَسُولٌ أَمِينٌ ﴿١٧٨﴾ فَٱتَّقُوا۟ ٱللَّهَ وَأَطِيعُونِ ﴿١٧٩﴾ وَمَآ أَسْـَٔلُكُمْ عَلَيْهِ مِنْ أَجْرٍ ۖ إِنْ أَجْرِىَ إِلَّا عَلَىٰ رَبِّ ٱلْعَٰلَمِينَ ﴿١٨٠﴾ ۞ أَوْفُوا۟ ٱلْكَيْلَ وَلَا تَكُونُوا۟ مِنَ ٱلْمُخْسِرِينَ ﴿١٨١﴾ وَزِنُوا۟ بِٱلْقِسْطَاسِ ٱلْمُسْتَقِيمِ ﴿١٨٢﴾ وَلَا تَبْخَسُوا۟ ٱلنَّاسَ أَشْيَآءَهُمْ وَلَا تَعْثَوْا۟ فِى ٱلْأَرْضِ مُفْسِدِينَ ﴿١٨٣﴾ وَٱتَّقُوا۟ ٱلَّذِى خَلَقَكُمْ وَٱلْجِبِلَّةَ ٱلْأَوَّلِينَ ﴿١٨٤﴾ قَالُوٓا۟ إِنَّمَآ أَنتَ مِنَ ٱلْمُسَحَّرِينَ ﴿١٨٥﴾ وَمَآ أَنتَ إِلَّا بَشَرٌ مِّثْلُنَا وَإِن نَّظُنُّكَ لَمِنَ ٱلْكَٰذِبِينَ

۞ فَأَسْقِطْ عَلَيْنَا كِسَفًا مِّنَ ٱلسَّمَآءِ إِن كُنتَ مِنَ ٱلصَّٰدِقِينَ ۝١٨٦ قَالَ رَبِّىٓ أَعْلَمُ بِمَا تَعْمَلُونَ ۝١٨٨ فَكَذَّبُوهُ فَأَخَذَهُمْ عَذَابُ يَوْمِ ٱلظُّلَّةِ ۚ إِنَّهُۥ كَانَ عَذَابَ يَوْمٍ عَظِيمٍ ۝١٨٩ إِنَّ فِى ذَٰلِكَ لَءَايَةً ۖ وَمَا كَانَ أَكْثَرُهُم مُّؤْمِنِينَ ۝١٩٠ وَإِنَّ رَبَّكَ لَهُوَ ٱلْعَزِيزُ ٱلرَّحِيمُ ۝١٩١ وَإِنَّهُۥ لَتَنزِيلُ رَبِّ ٱلْعَٰلَمِينَ ۝١٩٢ نَزَلَ بِهِ ٱلرُّوحُ ٱلْأَمِينُ ۝١٩٣ عَلَىٰ قَلْبِكَ لِتَكُونَ مِنَ ٱلْمُنذِرِينَ ۝١٩٤ بِلِسَانٍ عَرَبِىٍّ مُّبِينٍ ۝١٩٥ وَإِنَّهُۥ لَفِى زُبُرِ ٱلْأَوَّلِينَ ۝١٩٦ أَوَلَمْ يَكُن لَّهُمْ ءَايَةً أَن يَعْلَمَهُۥ عُلَمَٰٓؤُا۟ بَنِىٓ إِسْرَٰٓءِيلَ ۝١٩٧ وَلَوْ نَزَّلْنَٰهُ عَلَىٰ بَعْضِ ٱلْأَعْجَمِينَ ۝١٩٨ فَقَرَأَهُۥ عَلَيْهِم مَّا كَانُوا۟ بِهِۦ مُؤْمِنِينَ ۝١٩٩ كَذَٰلِكَ سَلَكْنَٰهُ فِى قُلُوبِ ٱلْمُجْرِمِينَ ۝٢٠٠ لَا يُؤْمِنُونَ بِهِۦ حَتَّىٰ يَرَوُا۟ ٱلْعَذَابَ ٱلْأَلِيمَ ۝٢٠١ فَيَأْتِيَهُم بَغْتَةً وَهُمْ لَا يَشْعُرُونَ ۝٢٠٢ فَيَقُولُوا۟ هَلْ نَحْنُ مُنظَرُونَ ۝٢٠٣ أَفَبِعَذَابِنَا يَسْتَعْجِلُونَ ۝٢٠٤ أَفَرَءَيْتَ إِن مَّتَّعْنَٰهُمْ سِنِينَ ۝٢٠٥ ثُمَّ جَآءَهُم مَّا كَانُوا۟ يُوعَدُونَ ۝٢٠٦ مَآ أَغْنَىٰ عَنْهُم مَّا كَانُوا۟ يُمَتَّعُونَ ۝٢٠٧ وَمَآ أَهْلَكْنَا مِن قَرْيَةٍ إِلَّا لَهَا مُنذِرُونَ ۝٢٠٨ ذِكْرَىٰ وَمَا كُنَّا ظَٰلِمِينَ ۝٢٠٩ وَمَا تَنَزَّلَتْ بِهِ ٱلشَّيَٰطِينُ ۝٢١٠ وَمَا يَنۢبَغِى لَهُمْ وَمَا يَسْتَطِيعُونَ ۝٢١١ إِنَّهُمْ عَنِ ٱلسَّمْعِ لَمَعْزُولُونَ ۝٢١٢ فَلَا تَدْعُ مَعَ ٱللَّهِ إِلَٰهًا ءَاخَرَ فَتَكُونَ مِنَ ٱلْمُعَذَّبِينَ ۝٢١٣ وَأَنذِرْ عَشِيرَتَكَ ٱلْأَقْرَبِينَ ۝٢١٤ وَٱخْفِضْ جَنَاحَكَ لِمَنِ ٱتَّبَعَكَ مِنَ ٱلْمُؤْمِنِينَ ۝٢١٥ فَإِنْ عَصَوْكَ فَقُلْ إِنِّى بَرِىٓءٌ مِّمَّا تَعْمَلُونَ ۝٢١٦ وَتَوَكَّلْ عَلَى ٱلْعَزِيزِ ٱلرَّحِيمِ ۝٢١٧ ٱلَّذِى يَرَىٰكَ حِينَ تَقُومُ ۝٢١٨ وَتَقَلُّبَكَ فِى ٱلسَّٰجِدِينَ ۝٢١٩ إِنَّهُۥ هُوَ ٱلسَّمِيعُ ٱلْعَلِيمُ ۝٢٢٠ هَلْ أُنَبِّئُكُمْ عَلَىٰ مَن تَنَزَّلُ ٱلشَّيَٰطِينُ ۝٢٢١ تَنَزَّلُ عَلَىٰ كُلِّ أَفَّاكٍ أَثِيمٍ ۝٢٢٢ يُلْقُونَ ٱلسَّمْعَ وَأَكْثَرُهُمْ كَٰذِبُونَ ۝٢٢٣ وَٱلشُّعَرَآءُ يَتَّبِعُهُمُ ٱلْغَاوُۥنَ ۝٢٢٤ أَلَمْ تَرَ أَنَّهُمْ فِى كُلِّ وَادٍ يَهِيمُونَ ۝٢٢٥ وَأَنَّهُمْ يَقُولُونَ مَا لَا يَفْعَلُونَ ۝٢٢٦ إِلَّا ٱلَّذِينَ ءَامَنُوا۟ وَعَمِلُوا۟ ٱلصَّٰلِحَٰتِ وَذَكَرُوا۟ ٱللَّهَ كَثِيرًا

(Ash-Shu'araa 001-227)

Chapter (Surah) 27: An-Naml 001-055

بِسْمِ اللَّهِ الرَّحْمَنِ الرَّحِيمِ

طس ۚ تِلْكَ ءَايَـٰتُ ٱلْقُرْءَانِ وَكِتَابٍ مُّبِينٍ ۝ هُدًى وَبُشْرَىٰ لِلْمُؤْمِنِينَ ۝ ٱلَّذِينَ يُقِيمُونَ ٱلصَّلَوٰةَ وَيُؤْتُونَ ٱلزَّكَوٰةَ وَهُم بِٱلْـَٔاخِرَةِ هُمْ يُوقِنُونَ ۝ إِنَّ ٱلَّذِينَ لَا يُؤْمِنُونَ بِٱلْـَٔاخِرَةِ زَيَّنَّا لَهُمْ أَعْمَـٰلَهُمْ فَهُمْ يَعْمَهُونَ ۝ أُوْلَـٰٓئِكَ ٱلَّذِينَ لَهُمْ سُوٓءُ ٱلْعَذَابِ وَهُمْ فِى ٱلْـَٔاخِرَةِ هُمُ ٱلْأَخْسَرُونَ ۝ وَإِنَّكَ لَتُلَقَّى ٱلْقُرْءَانَ مِن لَّدُنْ حَكِيمٍ عَلِيمٍ ۝ إِذْ قَالَ مُوسَىٰ لِأَهْلِهِ إِنِّىٓ ءَانَسْتُ نَارًا سَـَٔاتِيكُم مِّنْهَا بِخَبَرٍ أَوْ ءَاتِيكُم بِشِهَابٍ قَبَسٍ لَّعَلَّكُمْ تَصْطَلُونَ ۝ فَلَمَّا جَآءَهَا نُودِىَ أَن بُورِكَ مَن فِى ٱلنَّارِ وَمَنْ حَوْلَهَا وَسُبْحَـٰنَ ٱللَّهِ رَبِّ ٱلْعَـٰلَمِينَ ۝ يَـٰمُوسَىٰٓ إِنَّهُۥٓ أَنَا ٱللَّهُ ٱلْعَزِيزُ ٱلْحَكِيمُ ۝ وَأَلْقِ عَصَاكَ ۚ فَلَمَّا رَءَاهَا تَهْتَزُّ كَأَنَّهَا جَآنٌّ وَلَّىٰ مُدْبِرًا وَلَمْ يُعَقِّبْ ۚ يَـٰمُوسَىٰ لَا تَخَفْ إِنِّى لَا يَخَافُ لَدَىَّ ٱلْمُرْسَلُونَ ۝ إِلَّا مَن ظَلَمَ ثُمَّ بَدَّلَ حُسْنًۢا بَعْدَ سُوٓءٍ فَإِنِّى غَفُورٌ رَّحِيمٌ ۝ وَأَدْخِلْ يَدَكَ فِى جَيْبِكَ تَخْرُجْ بَيْضَآءَ مِنْ غَيْرِ سُوٓءٍ ۖ فِى تِسْعِ ءَايَـٰتٍ إِلَىٰ فِرْعَوْنَ وَقَوْمِهِۦٓ ۚ إِنَّهُمْ كَانُواْ قَوْمًا فَـٰسِقِينَ ۝ فَلَمَّا جَآءَتْهُمْ ءَايَـٰتُنَا مُبْصِرَةً قَالُواْ هَـٰذَا سِحْرٌ مُّبِينٌ ۝ وَجَحَدُواْ بِهَا وَٱسْتَيْقَنَتْهَآ أَنفُسُهُمْ ظُلْمًا وَعُلُوًّا ۚ فَٱنظُرْ كَيْفَ كَانَ عَـٰقِبَةُ ٱلْمُفْسِدِينَ ۝ وَلَقَدْ ءَاتَيْنَا دَاوُۥدَ وَسُلَيْمَـٰنَ عِلْمًا ۖ وَقَالَا ٱلْحَمْدُ لِلَّهِ ٱلَّذِى فَضَّلَنَا عَلَىٰ كَثِيرٍ مِّنْ عِبَادِهِ ٱلْمُؤْمِنِينَ ۝ وَوَرِثَ سُلَيْمَـٰنُ دَاوُۥدَ ۖ وَقَالَ يَـٰٓأَيُّهَا ٱلنَّاسُ عُلِّمْنَا مَنطِقَ ٱلطَّيْرِ وَأُوتِينَا مِن كُلِّ شَىْءٍ ۖ إِنَّ هَـٰذَا لَهُوَ ٱلْفَضْلُ ٱلْمُبِينُ ۝ وَحُشِرَ لِسُلَيْمَـٰنَ جُنُودُهُۥ مِنَ ٱلْجِنِّ وَٱلْإِنسِ وَٱلطَّيْرِ فَهُمْ يُوزَعُونَ ۝

حَتَّىٰ إِذَآ أَتَوْا۟ عَلَىٰ وَادِ ٱلنَّمْلِ قَالَتْ نَمْلَةٌ يَـٰٓأَيُّهَا ٱلنَّمْلُ ٱدْخُلُوا۟ مَسَـٰكِنَكُمْ لَا يَحْطِمَنَّكُمْ سُلَيْمَـٰنُ وَجُنُودُهُۥ وَهُمْ لَا يَشْعُرُونَ ۝ فَتَبَسَّمَ ضَاحِكًۭا مِّن قَوْلِهَا وَقَالَ رَبِّ أَوْزِعْنِىٓ أَنْ أَشْكُرَ نِعْمَتَكَ ٱلَّتِىٓ أَنْعَمْتَ عَلَىَّ وَعَلَىٰ وَٰلِدَىَّ وَأَنْ أَعْمَلَ صَـٰلِحًۭا تَرْضَىٰهُ وَأَدْخِلْنِى بِرَحْمَتِكَ فِى عِبَادِكَ ٱلصَّـٰلِحِينَ ۝ وَتَفَقَّدَ ٱلطَّيْرَ فَقَالَ مَا لِىَ لَآ أَرَى ٱلْهُدْهُدَ أَمْ كَانَ مِنَ ٱلْغَآئِبِينَ ۝ لَأُعَذِّبَنَّهُۥ عَذَابًۭا شَدِيدًا أَوْ لَأَا۟ذْبَحَنَّهُۥٓ أَوْ لَيَأْتِيَنِّى بِسُلْطَـٰنٍ مُّبِينٍۢ ۝ فَمَكَثَ غَيْرَ بَعِيدٍۢ فَقَالَ أَحَطتُ بِمَا لَمْ تُحِطْ بِهِۦ وَجِئْتُكَ مِن سَبَإٍۭ بِنَبَإٍۢ يَقِينٍ ۝ إِنِّى وَجَدتُّ ٱمْرَأَةًۭ تَمْلِكُهُمْ وَأُوتِيَتْ مِن كُلِّ شَىْءٍۢ وَلَهَا عَرْشٌ عَظِيمٌۭ ۝ وَجَدتُّهَا وَقَوْمَهَا يَسْجُدُونَ لِلشَّمْسِ مِن دُونِ ٱللَّهِ وَزَيَّنَ لَهُمُ ٱلشَّيْطَـٰنُ أَعْمَـٰلَهُمْ فَصَدَّهُمْ عَنِ ٱلسَّبِيلِ فَهُمْ لَا يَهْتَدُونَ ۝ أَلَّا يَسْجُدُوا۟ لِلَّهِ ٱلَّذِى يُخْرِجُ ٱلْخَبْءَ فِى ٱلسَّمَـٰوَٰتِ وَٱلْأَرْضِ وَيَعْلَمُ مَا تُخْفُونَ وَمَا تُعْلِنُونَ ۝ ٱللَّهُ لَآ إِلَـٰهَ إِلَّا هُوَ رَبُّ ٱلْعَرْشِ ٱلْعَظِيمِ ۩ ۝ ۞ قَالَ سَنَنظُرُ أَصَدَقْتَ أَمْ كُنتَ مِنَ ٱلْكَـٰذِبِينَ ۝ ٱذْهَب بِّكِتَـٰبِى هَـٰذَا فَأَلْقِهْ إِلَيْهِمْ ثُمَّ تَوَلَّ عَنْهُمْ فَٱنظُرْ مَاذَا يَرْجِعُونَ ۝ قَالَتْ يَـٰٓأَيُّهَا ٱلْمَلَؤُا۟ إِنِّىٓ أُلْقِىَ إِلَىَّ كِتَـٰبٌۭ كَرِيمٌ ۝ إِنَّهُۥ مِن سُلَيْمَـٰنَ وَإِنَّهُۥ بِسْمِ ٱللَّهِ ٱلرَّحْمَـٰنِ ٱلرَّحِيمِ ۝ أَلَّا تَعْلُوا۟ عَلَىَّ وَأْتُونِى مُسْلِمِينَ ۝ قَالَتْ يَـٰٓأَيُّهَا ٱلْمَلَؤُا۟ أَفْتُونِى فِىٓ أَمْرِى مَا كُنتُ قَاطِعَةً أَمْرًا حَتَّىٰ تَشْهَدُونِ ۝ قَالُوا۟ نَحْنُ أُو۟لُوا۟ قُوَّةٍۢ وَأُو۟لُوا۟ بَأْسٍۢ شَدِيدٍۢ وَٱلْأَمْرُ إِلَيْكِ فَٱنظُرِى مَاذَا تَأْمُرِينَ ۝ قَالَتْ إِنَّ ٱلْمُلُوكَ إِذَا دَخَلُوا۟ قَرْيَةً أَفْسَدُوهَا وَجَعَلُوٓا۟ أَعِزَّةَ أَهْلِهَآ أَذِلَّةًۭ ۚ وَكَذَٰلِكَ يَفْعَلُونَ ۝ وَإِنِّى مُرْسِلَةٌ إِلَيْهِم بِهَدِيَّةٍۢ فَنَاظِرَةٌۢ بِمَ يَرْجِعُ ٱلْمُرْسَلُونَ ۝ فَلَمَّا جَآءَ سُلَيْمَـٰنَ قَالَ أَتُمِدُّونَنِ بِمَالٍۢ فَمَآ ءَاتَىٰنِۦَ ٱللَّهُ خَيْرٌۭ مِّمَّآ ءَاتَىٰكُم بَلْ أَنتُم بِهَدِيَّتِكُمْ تَفْرَحُونَ ۝ ٱرْجِعْ إِلَيْهِمْ فَلَنَأْتِيَنَّهُم بِجُنُودٍۢ لَّا قِبَلَ لَهُم بِهَا

وَلَنُخْرِجَنَّهُم مِّنْهَا أَذِلَّةً وَهُمْ صَـٰغِرُونَ ۝ قَالَ يَـٰٓأَيُّهَا ٱلْمَلَؤُاْ أَيُّكُمْ يَأْتِينِى بِعَرْشِهَا قَبْلَ أَن يَأْتُونِى مُسْلِمِينَ ۝ قَالَ عِفْرِيتٌ مِّنَ ٱلْجِنِّ أَنَا۠ ءَاتِيكَ بِهِۦ قَبْلَ أَن تَقُومَ مِن مَّقَامِكَ ۖ وَإِنِّى عَلَيْهِ لَقَوِىٌّ أَمِينٌ ۝ قَالَ ٱلَّذِى عِندَهُۥ عِلْمٌ مِّنَ ٱلْكِتَـٰبِ أَنَا۠ ءَاتِيكَ بِهِۦ قَبْلَ أَن يَرْتَدَّ إِلَيْكَ طَرْفُكَ ۚ فَلَمَّا رَءَاهُ مُسْتَقِرًّا عِندَهُۥ قَالَ هَـٰذَا مِن فَضْلِ رَبِّى لِيَبْلُوَنِىٓ ءَأَشْكُرُ أَمْ أَكْفُرُ ۖ وَمَن شَكَرَ فَإِنَّمَا يَشْكُرُ لِنَفْسِهِۦ ۖ وَمَن كَفَرَ فَإِنَّ رَبِّى غَنِىٌّ كَرِيمٌ ۝ قَالَ نَكِّرُواْ لَهَا عَرْشَهَا نَنظُرْ أَتَهْتَدِىٓ أَمْ تَكُونُ مِنَ ٱلَّذِينَ لَا يَهْتَدُونَ ۝ فَلَمَّا جَآءَتْ قِيلَ أَهَـٰكَذَا عَرْشُكِ ۖ قَالَتْ كَأَنَّهُۥ هُوَ ۚ وَأُوتِينَا ٱلْعِلْمَ مِن قَبْلِهَا وَكُنَّا مُسْلِمِينَ ۝ وَصَدَّهَا مَا كَانَت تَّعْبُدُ مِن دُونِ ٱللَّهِ ۖ إِنَّهَا كَانَتْ مِن قَوْمٍ كَـٰفِرِينَ ۝ قِيلَ لَهَا ٱدْخُلِى ٱلصَّرْحَ ۖ فَلَمَّا رَأَتْهُ حَسِبَتْهُ لُجَّةً وَكَشَفَتْ عَن سَاقَيْهَا ۚ قَالَ إِنَّهُۥ صَرْحٌ مُّمَرَّدٌ مِّن قَوَارِيرَ ۗ قَالَتْ رَبِّ إِنِّى ظَلَمْتُ نَفْسِى وَأَسْلَمْتُ مَعَ سُلَيْمَـٰنَ لِلَّهِ رَبِّ ٱلْعَـٰلَمِينَ ۝ وَلَقَدْ أَرْسَلْنَآ إِلَىٰ ثَمُودَ أَخَاهُمْ صَـٰلِحًا أَنِ ٱعْبُدُواْ ٱللَّهَ فَإِذَا هُمْ فَرِيقَانِ يَخْتَصِمُونَ ۝ قَالَ يَـٰقَوْمِ لِمَ تَسْتَعْجِلُونَ بِٱلسَّيِّئَةِ قَبْلَ ٱلْحَسَنَةِ ۖ لَوْلَا تَسْتَغْفِرُونَ ٱللَّهَ لَعَلَّكُمْ تُرْحَمُونَ ۝ قَالُواْ ٱطَّيَّرْنَا بِكَ وَبِمَن مَّعَكَ ۚ قَالَ طَـٰٓئِرُكُمْ عِندَ ٱللَّهِ ۖ بَلْ أَنتُمْ قَوْمٌ تُفْتَنُونَ ۝ وَكَانَ فِى ٱلْمَدِينَةِ تِسْعَةُ رَهْطٍ يُفْسِدُونَ فِى ٱلْأَرْضِ وَلَا يُصْلِحُونَ ۝ قَالُواْ تَقَاسَمُواْ بِٱللَّهِ لَنُبَيِّتَنَّهُۥ وَأَهْلَهُۥ ثُمَّ لَنَقُولَنَّ لِوَلِيِّهِۦ مَا شَهِدْنَا مَهْلِكَ أَهْلِهِۦ وَإِنَّا لَصَـٰدِقُونَ ۝ وَمَكَرُواْ مَكْرًا وَمَكَرْنَا مَكْرًا وَهُمْ لَا يَشْعُرُونَ ۝ فَٱنظُرْ كَيْفَ كَانَ عَـٰقِبَةُ مَكْرِهِمْ أَنَّا دَمَّرْنَـٰهُمْ وَقَوْمَهُمْ أَجْمَعِينَ ۝ فَتِلْكَ بُيُوتُهُمْ خَاوِيَةً بِمَا ظَلَمُوٓاْ ۗ إِنَّ فِى ذَٰلِكَ لَـَٔايَةً لِّقَوْمٍ يَعْلَمُونَ ۝ وَأَنجَيْنَا ٱلَّذِينَ ءَامَنُواْ وَكَانُواْ يَتَّقُونَ

﴿ وَلُوطًا إِذْ قَالَ لِقَوْمِهِ أَتَأْتُونَ ٱلْفَٰحِشَةَ وَأَنتُمْ تُبْصِرُونَ ﴾ ﴿ أَئِنَّكُمْ لَتَأْتُونَ ٱلرِّجَالَ شَهْوَةً مِّن دُونِ ٱلنِّسَآءِ ۚ بَلْ أَنتُمْ قَوْمٌ تَجْهَلُونَ ﴾

(An-Naml 001-055)

CHAPTER (SURAH) 25: AL-FURQAN (THE CRITERION, THE STANDARD), VERSES 021 – 077

Surah: 25 Ayah: 21, Ayah: 22, Ayah: 23 & Ayah: 24

﴿ وَقَالَ ٱلَّذِينَ لَا يَرْجُونَ لِقَآءَنَا لَوْلَآ أُنزِلَ عَلَيْنَا ٱلْمَلَٰٓئِكَةُ أَوْ نَرَىٰ رَبَّنَا ۗ لَقَدِ ٱسْتَكْبَرُوا۟ فِىٓ أَنفُسِهِمْ وَعَتَوْ عُتُوًّا كَبِيرًا ﴾

21. And those who expect not a Meeting with Us (i.e. those who deny the Day of Resurrection and the life of the Hereafter), said: "Why are not the angels sent down to us, or why do we not see our Lord?" Indeed they think too highly of themselves, and are scornful with great pride.

﴿ يَوْمَ يَرَوْنَ ٱلْمَلَٰٓئِكَةَ لَا بُشْرَىٰ يَوْمَئِذٍ لِّلْمُجْرِمِينَ وَيَقُولُونَ حِجْرًا مَّحْجُورًا ﴾

22. On the Day they will see the angels - no glad tidings will there be for the Mujrimûn (criminals, disbelievers, polytheists, sinners) that day. And they (angels) will say: "All kinds of glad tidings are forbidden for you," (None will be allowed to enter Paradise except the one who said: Lâ ilâha illallâh, "(none has the right to be worshipped but Allâh) and acted practically on its legal orders and obligations).

﴿ وَقَدِمْنَآ إِلَىٰ مَا عَمِلُوا۟ مِنْ عَمَلٍ فَجَعَلْنَٰهُ هَبَآءً مَّنثُورًا ﴾

23. And We shall turn to whatever deeds they (disbelievers, polytheists, sinners) did, and We shall make such deeds as scattered floating particles of dust.

﴿ أَصْحَٰبُ ٱلْجَنَّةِ يَوْمَئِذٍ خَيْرٌ مُّسْتَقَرًّا وَأَحْسَنُ مَقِيلًا ﴾

24. The dwellers of Paradise (i.e. those who deserved it through their Islamic

Transliteration

21. Waqala allatheena la yarjoona liqaana lawla onzila AAalayna almala-ikatu aw nara rabbana laqadi istakbaroo fee anfusihim waAAataw AAutuwwan kabeeran 22. Yawma yarawna almala-ikata la bushra yawma-ithin lilmujrimeena wayaqooloona hijran mahjooran 23. Waqadimna ila ma AAamiloo min AAamalin fajaAAalnahu habaan manthooran 24. As-habu aljannati yawma-ithin khayrun mustaqarran waahsanu maqeelan

Tafsir Ibn Kathir

The Stubbornness of the Disbelievers

Allah describes how stubborn the disbelievers were in their disbelief when they said:

(Why are not the angels sent down to us,) meaning, `so that we may see them with our own eyes and they may tell us that Muhammad is the Messenger of Allah.' This is like when they said:

(or you bring Allah and the angels before (us) face to face) (17:92). Hence they also said:

(or why do we not see our Lord) Allah said:

(Indeed they think too highly of themselves, and are scornful with great pride.) And Allah says:

(And even if We had sent down unto them angels, and the dead had spoken unto them...) (6:111)

(On the Day they will see the angels -- no good news will there be for the criminals that day. And they will say: "Hijran Mahjura.") means, when they do see the angels, it will not be a good day for them, for on that day there will be no good news for them. This is also confirmed at the time when they are dying, when the angels bring them the tidings of Hell and the wrath of the Compeller, and when the disbeliever's soul is being taken out, the angels say to it, "Come out, O evil soul from an evil body, come out to fierce hot wind and boiling water, and the shadow of black smoke." It refuses to come out and it scatters throughout his body, so they beat him, as Allah says:

(And if you could see when the angels take away the souls of those who disbelieve; they smite their faces and their backs...") (8:50)

(And if you could but see when the wrongdoers are in the agonies of death, while the angels are stretching forth their hands.) that is, to beat them:

((saying): "Deliver your souls! This day you shall be recompensed with the torment of degradation because of what you used to utter against Allah other than the truth. And you used to reject His Ayat with disrespect!") (6: 93) Hence in this Ayah Allah says:

(On the Day they will see the angels -- no good news will there be for the criminals) This is in contrast to the state of the believers when death approaches them, for they are given glad tidings of joy and delight. Allah says:

(Verily, those who say: "Our Lord is Allah," and then they stand firm, on them the angels will descend (saying): "Fear not, nor grieve! But receive the good news of Paradise which you have been promised! We have been your friends in the life of this world and are (so) in the Hereafter. Therein you shall have what your souls desire, and therein you shall have what you ask for. Entertainment from, the Oft-Forgiving, Most Merciful.") (41:30-32) According to an authentic Hadith narrated from Al-Bara' bin `Azib, the angels say to the believer's soul (at the time of death): "Come out, O

Chapter 25: Al-Furqan (The Criterion, The Standard), Verses 021-077

good soul in a good body, as you were dwelling in it. Come out to rest and pleasant fragrances and a Lord Who is not angry." Other scholars said that the Ayah:

(On the Day they will see the angels -- no good news) vrefers to the Day of Resurrection. This was the view of Mujahid, Ad-Dahhak and others. But there is no contradiction between these two views, because on both of these days -- the day of death and the Day of Resurrection -- the angels will appear to the believers and disbelievers, and they will give glad tidings of divine mercy and pleasure to the believers, while they will give the disbelievers news that will bring regret and sorrow, so there will be no glad tidings for the evildoers and criminals on that Day.

(And they (angels) will say: "Hijran Mahjura.") The angels will say to the disbelievers: `success is forbidden to you this day.' The basic meaning of Al-Hijr is preventing or prohibition, hence the word is used in the phrase "Hajara Al-Qadi `Ala Fulan" (or, "The judge prohibited so and so.") when he forbids him to dispose of his wealth in cases of bankruptcy, folly, being underage, etc. The name of Al-Hijr (the low semicircular wall near the Ka`bah) is also derived from this root, because it prevents people from Tawaf inside it, since they have to go behind it. The mind is also called Al-Hijr, because it prevents a person from indulging in things that do not befit him. In conclusion, the pronoun in the phrase.

(And they will say) refers to the angels. This was the view of Mujahid, `Ikrimah, Al-Hasan, Ad-Dahhak, Qatadah, `Atiyyah Al-`Awfi, `Ata' Al-Khurasani, Khusayf and others; it was also the view favored by Ibn Jarir. Ibn Jarir recorded that Ibn Jurayj said that this referred to the words of the idolators.

(On the Day they will see the angels) means, they will seek refuge from the angels. This is because when disaster and hardship struck, the Arabs would say:

("Hijran Mahjura.") Although there is a point to what Ibn Jurayj said, from the context it is unlikely that this is what was meant, and the majority of scholars said something different.

(And We shall turn to whatever deeds they did,) This refers to the Day of Resurrection, when Allah will bring mankind to account for their deeds, good and bad alike. Allah tells us that the deeds which these idolators thought would bring them salvation will be of no avail to them, because they were not in accordance with the Shari`ah or Laws of Allah, whether in terms of sincere intention or in terms of following the Laws set out by Allah. Every deed that is neither sincere nor in accordance with the Laws of Allah is futile, and the deeds of the disbelievers are either one or the other, or they may include both, in which case they are even less likely to be accepted. Allah says:

(And We shall turn to whatever deeds they did, and We shall make such deeds as scattered floating particles of dust.) Sufyan Ath-Thawri, narrated from Abu Ishaq, from Al-Harith that `Ali, may Allah be pleased with him, commented on Allah's saying:

(and We shall make such deeds as scattered floating particles of dust (Haba').) "The rays of the sun when they pass through a small aperture." A similar view was also narrated through a different chain of narrators from `Ali, and something similar was also narrated from Ibn `Abbas, Mujahid, `Ikrimah, Sa`id bin Jubayr, As-Suddi, Ad-Dahhak and others. Al-Hasan Al-Basri said, "This refers to the rays coming through a small window, and if anyone tries to grasp them, he cannot." Abu Al-Ahwas narrated from Abu Ishaq from Al-Harith that `Ali said: "Haba' refers to the dust raised by animals. " A similar view was also narrated from Ibn `Abbas and Ad-Dahhak, and this was also said by `Abdur-Rahman bin Zayd bin Aslam.

(scattered floating particles of dust (Haba').) Qatadah said: "Have you not seen dry trees when they are blown by the wind This refers to those leaves." It was narrated that Ya`la bin `Ubayd said: "Ashes or dust when it is stirred up by the wind." In conclusion, all of these views are pointing out that the deeds of the disbelievers will be like some worthless scattered thing, and will be of no avail to them whatsoever. As Allah says:

(The parable of those who disbelieved in their Lord is that their works are as ashes, on which the wind blows furiously) (14:18).

(O you who believe! Do not render in vain your charity by reminders of your generosity or by injury,) until His saying:

(They are not able to do anything with what they have earned) (2:264).

(As for those who disbelieved, their deeds are like a mirage in a desert. The thirsty one thinks it to be water, until he comes up to it, he finds it to be nothing) (24:39).

The Abode of the People of Paradise

Allah says:

(The dwellers of Paradise will, on that Day, have the best abode, and have the fairest of places for repose.) meaning, on the Day of Resurrection.

(Not equal are the dwellers of the Fire and the dwellers of the Paradise. It is the dwellers of Paradise that will be successful) (59:20). That is because the people of Paradise will ascend to lofty degrees and secure dwellings, so they will be in a place of safety, beauty and goodness,

(Abiding therein -- excellent it is as an abode, and as a place to rest in.) (25:76) The people of Hell will go down to the lowest levels and continual regret, with all kinds of punishments and torments.

(Evil indeed it (Hell) is as an abode and as a place to rest in.)(25:66) means, how evil a dwelling place to look at, and how evil an abode in which to stay. Allah says:

(The dwellers of Paradise will, on that Day, have the best abode, and have the fairest of places for repose.) meaning, in return for what they have done of acceptable deeds, they will attain what they will attain and reach the status they will reach, in contrast to the people of Hell, who will not have even one deed to their credit that would qualify them to enter Paradise and be saved from the Fire. Allah points out the situation of the blessed in contrast to that of the doomed, who will not enjoy any goodness at all. Sa`id bin Jubayr said: "Allah will finish the Judgement halfway through the Day, and the people of Paradise will take their mid day rest in Paradise and the people of Hell in Hell. Allah says:

(The dwellers of Paradise will, on that Day, have the best abode, and have the fairest of places for repose.) `Ikrimah said, "I know the time when the people of Paradise will enter Paradise and the people of Hell will enter Hell. It is the time which in this world is the time when the late forenoon starts and people go back to their families to take a siesta. The people of Hell will go to Hell, but the people of Paradise will be taken to Paradise and will have their siesta in Paradise, and they will be fed the liver of a whale and they will all eat their fill. This is what Allah says:

(The dwellers of Paradise will, on that Day, have the best abode, and have the fairest of places for repose.)

Surah: 25 Ayah: 25, Ayah: 26, Ayah: 27, Ayah: 28 & Ayah: 29

وَيَوْمَ تَشَقَّقُ ٱلسَّمَآءُ بِٱلْغَمَٰمِ وَنُزِّلَ ٱلْمَلَٰٓئِكَةُ تَنزِيلًا ﴿٢٥﴾

25. And (remember) the Day when the heaven shall be rent asunder with clouds, and the angels will be sent down, with a grand descending.

ٱلْمُلْكُ يَوْمَئِذٍ ٱلْحَقُّ لِلرَّحْمَٰنِ ۚ وَكَانَ يَوْمًا عَلَى ٱلْكَٰفِرِينَ عَسِيرًا ﴿٢٦﴾

26. The sovereignty on that Day will be the true (sovereignty), belonging to the Most Gracious (Allâh), and it will be a hard Day for the disbelievers (those who disbelieve in the Oneness of Allâh - Islâmic Monotheism).

وَيَوْمَ يَعَضُّ ٱلظَّالِمُ عَلَىٰ يَدَيْهِ يَقُولُ يَٰلَيْتَنِى ٱتَّخَذْتُ مَعَ ٱلرَّسُولِ سَبِيلًا ﴿٢٧﴾

27. And (remember) the Day when the Zâlim (wrong-doer, oppressor, polytheist) will bite at his hands, he will say: "Oh! Would that I had taken a path with the Messenger (Muhammad (peace be upon him))

يَٰوَيْلَتَىٰ لَيْتَنِى لَمْ أَتَّخِذْ فُلَانًا خَلِيلًا ﴿٢٨﴾

28. "Ah! Woe to me! Would that I had never taken so-and-so as a Khalîl (an intimate friend)!

لَّقَدْ أَضَلَّنِى عَنِ ٱلذِّكْرِ بَعْدَ إِذْ جَآءَنِى ۗ وَكَانَ ٱلشَّيْطَٰنُ لِلْإِنسَٰنِ خَذُولًا ﴿٢٩﴾

29. "He indeed led me astray from the Reminder (this Qur'ân) after it had come to me. And Shaitân (Satan) is to man ever deserter in the hour of need."

Transliteration

25. Wayawma tashaqqaqu alssamao bialghamami wanuzzila almala-ikatu tanzeelan 26. Almulku yawma-ithin alhaqqu lilrrahmani wakana yawman AAala alkafireena AAaseeran 27. Wayawma yaAAaddu aththalimu AAala yadayhi yaqoolu ya laytanee ittakhathtu maAAa alrrasooli sabeelan 28. Ya waylata laytanee lam attakhith fulanan khaleelan 29. Laqad adallanee AAani aththikri baAAda ith jaanee wakana alshshaytanu lil-insani khathoolan

Tafsir Ibn Kathir

The Terrors of the Day of Resurrection, and how the Wrongdoers will wish that They had taken a Path with the Messenger

Here Allah tells us about the terror of the Day of Resurrection and the tremendous events that will happen, including the splitting of heavens when they are pierced by the clouds, that is the shadow of the magnificent light which dazzles all sight. The angels of heaven will come down on that Day and surround all creatures at the place of gathering, then the Lord, may He be blessed and exalted, will come to pass judgement. Mujahid said, "This is as Allah says:

(Do they then wait for anything other than that Allah should come to them in the shadows of the clouds and the angels)" (2:210)

(The sovereignty on that Day will be the true (sovereignty) of the Most Gracious,) This is like the Ayah,

(Whose is the kingdom this Day: It is Allah's, the One, the Irresistable!) (40:16) In the Sahih it says:

«أَنَّ اللهَ تَعَالَى يَطْوِي السَّمَوَاتِ بِيَمِينِهِ، وَيَأْخُذُ الْأَرَضِينَ بِيَدِهِ الْأُخْرَى، ثُمَّ يَقُولُ: أَنَا الْمَلِكُ أَنَا الدَّيَّانُ، أَيْنَ مُلُوكُ الْأَرْضِ؟ أَيْنَ الْجَبَّارُونَ؟ أَيْنَ الْمُتَكَبِّرُونَ؟»

(Allah, may He be exalted, will fold up the heavens in His Right Hand, and will take the earths in His other Hand, then He will say: "I am the Sovereign, I am the Judge. Where are the kings of the earth Where are the tyrants Where are the arrogants")

(and it will be a hard Day for the disbelievers.) means it will be very difficult, because it will be the Day of justice and the decisive judgement, as Allah says:

(Truly, that Day will be a hard Day -- Far from easy for the disbelievers) (74:9-10). This is how the disbelievers will be on the Day of Resurrection. As for the believers, Allah says:

(The greatest terror will not grieve them.)

(And (remember) the Day when the wrongdoer will bite at his hands, he will say: "O! Would that I had taken a path with the Messenger.") Here Allah tells us of the regret felt by the wrongdoer who rejected the path of the Messenger and what he brought from Allah of clear truth concerning which there is no doubt, and followed another path. When the Day of Resurrection comes, he will feel regret but his regret will avail him nothing, and he will bite on his hands in sorrow and grief. Whether this Ayah was revealed concerning `Uqbah bin Abi Mu`it or someone else among the doomed, it applies to every wrongdoer, as Allah says:

(On the Day when their faces will be turned over in the Fire) as mentioned in those two Ayat (33:66) Every wrongdoer will feel the ultimate regret on the Day of Resurrection, and will bite at his hands, saying:

(O! Would that I had taken a path with the Messenger. Ah! Woe to me! Would that I had never taken so-and-so as an intimate friend!) meaning, the one among the propagators of misguidance who diverted him from true guidance and led him to follow the path of misguidance, whether this refers to Umayyah bin Khalaf or his brother Ubayy bin Khalaf, or to someone else.

(He indeed led me astray from the Reminder) means the Qur'an,

(after it had come to me.) means, after it had reached me. Allah says:

(And Shaytan is to man ever a deserter (in the hour of need).) meaning, he leads him away from the truth and diverts him from it, and uses him for the purposes of falsehood and calls him to it.

Surah: 25 Ayah: 30 & Ayah: 31

وَقَالَ ٱلرَّسُولُ يَـٰرَبِّ إِنَّ قَوْمِى ٱتَّخَذُواْ هَـٰذَا ٱلْقُرْءَانَ مَهْجُورًا ﴿٣٠﴾

30. And the Messenger (Muhammad (peace be upon him)) will say: "O my Lord! Verily, my people deserted this Qur'ân (neither listened to it, nor acted on its laws and teachings).

وَكَذَٰلِكَ جَعَلْنَا لِكُلِّ نَبِىٍّ عَدُوًّا مِّنَ ٱلْمُجْرِمِينَ ۗ وَكَفَىٰ بِرَبِّكَ هَادِيًا وَنَصِيرًا ﴿٣١﴾

31. Thus have We made for every Prophet an enemy among the Mujrimûn (disbelievers, polytheists, criminals). But Sufficient is your Lord as a Guide and Helper.

Transliteration

30. Waqala alrrasoolu ya rabbi inna qawmee ittakhathoo hatha alqur-ana mahjooran
31. Wakathalika jaAAalna likulli nabiyyin AAaduwwan mina almujrimeena wakafa birabbika hadiyan wanaseeran

Tafsir Ibn Kathir

The Messenger will complain against His Opponents

Allah tells how His Messenger and Prophet Muhammad will say: "O my Lord! Verily, my people deserted this Qur'an." The idolators would not listen to the Qur'an, as Allah says:

(And those who disbelieve say: "Listen not to this Qur'an, and make noise in the midst of it.") (41:26). When he would recite Qur'an to them, they would talk nonsense or speak about something else, so that they would not hear it. This is a form of forsaking it and rejecting it, and not believing in it is the same as forsaking it, and not pondering its meanings and trying to understand it is the same as forsaking it, and not acting upon it and following its commandments and heeding its prohibitions is the same as forsaking it, and turning away from it in favor of poetry or other words or songs or idle talk or some other way is the same as forsaking it. We ask Allah, the Most Generous, the Bestower of bounty, the One Who is able to do what He wills, to keep us safe from doing that which earns His wrath and to use us to do that which will earn His pleasure of preserving and understanding His Book, following its commandments night and day in the manner which He loves and which pleases Him, for He is Generous and Kind.

(Thus have We made for every Prophet an enemy among the criminals.) means, `just as there is for you, O Muhammad, those people who scorned the Qur'an, so in all the previous nations did Allah make for every Prophet an enemy among the criminals, who called people to their misguidance and disbelief,' as Allah says:

(And so We have appointed for every Prophet enemies -- Shayatin among mankind and Jinn) as stated in these two Ayat. (6:112) Allah says here:

(But sufficient is your Lord as a Guide and Helper.) meaning, for the one who follows His Messenger and believes in His Book, Allah will be his Guide and Helper in this world and the Hereafter. Allah says

(a Guide and Helper.) because the idolators used to try to prevent people from following the Qur'an lest anyone be guided by it. They wanted their way to prevail over the way of the Qur'an. Allah says:

(Thus have We made for every Prophet an enemy among the criminals.)

Surah: 25 Ayah: 32, Ayah: 33 & Ayah: 34

وَقَالَ ٱلَّذِينَ كَفَرُواْ لَوْلَا نُزِّلَ عَلَيْهِ ٱلْقُرْءَانُ جُمْلَةً وَٰحِدَةً ۚ كَذَٰلِكَ لِنُثَبِّتَ بِهِۦ فُؤَادَكَ ۖ وَرَتَّلْنَٰهُ تَرْتِيلًا ۝

32. And those who disbelieve say: "Why is not the Qur'ân revealed to him all at once?" Thus (it is sent down in parts), that We may strengthen your heart thereby. And We have revealed it to you gradually, in stages. (It was revealed to the Prophet (peace be upon him) in 23 years.).

$$\text{وَلَا يَأْتُونَكَ بِمَثَلٍ إِلَّا جِئْنَاكَ بِالْحَقِّ وَأَحْسَنَ تَفْسِيرًا ۝}$$

33. And no example or similitude do they bring (to oppose or to find fault in you or in this Qur'ân), but We reveal to you the truth (against that similitude or example), and the better explanation thereof.

$$\text{ٱلَّذِينَ يُحْشَرُونَ عَلَىٰ وُجُوهِهِمْ إِلَىٰ جَهَنَّمَ أُو۟لَٰٓئِكَ شَرٌّ مَّكَانًا وَأَضَلُّ سَبِيلًا ۝}$$

34. Those who will be gathered to Hell (prone) on their faces, such will be in an evil state, and most astray from the (Straight) Path.

Transliteration

32. Waqala allatheena kafaroo lawla nuzzila AAalayhi alqur-anu jumlatan wahidatan kathalika linuthabbita bihi fu-adaka warattalnahu tarteelan 33. Wala ya/toonaka bimathalin illa ji/naka bialhaqqi waahsana tafseeran 34. Allatheena yuhsharoona AAala wujoohihim ila jahannama ola-ika sharrun makanan waadallu sabeelan

Tafsir Ibn Kathir

The Reason why the Qur'an was revealed in Stages, the Refutation of the Disbelievers, and their Evil End

Allah tells us about the many objections raised by the disbelievers, their stubbornness, and how they spoke of things which were none of their concern. They said:

("Why is not the Qur'an revealed to him all at once") meaning, why was this Qur'an, which was revealed to him, not sent down all at one time, as the previous Books, the Tawrah, Injil, Zabur and other Divine Books Allah answered them, telling them that it was revealed in stages over twenty-three years, according to events and circumstances, and whatever rulings were needed, in order to strengthen the hearts of the believers, as He says:

(And (it is) a Qur'an which We have divided (into parts)...) (17:106). Allah says:

(that We may strengthen your heart thereby. And We have revealed it to you gradually, in stages.) Qatadah said it means: "We have explained it." `Abdur-Rahman bin Zayd bin Aslam said it means: "We have given its interpretation."

(And no example or similitude do they bring,) This means no arguments or doubts,

(but We reveal to you the truth, and the better explanation thereof.) They do not say anything in an attempt to oppose the truth, but We respond to them with the truth of that same matter, more clearly and more eloquently than anything they say. Abu `Abdur-Rahman An-Nasa'i recorded that Ibn `Abbas said, "The Qur'an was sent down all at once to the first heaven on Laylatul-Qadr (the Night of Power), then it was revealed over twenty years." Allah says:

(And no example or similitude do they bring, but We reveal to you the truth, and the better explanation thereof.) and:

(And (it is) a Qur'an which We have divided (into parts), in order that you might recite it to men at intervals. And We have revealed it by stages) (17:106). Then Allah tells us about the terrible state of the disbelievers when they are raised on the Day of Resurrection and gathered into Hell:

(Those who will be gathered to Hell on their faces, such will be in an evil state, and most astray from the path.) In the Sahih, it is reported from Anas that a man said, "O Messenger of Allah, how will the disbeliever be gathered on his face on the Day of Resurrection" The Prophet said:

«إِنَّ الَّذِي أَمْشَاهُ عَلَى رِجْلَيْهِ قَادِرٌ أَنْ يُمْشِيَهُ عَلَى وَجْهِهِ يَوْمَ الْقِيَامَةِ»

(The One Who caused him to walk on his two feet is able to make him walk on his face on the Day of Resurrection.)

Surah: 25 Ayah: 35, Ayah: 36, Ayah: 37, Ayah: 38, Ayah: 39 & Ayah: 40

وَلَقَدْ ءَاتَيْنَا مُوسَى ٱلْكِتَبَ وَجَعَلْنَا مَعَهُ أَخَاهُ هَٰرُونَ وَزِيرًا ۝

35. And indeed We gave Mûsâ (Moses) the Scripture (the Taurât (Torah)) and placed his brother Hârûn (Aaron) with him as a helper;

فَقُلْنَا ٱذْهَبَا إِلَى ٱلْقَوْمِ ٱلَّذِينَ كَذَّبُوا۟ بِـَٔايَٰتِنَا فَدَمَّرْنَٰهُمْ تَدْمِيرًا ۝

36. And We said: "Go you both to the people who have denied Our Ayât (proofs, evidences, verses, lessons, signs, revelations, etc.)." Then We destroyed them with utter destruction.

وَقَوْمَ نُوحٍ لَّمَّا كَذَّبُوا۟ ٱلرُّسُلَ أَغْرَقْنَٰهُمْ وَجَعَلْنَٰهُمْ لِلنَّاسِ ءَايَةً ۖ وَأَعْتَدْنَا لِلظَّٰلِمِينَ عَذَابًا أَلِيمًا ۝

37. And Nûh's (Noah) people, when they denied the Messengers, We drowned them, and We made them as a sign for mankind. And We have prepared a painful torment for the Zâlimûn (polytheists and wrong-doers).

وَعَادًا وَثَمُودَا۟ وَأَصْحَٰبَ ٱلرَّسِّ وَقُرُونًۢا بَيْنَ ذَٰلِكَ كَثِيرًا ۝

38. And (also) 'Ad and Thamûd, and the dwellers of Ar-Rass, and many generations in between.

وَكُلًّا ضَرَبْنَا لَهُ ٱلْأَمْثَٰلَ وَكُلًّا تَبَّرْنَا تَتْبِيرًا ۝

39. And for each (of them) We put forward examples (as proofs and lessons), and each (of them) We brought to utter ruin (because of their disbelief and evil deeds).

وَلَقَدْ أَتَوْا۟ عَلَى ٱلْقَرْيَةِ ٱلَّتِىٓ أُمْطِرَتْ مَطَرَ ٱلسَّوْءِ ۚ أَفَلَمْ يَكُونُوا۟ يَرَوْنَهَا ۚ بَلْ كَانُوا۟ لَا يَرْجُونَ نُشُورًا ۝

40. And indeed they have passed by the town (of Prophet Lût (Lot)) on which was rained the evil rain. Did they (disbelievers) not then see it (with their own eyes)? Nay ! But they used not to expect for any resurrection.

Transliteration

35. Walaqad atayna moosa alkitaba wajaAAalna maAAahu akhahu haroona wazeeran 36. Faqulna ithhaba ila alqawmi allatheena kaththaboo bi-ayatina fadammarnahum tadmeeran 37. Waqawma noohin lamma kaththaboo alrrusula aghraqnahum wajaAAalnahum lilnnasi ayatan waaAAtadna lilththalimeena AAathaban aleeman 38. WaAAadan wathamooda waas-haba alrrassi waquroonan bayna thalika katheeran 39. Wakullan darabna lahu al-amthala wakullan tabbarna tatbeeran 40. Walaqad ataw AAala alqaryati allatee omtirat matara alssaw-i afalam yakoonoo yarawnaha bal kanoo la yarjoona nushooran

Tafsir Ibn Kathir

Frightening the Idolators of Quraysh

Allah threatens the idolators who denied and opposed His Messenger Muhammad and He warns them of the punishment and painful torment He sent upon the previous nations who rejected their Messengers. Allah begins by mentioning Musa, upon him be peace, whom He sent along with his brother Harun as a helper -- i.e., as another Prophet who helped and supported him -- but Fir`awn and his chiefs denied them both:

(Allah destroyed them completely, and similar (awaits) the disbelievers) (47:10). And when the people of Nuh denied him, Allah destroyed them likewise, for whoever denies one Messenger denies all the Messengers, because there is no difference between one Messenger and another. If it had so happened that Allah had sent all His Messengers to them, they would have denied them all. Allah says:

(And Nuh's people, when they denied the Messengers,) although Allah sent only Nuh to them, and he stayed among them for 950 years, calling them to Allah and warning them of His punishment,

(And none believed with him, except a few) (11:40). For this reason Allah drowned them all and left no one among the sons of Adam alive on earth apart from those who boarded the boat,

(and We made them a sign for mankind.) meaning a lesson to be learned. This is like the Ayah,

(Verily, when the water rose beyond its limits, We carried you in the boat. That We might make it a remembrance for you, and the keen ear may understand it) (69:11-12), which means: `We left for you ships that you ride upon to travel across the depths of the seas, so that you may remember the blessing of Allah towards you when He saved you from drowning, and made you the descendants of those who believed in Allah and followed His commandments.'

(And (also) `Ad and Thamud, and the Dwellers of Ar-Rass,) We have already discussed their story, which is referred to in more than one Surah, such as Surat Al-A`raf, and there is no need to repeat it here. As for the Dwellers of Ar-Rass, Ibn Jurayj narrated from Ibn `Abbas about the Dwellers of Ar-Rass that they were the people of one of the villages of Thamud. Ath-Thawri narrated from Abu Bukayr from `Ikrimah that Ar-Rass was a well where they buried (Rassu) their Prophet.

(and many generations in between.) means nations, many more than have been mentioned here, whom We destroyed. Allah said:

(And for each We put forward examples,) meaning, `We showed them the proof and gave them clear evidence,' as Qatadah said, "They had no excuse."

(and each (of them) We brought to utter ruin.) means, `We destroyed them completely.' This is like the Ayah,

(And how many generations (Qurun) have We destroyed after Nuh!) (17:17). "Generations" (Qurun) here refers to nations among mankind. This is like the Ayah,

(Then, after them, We created other generations (Qurun).) (23:42) Some defined a generation as being 120 years, or it was said that a generation was one hundred years, or eighty, or forty, etc. The most correct view is that a generation refers to nations who are one another's contemporaries, living at the same time. When they go and others succeed them, this is another generation, as it was recorded in the Two Sahihs:

«خَيْرُ الْقُرُونِ قَرْنِي، ثُمَّ الَّذِينَ يَلُونَهُمْ، ثُمَّ الَّذِينَ يَلُونَهُمْ»

(The best of generations is my generation, then the one that follows it, then the one that follows that.)

(And indeed they have passed by the town on which was rained the evil rain.) refers to the town of the people of Lut, which was called Sodom, and the way in which Allah dealt with it, when He destroyed it by turning it upside down and by sending upon it the rain of stones of baked clay, as Allah says:

(And We rained on them a rain. And how evil was the rain of those who had been warned!) (26:176),

(Verily, you pass by them in the morning. And at night; will you not then reflect) (37:137-138),

(And verily, they were right on the highroad.) (15:76),

(They are both on an open highway, plain to see) (15:79). Allah says:

(Did they not then see it) meaning, so that they might learn a lesson from what happened to its inhabitants of punishment for denying the Messenger and going against the commands of Allah.

(Nay! But they used not to expect any resurrection.) means, the disbelievers who passed by it did not learn any lesson, because they did not expect any resurrection, i.e., on the Day of Judgement.

Surah: 25 Ayah: 41, Ayah: 42, Ayah: 43 & Ayah: 44

وَإِذَا رَأَوْكَ إِن يَتَّخِذُونَكَ إِلَّا هُزُوًا أَهَٰذَا ٱلَّذِى بَعَثَ ٱللَّهُ رَسُولًا ﴿٤١﴾

41. And when they see you (O Muhammad (peace be upon him)) they treat you only in mockery (saying): "Is this the one whom Allâh has sent as a Messenger?

إِن كَادَ لَيُضِلُّنَا عَنْ ءَالِهَتِنَا لَوْلَآ أَن صَبَرْنَا عَلَيْهَا ۚ وَسَوْفَ يَعْلَمُونَ حِينَ يَرَوْنَ ٱلْعَذَابَ مَنْ أَضَلُّ سَبِيلًا ﴿٤٢﴾

42. "He would have nearly misled us from our âliha (gods), had it not been that we were patient and constant in their worship!" And they will know when they see the torment, who it is that is most astray from the (Right) Path!

أَرَءَيْتَ مَنِ ٱتَّخَذَ إِلَٰهَهُ هَوَىٰهُ أَفَأَنتَ تَكُونُ عَلَيْهِ وَكِيلًا ﴿٤٣﴾

43. Have you (O Muhammad (peace be upon him)) seen him who has taken as his ilâh (god) his own desire? Would you then be a Wakîl (a disposer of his affairs or a watcher) over him?

أَمْ تَحْسَبُ أَنَّ أَكْثَرَهُمْ يَسْمَعُونَ أَوْ يَعْقِلُونَ ۚ إِنْ هُمْ إِلَّا كَٱلْأَنْعَٰمِ ۖ بَلْ هُمْ أَضَلُّ سَبِيلًا ﴿٤٤﴾

44. Or do you think that most of them hear or understand? They are only like cattle- nay, they are even farther astray from the Path. (i.e. even worst than cattle).

Transliteration

41. Wa-itha raawka in yattakhithoonaka illa huzuwan ahatha allathee baAAatha Allahu rasoolan 42. In kada layudilluna AAan alihatina lawla an sabarna AAalayha wasawfa yaAAlamoona heena yarawna alAAathaba man adallu sabeelan 43. Araayta mani ittakhatha ilahahu hawahu afaanta takoonu AAalayhi wakeelan 44. Am tahsabu anna aktharahum yasmaAAoona aw yaAAqiloona in hum illa kaal-anAAami bal hum adallu sabeelan

Tafsir Ibn Kathir

How the Disbelievers mocked the Messenger

Allah tells us how the disbelievers mocked the Messenger when they saw him. This is like the Ayah,

(And when the disbelievers see you, they take you not except for mockery) (21:36), which means that they tried to find faults and shortcomings in him. Here Allah says:

(And when they see you, they treat you only in mockery (saying): "Is this the one whom Allah has sent as a Messenger") i.e., they said this by way of belittling and trying to undermine him, so Allah put them in their place, and said:

(And indeed Messengers before you were mocked at) (6:10)

(He would have nearly misled us from our gods,) They meant: `he nearly turned us away from worshipping idols, and he would have done so, had we not been patient and persevered in our ways.' So Allah said, warning and threatening them:

(And they will know, when they see the torment...)

They took Their Desires as their gods and were more astray than Cattle

Then Allah tells His Prophet that if Allah decrees that someone will be misguided and wretched, then no one can guide him except Allah, glory be to Him:

(Have you seen him who has taken as his god his own vain desire) meaning, whatever he admires and sees as good in his own desires becomes his religion and his way. As Allah says:

(Is he then, to whom the evil of his deeds is made fair seeming. So that he consider it as good. Verily, Allah sends astray whom he wills.) (35:8)

(Would you then be a guardian over him) Ibn `Abbas said: "During the Jahiliyyah, a man would worship a white rock for a while, then if he saw another that looked better, he would worship that and leave the first." Then Allah said:

(Or do you think that most of them hear or understand) meaning, they are worse than grazing cattle. Cattle only do what they were created to do, but these people were created to worship Allah Alone without associating partners with Him, but they worship others with Him, even though evidence has been established against them and Messengers have been sent to them.

Surah: 25 Ayah: 45, Ayah: 46 & Ayah: 47

أَلَمْ تَرَ إِلَىٰ رَبِّكَ كَيْفَ مَدَّ ٱلظِّلَّ وَلَوْ شَآءَ لَجَعَلَهُۥ سَاكِنًا ثُمَّ جَعَلْنَا ٱلشَّمْسَ عَلَيْهِ دَلِيلًا ۝

45. Have you not seen how your Lord spread the shadow. If He willed, He could have made it still - but We have made the sun its guide (i.e. after the sunrise, the shadow shrinks and vanishes at midnoon and then again appears in the afternoon with the decline of the sun, and had there been no sun light, there would have been no shadow).

$$ثُمَّ قَبَضْنَٰهُ إِلَيْنَا قَبْضًا يَسِيرًا ۝$$

46. Then We withdraw it to Us a gradual concealed withdrawal.

$$وَهُوَ ٱلَّذِى جَعَلَ لَكُمُ ٱلَّيْلَ لِبَاسًا وَٱلنَّوْمَ سُبَاتًا وَجَعَلَ ٱلنَّهَارَ نُشُورًا ۝$$

47. And it is He Who makes the night a covering for you, and the sleep (as) a repose, and makes the day Nushûr (i.e. getting up and going about here and there for daily work, etc. after one's sleep at night, or like resurrection after one's death).

Transliteration

45. Alam tara ila rabbika kayfa madda alththilla walaw shaa lajaAAalahu sakinan thumma jaAAalna alshshamsa AAalayhi daleelan   46. Thumma qabadnahu ilayna qabdan yaseeran   47. Wahuwa allathee jaAAala lakumu allayla libasan waalnnawma subatan wajaAAala alnnahara nushooran

Tafsir Ibn Kathir

Evidence of the existence of the Creator and the extent of His Power

Here Allah begins explaining the evidence for His existence and His perfect power to create various things and pairs of opposites. Allah says:

(Have you not seen how your Lord spread the shadow.) Ibn `Abbas, Ibn `Umar, Abu Al-`Aliyah, Abu Malik, Masruq, Mujahid, Sa`id bin Jubayr, An-Nakha`i, Ad-Dahhak, Al-Hasan, Qatadah, As-Suddi and others said, "This refers to the period from the beginning of the dawn until the sun rises."

(If He willed, He could have made it still) meaning, immobile, never changing. This is like the Ayat:

(Say : "Tell me! If Allah made the night continuous for you...") (28:71)

(but We have made the sun its guide.) means, were it not for the sun rising, it would not be there, for a thing can only be known in contrast to its opposite. Qatadah and As-Suddi said, "The sun is a guide which follows the shade until the shade disappears."

(Then We withdraw it towards Ourselves -- a gradual withdrawal.) This refers to the shade.

(gradual) meaning slowly. As-Suddi said: "A gentle, concealed, withdrawal until there is no shade left on earth except under a roof or a tree, and the sun is shining on whatever is above it."

(a gradual withdrawal.) Ayyub bin Musa said: "Little by little.

(And it is He Who makes the night a covering for you,) It covers and conceals all things. This is like the Ayah:

(By the night as it envelops) (92:1).

(and the sleep a repose,) means, a halt to movement so that bodies may rest. For the faculties and limbs get tired from their constant movement during the day when one goes out to earn a living. When night comes, and it becomes quiet, they stop moving, and rest; so sleep provides a rejuvenation for both the body and the soul.

(and makes the day Nushur) meaning, people get up and go out to earn a living and attend to their business. This is like the Ayah:

(It is out of His mercy that He has made for you the night and the day that you may rest therein and that you may seek of His bounty...) (28:73)

Surah: 25 Ayah: 48, Ayah: 48 & Ayah: 50

وَهُوَ ٱلَّذِىٓ أَرْسَلَ ٱلرِّيَـٰحَ بُشْرًۢا بَيْنَ يَدَىْ رَحْمَتِهِۦ ۚ وَأَنزَلْنَا مِنَ ٱلسَّمَآءِ مَآءً طَهُورًا ۝

48. And it is He Who sends the winds as heralds of glad tidings, going before His Mercy (rain) and We send down pure water from the sky.

لِّنُحْـِۧىَ بِهِۦ بَلْدَةً مَّيْتًا وَنُسْقِيَهُۥ مِمَّا خَلَقْنَآ أَنْعَـٰمًا وَأَنَاسِىَّ كَثِيرًا ۝

49. That We may give life thereby to a dead land, and We give to drink thereof many of the cattle and men that We had created.

وَلَقَدْ صَرَّفْنَـٰهُ بَيْنَهُمْ لِيَذَّكَّرُوا۟ فَأَبَىٰٓ أَكْثَرُ ٱلنَّاسِ إِلَّا كُفُورًا ۝

50. And indeed We have distributed it (rain or water) amongst them in order that they may remember (the Grace of Allâh,) but most men (refuse to accept the Truth or Faith and) accept nothing but disbelief or ingratitude.

Transliteration

48. Wahuwa allathee arsala alrriyaha bushran bayna yaday rahmatihi waanzalna mina alssama-i maan tahooran 49. Linuhyiya bihi baldatan maytan wanusqiyahu mimma khalaqna anAAaman waanasiyya katheeran 50. Walaqad sarrafnahu baynahum liyaththakkaroo faaba aktharu alnnasi illa kufooran

Tafsir Ibn Kathir

This is also part of His complete power and supreme authority:

Allah sends the winds as heralds of glad tidings, i.e., they bring the clouds behind them. The winds are of many different types, depending on the purpose for which they are sent. Some of them form the clouds, others carry the clouds or drive them, and others come ahead of the clouds as heralds announcing their coming. Some of them come before that to stir up the earth, and some of them fertilize or "seed" the clouds to make it rain. Allah says:

(and We send down pure water from the sky), meaning, as a means of purifying it. Abu Sa`id said, "It was said: "O Messenger of Allah, can we perform Wudu' with the water of the well of Buda`ah For it is a well in which rubbish and the flesh of dogs are thrown. He said:

»إِنَّ الْمَاءَ طَهُورٌ لَا يُنَجِّسُهُ شَيْءٌ«

(Water is pure and nothing makes it impure.) This was recorded by Ash-Shafi`i and Ahmad, who graded it Sahih, and also by Abu Dawud and At-Tirmidhi, who graded it Hasan, and by An-Nasa'i. His saying:

(That We may give life thereby to a dead land,) means, a land that waited a long time for rain. It is devoid of vegetation or anything at all. When the rain comes to it, it becomes alive and its hills are covered with all kinds of colorful flowers, as Allah says:

(but when We send down water to it, it is stirred to life and growth...) (41:39). His saying:

(and We give to drink thereof many of the cattle and men that We had created.) means, so that animals such as cattle can drink from it, and people who are in desperate need of water can drink from it and water their crops and fruits. This is like the Ayah:

(And He it is Who sends down the rain after they have despaired,) (42:28)

(Look then at the effects of Allah's mercy, how He revives the earth after its death.) (30:50) His saying:

(And indeed We have distributed it among them in order that they may remember) means, `We cause rain to fall on this land and not on that, and We cause the clouds to pass over one land and go to another, where We cause sufficient rain to fall so that its people have plenty, but not one drop falls on the first land.' There is a reason and great wisdom behind this. Ibn `Abbas and Ibn Mas`ud, may Allah be pleased with them said: "One year does not have more rain than another, but Allah distributes the rain as He wills. Then he recited this Ayah:

(And indeed We have distributed it (rain or water) amongst them in order that they may remember the grace of Allah, but most men refuse (out of) ingratitude.)"

meaning, so that they may be reminded, when Allah brings the dead earth back to life, that He is able to bring the dead and dry bones back to life, or that those from whom rain is withheld are suffering this because of some sin they have committed, so that they may give it up.

(but most men refuse (out of) ingratitude.) `Ikrimah said, "This refers to those who say that rain comes because of such and such a star." This view of `Ikrimah is similar to the authentic Hadith recorded in Sahih Muslim; one day after a night's rain, the Messenger of Allah said to his Companions:

«أَتَدْرُونَ مَاذَا قَالَ رَبُّكُمْ؟»

(Do you know what your Lord says) They said: "Allah and His Messenger know best." He said:

«قَالَ: أَصْبَحَ مِنْ عِبَادِي مُؤْمِنٌ بِي وَكَافِرٌ، فَأَمَّا مَنْ قَالَ: مُطِرْنَا بِفَضْلِ اللهِ وَرَحْمَتِهِ فَذَاكَ مُؤْمِنٌ بِي، كَافِرٌ بِالْكَوْكَبِ، وَأَمَّا مَنْ قَالَ: مُطِرْنَا بِنَوْءِ كَذَا وَكَذَا، فَذَاكَ كَافِرٌ بِي، مُؤْمِنٌ بِالْكَوْكَبِ»

(He says: "This morning some of My servants became believers in Me, and some became disbelievers. As for the one who said, `We have been given rain by the mercy and grace of Allah,' he is a believer in Me and a disbeliever in the stars. As for the one who said, `We have been given rain by such and such a star,' he is a disbeliever in Me and a believer in the stars.")

Surah: 25 Ayah: 51, Ayah: 52, Ayah: 53 & Ayah: 54

وَلَوْ شِئْنَا لَبَعَثْنَا فِى كُلِّ قَرْيَةٍ نَّذِيرًا ۝

51. And had We willed, We would have raised a warner in every town.

فَلَا تُطِعِ ٱلْكَٰفِرِينَ وَجَٰهِدْهُم بِهِۦ جِهَادًا كَبِيرًا ۝

52. So obey not the disbelievers, but strive against them (by preaching) with the utmost endeavor with it (the Qur'ân).

۞ وَهُوَ ٱلَّذِى مَرَجَ ٱلْبَحْرَيْنِ هَٰذَا عَذْبٌ فُرَاتٌ وَهَٰذَا مِلْحٌ أُجَاجٌ وَجَعَلَ بَيْنَهُمَا بَرْزَخًا وَحِجْرًا مَّحْجُورًا ۝

53. And it is He Who has let free the two seas (kinds of water): one palatable and sweet, and the other salt and bitter; and He has set a barrier and a complete partition between them.

$$\text{وَهُوَ ٱلَّذِى خَلَقَ مِنَ ٱلْمَآءِ بَشَرًا فَجَعَلَهُۥ نَسَبًا وَصِهْرًا ۗ وَكَانَ رَبُّكَ قَدِيرًا}$$

54. And it is He Who has created man from water, and has appointed for him kindred by blood, and kindred by marriage. And your Lord is Ever All-Powerful to do what He wills.

Transliteration

51. Walaw shi/na labaAAathna fee kulli qaryatin natheeran 52. Fala tutiAAi alkafireena wajahidhum bihi jihadan kabeeran 53. Wahuwa allathee maraja albahrayni hatha AAathbun furatun wahatha milhun ojajun wajaAAala baynahuma barzakhan wahijran mahjooran 54. Wahuwa allathee khalaqa mina alma-i basharan fajaAAalahu nasaban wasihran wakana rabbuka qadeeran

Tafsir Ibn Kathir

The universality of the Prophet's Message, how He was supported in His Mission and Allah's Blessings to Mankind

Allah says:

(And had We willed, We would have raised a warner in every town.) `Calling them to Allah, but We have singled you out, O Muhammad, to be sent to all the people of earth, and We have commanded you to convey the Qur'an,'

(that I may therewith warn you and whomsoever it may reach) (6:19).

(but those of the sects that reject it, the Fire will be their promised meeting place) (11:17).

(that you may warn the Mother of the Towns and all around it) (42:7).

(Say: "O mankind! Verily, I am sent to you all as the Messenger of Allah...") (7:158). In the Two Sahihs (it is reported that the Prophet said:)

$$\text{«بُعِثْتُ إِلَى الْأَحْمَرِ وَالْأَسْوَدِ»}$$

(I have been sent to the red and the black.) And:

$$\text{«وَكَانَ النَّبِيُّ يُبْعَثُ إِلَى قَوْمِهِ خَاصَّةً، وَبُعِثْتُ إِلَى النَّاسِ عَامَّةً»}$$

(...A Prophet would be sent to his own people, but I have been sent to all of mankind.) Allah says:

(So obey not the disbelievers, but strive hard against them with it.) meaning, with the Qur'an. This was the view of Ibn `Abbas.

(with the utmost endeavour.) This is like the Ayah,

(O Prophet! Strive hard against the disbelievers and the hypocrites,) (9:73)

(And it is He Who has let free the two seas, this is palatable and sweet, and that is salty and bitter;) means, He has created the two kinds of water, sweet and salty. The sweet water is like that in rivers, springs and wells, which is fresh, sweet, palatable water. This was the view of Ibn Jurayj and of Ibn Jarir, and this is the meaning without a doubt, for nowhere in creation is there a sea which is fresh and sweet. Allah has told us about reality so that His servants may realize His blessings to them and give thanks to Him. The sweet water is that which flows amidst people. Allah has portioned it out among His creatures according to their needs; rivers and springs in every land, according to what they need for themselves and their lands.

(and that is salty and bitter;) meaning that it is salty, bitter and not easy to swallow. This is like the seas that are known in the east and the west, the Atlantic Ocean and the Straits that lead to it, the Red Sea, the Arabian Sea, the Persian Gulf, the China Sea, the Indian Ocean, the Mediterranean Sea, the Black Sea and so on, all the seas that are stable and do not flow, but they swell and surge in the winter and when the winds are strong, and they have tides that ebb and flow. At the beginning of each month the tides ebb and flood, and when the month starts to wane they retreat until they go back to where they started. When the crescent of the following month appears, the tide begins to ebb again until the fourteenth of the month, then it decreases. Allah, may He be glorified, the One Whose power is absolute, has set these laws in motion, so all of these seas are stationary, and He has made their water salty lest the air turn putrid because of them and the whole earth turn rotten as a result, and lest the earth spoil because of the animals dying on it. Because its water is salty, its air is healthy and its dead are good (to eat), hence when the Messenger of Allah was asked whether sea water can be used for Wudu', he said:

«هُوَ الطَّهُورُ مَاؤُهُ، الْحِلُّ مَيْتَتُهُ»

(Its water is pure and its dead are lawful.) This was recorded by Malik, Ash-Shafi`i and Ahmad, and by the scholars of Sunan with a good (Jayyid) chain of narration.

(and He has set a barrier and a complete partition between them.) meaning, between the sweet water and the saltwater.

(a barrier) means a partition, which is dry land.

(and a complete partition) means, a barrier, to prevent one of them from reaching the other. This is like the Ayat:

(He has let loose the two seas meeting together. Between them is a barrier which none of them can transgress. Then which of the blessings of your Lord will you both deny) (55:19-21)

(Is not He Who has made the earth as a fixed abode, and has placed rivers in its midst, and placed firm mountains therein, and set a barrier between the two seas Is there any god with Allah Nay, but most of them know not!) (27:61)

(And it is He Who has created man from water,) means, He created man from a weak Nutfah, then gave him shape and formed him, and completed his form, male and female, as He willed.

(and has appointed for him kindred by blood, and kindred by marriage.) in the beginning, he is someone's child, then he gets married and becomes a son-in-law, then he himself has sons-in-law and other relatives through marriage. All of this comes from a despised liquid, Allah says:

(And your Lord is Ever All-Powerful to do what He wills.)

Surah: 25 Ayah: 55, Ayah: 56, Ayah: 57, Ayah: 58, Ayah: 59 & Ayah: 60

وَيَعْبُدُونَ مِن دُونِ ٱللَّهِ مَا لَا يَنفَعُهُمْ وَلَا يَضُرُّهُمْ ۗ وَكَانَ ٱلْكَافِرُ عَلَىٰ رَبِّهِۦ ظَهِيرًا ﴿٥٥﴾

55. And they (disbelievers, polytheists) worship besides Allâh that which can neither profit them nor harm them; and the disbeliever is ever a helper (of the Satan) against his Lord.

وَمَآ أَرْسَلْنَٰكَ إِلَّا مُبَشِّرًا وَنَذِيرًا ﴿٥٦﴾

56. And We have sent you (O Muhammad (peace be upon him)) only as a bearer of glad tidings and a warner.

قُلْ مَآ أَسْـَٔلُكُمْ عَلَيْهِ مِنْ أَجْرٍ إِلَّا مَن شَآءَ أَن يَتَّخِذَ إِلَىٰ رَبِّهِۦ سَبِيلًا ﴿٥٧﴾

57. Say: "No reward do I ask of you for this (that which I have brought from my Lord and its preaching), save that whosoever wills may take a Path to his Lord.

وَتَوَكَّلْ عَلَى ٱلْحَىِّ ٱلَّذِى لَا يَمُوتُ وَسَبِّحْ بِحَمْدِهِۦ ۚ وَكَفَىٰ بِهِۦ بِذُنُوبِ عِبَادِهِۦ خَبِيرًا ﴿٥٨﴾

58. And put your trust (O Muhammad (peace be upon him)) in the Ever Living One Who dies not, and glorify His Praises, and Sufficient is He as the All-Knower of the sins of His slaves,

ٱلَّذِى خَلَقَ ٱلسَّمَٰوَٰتِ وَٱلْأَرْضَ وَمَا بَيْنَهُمَا فِى سِتَّةِ أَيَّامٍ ثُمَّ ٱسْتَوَىٰ عَلَى ٱلْعَرْشِ ٱلرَّحْمَٰنُ فَسْـَٔلْ بِهِۦ خَبِيرًا ﴿٥٩﴾

59. Who created the heavens and the earth and all that is between them in six Days. Then He Istawâ (rose over) the Throne (in a manner that suits His Majesty). The Most Gracious (Allâh)! Ask Him (O Prophet Muhammad (peace be upon him)

concerning His Qualities: His rising over His Throne, His creations, etc.), as He is Al-Khabîr (The All-Knower of everything i.e. Allâh).

وَإِذَا قِيلَ لَهُمُ ٱسْجُدُواْ لِلرَّحْمَـٰنِ قَالُواْ وَمَا ٱلرَّحْمَـٰنُ أَنَسْجُدُ لِمَا تَأْمُرُنَا وَزَادَهُمْ نُفُورًا ۩ ۝

60. And when it is said to them: "Prostrate yourselves to the Most Gracious (Allâh)! They say: "And what is the Most Gracious? Shall we fall down in prostration to that which you (O Muhammad (peace be upon him)) command us?" And it increases in them only aversion.

Transliteration

55. WayaAAbudoona min dooni Allahi ma la yanfaAAuhum wala yadurruhum wakana alkafiru AAala rabbihi thaheeran 56. Wama arsalnaka illa mubashshiran wanatheeran 57. Qul ma as-alukum AAalayhi min ajrin illa man shaa an yattakhitha ila rabbihi sabeelan 58. Watawakkal AAala alhayyi allathee la yamootu wasabbih bihamdihi wakafa bihi bithunoobi AAibadihi khabeeran 59. Allathee khalaqa alssamawati waalarda wama baynahuma fee sittati ayyamin thumma istawa AAala alAAarshi alrrahmanu fais-al bihi khabeeran 60. Wa-itha qeela lahumu osjudoo lilrrahmani qaloo wama alrrahmanu anasjudu lima ta/muruna wazadahum nufooran

Tafsir Ibn Kathir

The Ignorance of the Idolators

Allah tells us how ignorant the idolators are; instead of worshipping Allah, they worship idols which do not possess the power either to harm or benefit. They do this with no evidence or proof; the only thing that led them to do this was their own whims and desires. So they take these idols as protectors and fight for their sake, and they oppose Allah and His Messenger and the believers for their sake. Similarly Allah says:

(and the disbeliever is ever a helper against his Lord.) meaning, he is a supporter of Shaytan against the party of Allah, but the party of Allah are the ones who will prevail, as Allah says:

(And they have taken besides Allah gods, hoping that they might be helped. They cannot help them, but they will be brought forward as a troop against those who worshipped them.) (36:74-75) meaning, the gods which they worshipped instead of Allah cannot help them. These ignorant people are troops for the idols and are ready to fight for their sake and protect their sanctuaries, but in the end the victory will be for Allah and His Messenger and the believers, in this world and the Hereafter.

(and the disbeliever is ever a helper against his Lord.) Mujahid said: "He supports and helps the Shaytan in disobedience towards Allah.

The Messenger brings Glad Tidings and Warnings

Then Allah tells His Messenger:

(And We have sent you only as a bearer of good news and a warner.) meaning, a bringer of good news to the believers, a warner to the disbelievers; bringing good news of Paradise to those who obey Allah, and bringing warnings of a dreadful punishment for those who go against the commandments of Allah.

(Say: "No reward do I ask of you for this...") `for conveying this message and this warning, I do not ask for any reward from your wealth; I am only doing this for the sake of Allah, may He be exalted.'

(To whomsoever among you who wills to walk straight) (81:28).

(save that whosoever wills, may take a path to his Lord.) means, a way and a methodology to be followed.

The Command to the Messenger to put his Trust in Allah, and some of His Qualities

Then Allah says:

(And put your trust in the Ever Living One Who dies not,) meaning, in all your affairs, put your trust in Allah, the Ever-Living Who never dies, the One Who

(is the First and the Last, the Most High and the Most Near. And He is the All-Knower of everything) (57:3). The Eternal, Ever-Lasting, Ever-Living, Self-Sufficient One, the Lord and Sovereign of all things, the One to Whom you should always turn. Allah is the One in Whom you should put your trust and to Whom you should turn for refuge, He will be sufficient for you and will be your helper and supporter, and will cause you to prevail. As Allah says:

(O Messenger! Proclaim which has been sent down to you from your Lord. And if you do not, then you have not conveyed His Message. Allah will protect you from mankind) (5:67).

(and glorify His praises,) means, combine praising Him with glorifying Him. Hence the Messenger of Allah used to say:

«سُبْحَانَكَ اللَّهُمَّ رَبَّنَا وَبِحَمْدِكَ»

(Glory be to You, O Allah, and with Your praise.) So the Ayah means: be sincere in worshipping Him and putting your trust in Him. This is like the Ayat:

(The Lord of the east and the west; there is no God but He. So take Him as a Trustee.) (73:9)

(So worship Him and put your trust in Him) (11:123).

(Say: "He is the Most Gracious, in Him we believe, and in Him we put our trust.") (67:29)

(and sufficient is He as the All-Knower of the sins of His servants) means, by His perfect knowledge nothing is hidden from Him nor can anything be hidden from Him, not even a speck of dust's weight.

(Who created the heavens and the earth...) means, He is the Ever-Living Who never dies, He is the Creator, Sustainer and Sovereign of all things, Who by His might and power created the seven heavens with their vast height and width, and the seven earths with their great depths and density.

(in six Days. Then He rose over the Throne.) means, He is running all affairs and He decrees according to the truth, and He is the best of those who decide.

(Then He rose over (Istawa) the Throne. The Most Gracious! Ask Him, as He is the All-Knower.) meaning, find out about Him from one who knows most about Him, and follow him and take him as your example. It is known that there is no one who knows more about Allah than His servant and Messenger Muhammad , the absolute leader of the sons of Adam in this world and the Hereafter, who does not speak of his own desire, but conveys revelation revealed to him. What he says is true, and he is the leader whose decision counts; when there is a dispute, people are obliged to refer to him, and whatever is in accordance with his words and deeds is right, and whatever goes against them should be rejected no matter who says or does it. Allah says:

((And) if you differ in anything among yourselves...) (4:59).

(And in whatsoever you differ, the decision thereof is with Allah) (42:10).

(And the Word of your Lord has been fulfilled in truth and in justice) (6: 115). meaning, He has spoken the truth and is fair and just in His commands and prohibitions. Allah says here:

(Ask Him, as He is Al-Knower.)

Condemnation of the Idolators

Then Allah rebukes the idolators who prostrate to idols and rivals instead of Allah:

(And when it is said to them: "Prostrate yourselves to Ar-Rahman!" They say: "And what is Ar-Rahman") meaning: we do not know Ar-Rahman. They did not like to call Allah by His Name Ar-Rahman (the Most Gracious), as they objected on the day of (the treaty of) Al-Hudaybiyyah, when the Prophet told the scribe:

«اكْتُبْ بِسْمِ اللهِ الرَّحْمَنِ الرَّحِيمِ»

(Write: "In the Name of Allah, Ar-Rahman (the Most Gracious), Ar-Rahim (the Most Merciful).") They said, "We do not know Ar-Rahman or Ar-Rahim. Write what you used to write: `Bismika Allahumma (in Your Name, O Allah).'" So Allah revealed the words:

(Say: "Invoke Allah or invoke Ar-Rahman, by whatever name you invoke Him (it is the same), for to Him belong the Best Names) (17:110). meaning, He is Allah and He is the Most Gracious. And in this Ayah, Allah said:

(And when it is said to them: "Prostrate yourselves to Ar-Rahman!" They say: "And what is the Ar-Rahman") meaning: we do not know or approve of this Name.

(Shall we fall down in prostration to that which you command us) means, "Just because you tell us to"

(And it increases in them only aversion.) As for the believers, they worship Allah Who is the Most Gracious, Most Merciful, and they attribute divinity to Him Alone and prostrate to Him. The scholars, agree that it is allowed and approved for the reader and the listener to prostrate when he reaches this mention of prostration in Surat Al-Furqan, and Allah knows best.

Surah: 25 Ayah: 61 & Ayah: 62

تَبَارَكَ ٱلَّذِى جَعَلَ فِى ٱلسَّمَآءِ بُرُوجًا وَجَعَلَ فِيهَا سِرَٰجًا وَقَمَرًا مُّنِيرًا ۝

61. Blessed is He Who has placed in the heaven big stars, and has placed therein a great lamp (sun), and a moon giving light.

وَهُوَ ٱلَّذِى جَعَلَ ٱلَّيْلَ وَٱلنَّهَارَ خِلْفَةً لِّمَنْ أَرَادَ أَن يَذَّكَّرَ أَوْ أَرَادَ شُكُورًا ۝

62. And He it is Who has put the night and the day in succession, for such who desires to remember or desires to show his gratitude.

Transliteration

61. Tabaraka allathee jaAAala fee alssama-i buroojan wajaAAala feeha sirajan waqamaran muneeran 62. Wahuwa allathee jaAAala allayla waalnnahara khilfatan liman arada an yaththakkara aw arada shukooran

Tafsir Ibn Kathir

Mentioning the Might and Power of Allah

Here Allah glorifies Himself and praises the beauty He created in the heavens of Al-Buruj, the giant stars, according to the view of Mujahid, Sa`id bin Jubayr, Abu Salih, Al-Hasan and Qatadah. This is like the Ayah,

(And indeed We have adorned the nearest heaven with lamps) (67:5). Allah says:

(Blessed be He Who has placed in the heaven Al-Buruj, and has placed therein a great lamp,) which is the sun which shines like a lamp, as Allah says:

(And We have made (therein) a shining lamp) (78:13).

(and a moon giving light.) means, shining and illuminated by the light of something else, different from the light of the sun, as Allah says:

(It is He Who made the sun a shining thing and the moon as a light) (10:5). And Allah tells us that Nuh, peace be upon him, said to his people:

(See you not how Allah has created the seven heavens one above another And has made the moon a light therein, and made the sun a lamp) (71:15-16). Then Allah says:

(And He it is Who has put the night and the day in succession (Khilfatan),) meaning, each one comes after the other, in a never-ending alternation. When one goes the other comes, and vice versa, as Allah says:

(And He has made the sun and the moon, both constantly pursuing their courses) (14:33).

(He brings the night as a cover over the day, seeking it rapidly) (7:54).

(It is not for the sun to overtake the moon) (36:40).

(for such who desires to remember or desires to show his gratitude.) means, He has caused them both to follow one another to show the times when His servants should worship Him. So whoever misses an act of worship during the night can make it up during the day, and whoever misses an act of worship during the day can make it up during the night. It was recorded in a Sahih Hadith:

»إِنَّ اللهَ عَزَّ وَجَلَّ يَبْسُطُ يَدَهُ بِاللَّيْلِ لِيَتُوبَ مُسِيءُ النَّهَارِ، وَيَبْسُطُ يَدَهُ بِالنَّهَارِ لِيَتُوبَ مُسِيءُ اللَّيْلِ«

(Allah spreads forth His Hand at night for the one who has done evil during the day to repent, and He spreads forth His Hand during the day for the one who has done evil during the night to repent.) Mujahid and Qatadah said: "Khilfatan means different, i.e., because one is dark and the other is light."

Surah: 25 Ayah: 63, Ayah: 64, Ayah: 65, Ayah: 66 & Ayah: 67

وَعِبَادُ ٱلرَّحْمَٰنِ ٱلَّذِينَ يَمْشُونَ عَلَى ٱلْأَرْضِ هَوْنًا وَإِذَا خَاطَبَهُمُ ٱلْجَٰهِلُونَ قَالُوا۟ سَلَٰمًا ۝

63. And the (faithful) slaves of the Most Gracious (Allâh) are those who walk on the earth in humility and sedateness, and when the foolish address them (with bad words) they reply back with mild words of gentleness.

وَٱلَّذِينَ يَبِيتُونَ لِرَبِّهِمْ سُجَّدًا وَقِيَٰمًا ۝

64. And those who spend the night in worship of their Lord, prostrate and standing.

وَٱلَّذِينَ يَقُولُونَ رَبَّنَا ٱصْرِفْ عَنَّا عَذَابَ جَهَنَّمَ إِنَّ عَذَابَهَا كَانَ غَرَامًا ﴿٦٥﴾

65. And those who say: "Our Lord! Avert from us the torment of Hell. Verily its torment is ever an inseparable, permanent punishment."

إِنَّهَا سَآءَتْ مُسْتَقَرًّا وَمُقَامًا ﴿٦٦﴾

66. Evil indeed it (Hell) is as an abode and as a place to rest in.

وَٱلَّذِينَ إِذَآ أَنفَقُوا۟ لَمْ يُسْرِفُوا۟ وَلَمْ يَقْتُرُوا۟ وَكَانَ بَيْنَ ذَٰلِكَ قَوَامًا ﴿٦٧﴾

67. And those who, when they spend, are neither extravagant nor niggardly, but hold a medium (way) between those (extremes).

Transliteration

63. WaAAibadu alrrahmani allatheena yamshoona AAala al-ardi hawnan wa-itha khatabahumu aljahiloona qaloo salaman 64. Waallatheena yabeetoona lirabbihim sujjadan waqiyaman 65. Waallatheena yaqooloona rabbana isrif AAanna AAathaba jahannama inna AAathabaha kana gharaman 66. Innaha saat mustaqarran wamuqaman 67. Waallatheena itha anfaqoo lam yusrifoo walam yaqturoo wakana bayna thalika qawaman

Tafsir Ibn Kathir

Attributes of the Servants of the Most Gracious

These are the attributes of the believing servants of Allah,

(those who walk on the earth Hawna,) meaning that they walk with dignity and humility, not with arrogance and pride. This is like the Ayah:

(And walk not on the earth with conceit and arrogance...) (17:37). So these people do not walk with conceit or arrogance or pride. This does not mean that they should walk like sick people, making a show of their humility, for the leader of the sons of Adam (the Prophet) used to walk as if he was coming downhill, and as if the earth were folded up beneath him. What is meant here by Hawn is serenity and dignity, as the Messenger of Allah said:

«إِذَا أَتَيْتُمُ الصَّلَاةَ فَلَا تَأْتُوهَا وَأَنْتُمْ تَسْعَوْنَ، وَأْتُوهَا وَعَلَيْكُمُ السَّكِينَةُ فَمَا أَدْرَكْتُمْ مِنْهَا فَصَلُّوا، وَمَا فَاتَكُمْ فَأَتِمُّوا»

(When you come to the prayer, do not come rushing in haste. Come calmly and with tranquility, and whatever you catch up with, pray, and whatever you miss, make it up.)

(and when the foolish address them they say: "Salama.") If the ignorant people insult them with bad words, they do not respond in kind, but they forgive and overlook, and say nothing but good words. This is what the Messenger of Allah did: the more ignorant the people, the more patient he would be. This is as Allah says:

(And when they hear Al-Laghw (evil or vain talk), they withdraw from it) (28:55). Then Allah says that their nights are the best of nights, as He says:

(And those who spend the night in worship of their Lord, prostrate and standing.) meaning, worshipping and obeying Him. This is like the Ayat:

(They used to sleep but little by night. And in the hours before dawn, they were asking for forgiveness) (51:17-18).

(Their sides forsake their beds...) (32:16).

(Is one who is obedient to Allah, prostrating himself or standing during the hours of the night, fearing the Hereafter and hoping for the mercy of his Lord...) (39:9). Allah says:

(And those who say: "Our Lord! Avert from us the torment of Hell. Verily, its torment is ever an inseparable punishment.") meaning, ever-present and never ending. Al-Hasan said concerning the Ayah,

(Verily, its torment is ever an inseparable, permanent punishment.) Everything that strikes the son of Adam, then disappears, does not constitute an inseparable, permanent punishment. The inseparable, permanent punishment is that which lasts as long as heaven and earth. This was also the view of Sulayman At-Taymi.

(Evil indeed it is as an abode and as a place to rest in.) means, how evil it looks as a place to dwell and how evil it is as a place to rest.

(And those who, when they spend, are neither extravagant nor stingy...) They are not extravagant, spending more than they need, nor are they miserly towards their families, not spending enough on their needs. But they follow the best and fairest way. The best of matters are those which are moderate, neither one extreme nor the other.

(but are in a just balance between them.) This is like the Ayah,

(And let not your hand be tied to your neck, nor stretch it forth to its utmost reach.)(17:29)

Surah: 25 Ayah: 68, Ayah: 69, Ayah: 70 & Ayah: 71

وَٱلَّذِينَ لَا يَدْعُونَ مَعَ ٱللَّهِ إِلَٰهًا ءَاخَرَ وَلَا يَقْتُلُونَ ٱلنَّفْسَ ٱلَّتِي حَرَّمَ ٱللَّهُ إِلَّا بِٱلْحَقِّ وَلَا يَزْنُونَ ۚ وَمَن يَفْعَلْ ذَٰلِكَ يَلْقَ أَثَامًا ۝

68. And those who invoke not any other ilâh (god) along with Allâh, nor kill such person as Allâh has forbidden, except for just cause, nor commit illegal sexual intercourse - and whoever does this shall receive the punishment.

يُضَـٰعَفْ لَهُ ٱلْعَذَابُ يَوْمَ ٱلْقِيَـٰمَةِ وَيَخْلُدْ فِيهِۦ مُهَانًا ۝

69. The torment will be doubled to him on the Day of Resurrection, and he will abide therein in disgrace;

إِلَّا مَن تَابَ وَءَامَنَ وَعَمِلَ عَمَلًا صَـٰلِحًا فَأُوْلَـٰٓئِكَ يُبَدِّلُ ٱللَّهُ سَيِّـَٔاتِهِمْ حَسَنَـٰتٍ ۗ وَكَانَ ٱللَّهُ غَفُورًا رَّحِيمًا ۝

70. Except those who repent and believe (in Islâmic Monotheism), and do righteous deeds; for those, Allâh will change their sins into good deeds, and Allâh is Oft-Forgiving, Most Merciful.

وَمَن تَابَ وَعَمِلَ صَـٰلِحًا فَإِنَّهُۥ يَتُوبُ إِلَى ٱللَّهِ مَتَابًا ۝

71. And whosoever repents and does righteous good deeds; then verily, he repents towards Allâh with true repentance.

Transliteration

68. Waallatheena la yadAAoona maAAa Allahi ilahan akhara wala yaqtuloona alnnafsa allatee harrama Allahu illa bialhaqqi wala yaznoona waman yafAAal thalika yalqa athaman 69. YudaAAaf lahu alAAathabu yawma alqiyamati wayakhlud feehi muhanan 70. Illa man taba waamana waAAamila AAamalan salihan faola-ika yubaddilu Allahu sayyi-atihim hasanatin wakana Allahu ghafooran raheeman 71. Waman taba waAAamila salihan fa-innahu yatoobu ila Allahi mataban

Tafsir Ibn Kathir

The Attributes of the Servants of the Most Gracious include avoiding Shirk, Murder and Zina

Imam Ahmad recorded that `Abdullah bin Mas`ud said, "The Messenger of Allah was asked which sin is the most serious'' He said:

«أَنْ تَجْعَلَ لِلهِ نِدًّا وَهُوَ خَلَقَكَ»

(That you appoint a rival to Allah when He has created you.) He asked, "Then what'' He said:

«أَنْ تَقْتُلَ وَلَدَكَ خَشْيَةَ أَنْ يَطْعَمَ مَعَكَ»

(That you kill your child for fear that he may eat with you.) He said, "Then what" He said:

$$«أَنْ تُزَانِي حَلِيلَةَ جَارِكَ»$$

(That you commit adultery with your neighbor's wife.) `Abdullah said, "Then Allah revealed, confirming that:

(And those who invoke not any other god along with Allah....)" This was also recorded by An-Nasa'i, and by Al-Bukhari and Muslim. It was narrated that Sa`id bin Jubayr heard Ibn `Abbas saying that some of the people of Shirk killed a great deal and committed Zina a great deal, then they came to Muhammad and said: "What you are saying and calling people to is good, if only you would tell us that there is a way to expiate for what we have done." Then the Ayah:

(And those who invoke not any other god along with Allah...) was revealed, as was the Ayah,

(Say: "O My servants who have transgressed against themselves!") (39:53).

(and whoever does this shall receive Athama.) It was recorded that `Abdullah bin `Amr said: "Athama is a valley in Hell." `Ikrimah also said that Athama refers to valleys in Hell in which those who commit unlawful sexual acts will be punished. This was also narrated from Sa`id bin Jubayr and Mujahid. As-Suddi said that Athama referred to punishment, which is closer to the apparent meaning of the Ayah. This interpretation makes it interchangeable with what comes next, the Ayah:

(The torment will be doubled for him on the Day of Resurrection,) i.e., repetitive and intensified.

(and he will abide therein in disgrace;) scorned and humiliated.

(Except those who repent and believe, and do righteous deeds;) means, those who do these evil deeds will be punished in the manner described,

(Except those who repent), that is; those who repent in this world to Allah from all of those deeds, for then Allah will accept their repentance. This is evidence that the repentance of the murderer is acceptable, and there is no contradiction between this and the Ayah in Surat An-Nisa':

(And whoever kills a believer intentionally) (4:93), because even though this was revealed in Al-Madinah, the meaning is general, and it could be interpreted to refer to one who does not repent, because this Ayah states that forgiveness is only for those who repent. Moreover Allah says:

(Verily, Allah forgives not that partners should be set up with Him, but He forgives except that to whom He wills) (4:48). And in the authentic Sunnah, it is reported from the Messenger of Allah that the repentance of a murderer is acceptable, as was stated

Chapter 25: Al-Furqan (The Criterion, The Standard), Verses 021-077

in the story of the person who killed one hundred men and then repented, and Allah accepted his repentance, and other Hadiths.

(for those, Allah will change their sins into good deeds, and Allah is Oft-Forgiving, Most Merciful.) Imam Ahmad recorded that Abu Dharr, may Allah be pleased with him, said, "The Messenger of Allah said:

«إِنِّي لَأَعْرِفُ آخِرَ أَهْلِ النَّارِ خُرُوجًا مِنَ النَّارِ، وَآخِرَ أَهْلِ الْجَنَّةِ دُخُولًا إِلَى الْجَنَّةِ، يُؤْتَى بِرَجُلٍ فَيَقُولُ: نَحُّوا عَنْهُ كِبَارَ ذُنُوبِهِ وَسَلُوهُ عَنْ صِغَارِهَا، قَالَ: فَيُقَالُ لَهُ: عَمِلْتَ يَوْمَ كَذَا، كَذَا وَكَذَا، وَعَمِلْتَ يَوْمَ كَذَا، كَذَا وَكَذَا، فَيَقُولُ: نَعَمْ لَا يَسْتَطِيعُ أَنْ يُنْكِرَ مِنْ ذَلِكَ شَيْئًا، فَيُقَالُ: فَإِنَّ لَكَ بِكُلِّ سَيِّئَةٍ حَسَنَةً، فَيَقُولُ: يَا رَبِّ عَمِلْتُ أَشْيَاءَ لَا أَرَاهَا هَهُنَا»

(I know the last person who will be brought forth from Hell, and the last person who will enter Paradise. A man will be brought and it will be said, "Take away his major sins and ask him about his minor sins." So it will be said to him: "On such and such a day, you did such and such, and on such and such a day, you did such and such." He will say, "Yes, and he will not be able to deny anything." Then it will be said to him: "For every evil deed you now have one good merit." He will say: "O Lord, I did things that I do not see here.") He (Abu Dharr) said: "And the Messenger of Allah smiled so broadly that his molars could be seen." Muslim recorded it. Ibn Abi Hatim recorded that Abu Jabir heard Makhul say, "A very old man with sunken eyes came and said, `O Messenger of Allah, a man betrayed others and did immoral deeds, and there was no evil deed which he did not do. If (his sins) were to be distributed among the whole of mankind, they would all be doomed. Is there any repentance for him" The Messenger of Allah said:

«أَأَسْلَمْتَ؟»

(Have you become Muslim) He said, "As for me, I bear witness that there is no God but Allah Alone, with no partner or associate, and that Muhammad is His servant and Messenger." The Prophet said:

«فَإِنَّ اللهَ غَافِرٌ لَكَ مَا كُنْتَ كَذَلِكَ، وَمُبَدِّلٌ سَيِّئَاتِكَ حَسَنَات»

(Allah will forgive you for whatever you have done like that, and will replace your evil deeds with good merits.) The man said: "O Messenger of Allah, even my betrayals and immoral actions" The Prophet said:

«وَغَدَرَاتُكَ وَفَجَرَاتُكَ»

(Even your betrayals and immoral actions.) "The man went away saying `La ilaha illallah' and `Allahu Akbar.'" Allah tells us how His mercy extends to all His creatrues, and that whoever among them repents to Him, He will accept his repentance for any sin, great or small. Allah says:

(And whosoever repents and does righteous good deeds; then indeed he has repented to Allah Mataba.) meaning, Allah will accept his repentance. This is like the Ayat:

(And whoever does evil or wrongs himself but afterwards seeks Allah's forgiveness, he will find Allah Oft-Forgiving, Most Merciful) (4:110).

(Know they not that Allah accepts repentance from His servants...) (9:104).

(Say: "O My servants who have transgressed against themselves! Despair not of the mercy of Allah.") (39:53) - for those who repent to Him.

Surah: 25 Ayah: 72, Ayah: 73 & Ayah: 74

وَٱلَّذِينَ لَا يَشْهَدُونَ ٱلزُّورَ وَإِذَا مَرُّوا۟ بِٱللَّغْوِ مَرُّوا۟ كِرَامًا ۝

72. And those who do not bear witness to falsehood, and if they pass by some evil play or evil talk, they pass by it with dignity.

وَٱلَّذِينَ إِذَا ذُكِّرُوا۟ بِـَٔايَٰتِ رَبِّهِمْ لَمْ يَخِرُّوا۟ عَلَيْهَا صُمًّا وَعُمْيَانًا ۝

73. And those who, when they are reminded of the Ayât (proofs, evidences, verses, lessons, signs, revelations, etc.) of their Lord, fall not deaf and blind thereat.

وَٱلَّذِينَ يَقُولُونَ رَبَّنَا هَبْ لَنَا مِنْ أَزْوَٰجِنَا وَذُرِّيَّٰتِنَا قُرَّةَ أَعْيُنٍ وَٱجْعَلْنَا لِلْمُتَّقِينَ إِمَامًا ۝

74. And those who say: "Our Lord! Bestow on us from our wives and our offspring the comfort of our eyes, and make us leaders of the Muttaqûn (the pious - see V.2:2)."

Transliteration

72. Waallatheena la yashhadoona alzzoora wa-itha marroo biallaghwi marroo kiraman 73. Waallatheena itha thukkiroo bi-ayati rabbihim lam yakhirroo AAalayha summan waAAumyanan 74. Waallatheena yaqooloona rabbana hab lana min azwajina wathurriyyatina qurrata aAAyunin waijAAalna lilmuttaqeena imaman

Tafsir Ibn Kathir

More Attributes of the Servants of the Most Gracious

These are further attributes of the servants of the Most Gracious. They do not bear witness to falsehood, including lies, immorality, disbelief, foul speech and false words. `Amr bin Qays said, this refers to gatherings of sexual immorality. It was said that the Ayah,

(And those who do not bear witness to falsehood,) refers to giving false testimony, which means lying deliberately to someone else. It was recorded in the Two Sahihs that Abu Bakrah said, "The Messenger of Allah said three times:

»أَلَا أُنَبِّئُكُمْ بِأَكْبَرِ الْكَبَائِرِ؟«

(Shall I not tell you of the greatest of major sins) We said, "Of course, O Messenger of Allah." The Messenger of Allah said:

»الشِّرْكُ بِاللهِ وَعُقُوقُ الْوَالِدَيْنِ«

(Associating others in worship with Allah and disobeying one's parents.) He was lying down, then he sat up and added:

»أَلَا وَقَوْلُ الزُّورِ، أَلَا وَشَهَادَةُ الزُّورِ«

(Beware false speech, and bearing witness to falsehood.) and he kept repeating it until we thought, would that he would stop." From the context it seems that what is meant by those who do not bear witness to falsehood is those who do not attend it or are not present when it happens. Allah says:

(and if they pass by some evil play or evil talk, they pass by it with dignity.) They do not attend where falsehood occurs, and if it so happens that they pass by it, they do not let it contaminate them in the slightest. Allah says:

(they pass by it with dignity.)

(And those who, when they are reminded of the Ayat of their Lord, fall not deaf and blind thereat.) This is also a characteristic of the believers,

(Those who, when Allah is mentioned, feel a fear in their hearts and when His Ayat are recited unto them, they increase their faith; and they put their trust in their Lord.) (8:2) Unlike the disbelievers. When they hear the Words of Allah, they are not affected by them or moved to change their ways. They persist in their disbelief, wrongdoing, ignorance and misguidance, as Allah says:

(And whenever there comes down a Surah, some of them say: "Which of you has had his faith increased by it" As for those who believe, it has increased their faith, and they rejoice. But as for those in whose hearts is a disease, it will add doubt to their doubt) (9:124-125).

(fall not deaf and blind thereat.) means, unlike the disbelievers who, when they hear the Ayat of Allah, are not moved by them, but continue as they are, as if they did not hear them but are deaf and blind. His saying:

(And those who say: "Our Lord! Bestow on us from our wives and our offspring the comfort of our eyes...") means those who ask Allah to bring forth from their loins offspring who will obey Him and worship Him and not associate anything in worship with Him. Ibn `Abbas said, "This means (offspring) who will strive to obey Allah and bring them joy in this world and the Hereafter." Imam Ahmad recorded that Jubayr bin Nufayr said: "We sat with Al-Miqdad bin Al-Aswad one day, and a man passed by and said, "How blessed are these two eyes which saw the Messenger of Allah ! Would that we had seen what you saw and witnessed what you witnessed." Al-Miqdad got angry, and I was surprised, because the man had not said anything but good. Then he turned to him and said, "What makes a man wish to be present when Allah had caused him to be absent, and he does not know how he would have behaved if he had been there By Allah, there are people who saw the Messenger of Allah , and Allah will throw them on their faces in Hell because they did not accept him or believe in him. Are you not grateful that Allah brought you forth from your mothers' wombs believing in your Lord and in what your Prophet brought, and that the test went to others and not to you Allah sent His Prophet during the most difficult time that any Prophet was ever sent, after a long period of ignorance, when the people could see no better religion than the worship of idols, and he brought the Criterion which distinguishes truth from falsehood and which would separate a father from his son. A man would realize that his father, son or brother was a disbeliever, and since Allah had opened his heart to Faith, he knew that if his relative died he would go to Hell, so he could not rest knowing that his loved one was in the Fire. This is what Allah referred to in the Ayah,

(And those who say: "Our Lord! Bestow on us from our wives and our offspring the comfort of our eyes...") Its chain of narrators is Sahih, although they did not report it.

(and make us leaders of those who have Taqwa.) Ibn `Abbas, Al-Hasan, As-Suddi, Qatadah and Rabi` bin Anas said: "Leaders who would be taken as examples in good." Others said: "Guides who would call others to goodness." They wanted their worship to be connected to the worship of their children and offspring, and their guidance to go beyond themselves and benefit others. This would be more rewarding and a better end, as it was recorded in Sahih Muslim from Abu Hurayrah, may Allah be pleased with him, that the Messenger of Allah said:

«إِذَا مَاتَ ابْنُ آدَمَ انْقَطَعَ عَمَلُهُ إِلَّا مِنْ ثَلَاثٍ: وَلَدٍ صَالِحٍ يَدْعُو لَهُ، أَوْ عِلْمٍ يُنْتَفَعُ بِهِ مِنْ بَعْدِهِ، أَوْ صَدَقَةٍ جَارِيَةٍ»

(When a son of Adam dies, his deeds cease apart from three: a righteous child who will pray for him, knowledge from which others may benefit after him, or ongoing charity.)

Surah: 25 Ayah: 75, Ayah: 76 & Ayah: 77

أُو۟لَـٰٓئِكَ يُجْزَوْنَ ٱلْغُرْفَةَ بِمَا صَبَرُوا۟ وَيُلَقَّوْنَ فِيهَا تَحِيَّةً وَسَلَـٰمًا ۝

75. Those will be rewarded with the highest place (in Paradise) because of their patience. Therein they shall be met with greetings and the word of peace and respect.

خَـٰلِدِينَ فِيهَا ۚ حَسُنَتْ مُسْتَقَرًّا وَمُقَامًا ۝

76. Abiding therein - excellent it is as an abode, and as a place to rest in.

قُلْ مَا يَعْبَؤُا۟ بِكُمْ رَبِّى لَوْلَا دُعَآؤُكُمْ ۖ فَقَدْ كَذَّبْتُمْ فَسَوْفَ يَكُونُ لِزَامًا ۝

77. Say (O Muhammad (peace be upon him) to the disbelievers): "My Lord pays attention to you only because of your invocation to Him. But now you have indeed denied (Him). So the torment will be yours for ever (inseparable permanent punishment)."

Transliteration

75. Ola-ika yujzawna alghurfata bima sabaroo wayulaqqawna feeha tahiyyatan wasalaman 76. Khalideena feeha hasunat mustaqarran wamuqaman 77. Qul ma yaAAbao bikum rabbee lawla duAAaokum faqad kaththabtum fasawfa yakoonu lizaman

Tafsir Ibn Kathir

The Reward of the Servants of the Most Gracious, and a Warning to the People of Makkah

After mentioning the beautiful attributes of His believing servants, and their fine words and deeds, Allah then says:

(Those) meaning, the people who are described in this manner,

(will be rewarded) on the Day of Resurrection,

(with the highest place), which is Paradise. Abu Ja`far Al-Baqir, Sa`id bin Jubayr, Ad-Dahhak and As-Suddi said, "It was so called because of its elevation."

(because of their patience.) means, their patience in doing what they did.

(Therein they shall be met) means, in Paradise.

(with greetings and the word of peace and respect.) This means that they will be greeted first with words of welcome and honor. Peace will be theirs and they will be wished peace. And angels shall enter unto them from every gate, saying, "Peace be upon you for that you persevered in patience! Excellent indeed is the final home!"

(Abiding therein) means, they will settle there and never leave or move or die, they will never exit or wish to move to somewhere else. This is like the Ayah,

(And those who are blessed, they will be in Paradise, abiding therein for all the time that the heavens and the earth endure) (11:108).

(excellent it is as an abode, and as a place to rest in.) Its appearance is beautiful and it is a good place in which to rest and to dwell. Then Allah says:

(Say: "My Lord pays attention to you only because of your invocation to Him...") meaning, He would not care to pay attention to you if you did not worship Him, for He only created mankind to worship Him Alone and to glorify Him morning and evening. His saying:

(But now you have indeed denied.) "O you disbelievers."

(So the torment will be yours forever.) So your denial will remain with you forever, i.e., it will lead to your punishment, doom and destruction in this world and the Hereafter. This also refers to the day of Badr, as it was interpreted by `Abdullah bin Mas`ud, Ubayy bin Ka`b, Muhammad bin Ka`b Al-Qurazi, Mujahid, Ad-Dahhak, Qatadah, As-Suddi and others.

(So the torment will be yours forever.) Al-Hasan Al-Basri said: "The Day of Resurrection." And there is no conflict between the two interpretations. This is the end of the Tafsir of Surat Al-Furqan, all praise and thanks are due to Allah.

CHAPTER (SURAH) 26: ASH-SHU'ARAA (THE POETS), VERSES 001 – 227

(بِسْمِ اللّهِ الرَّحْمَنِ الرَّحِيمِ)

In the Name of Allah, the Most Gracious, the Most Merciful.

> **Surah: 26 Ayah: 1, Ayah: 2, Ayah: 3, Ayah: 4, Ayah: 5, Ayah: 6, Ayah: 7, Ayah: 8 & Ayah: 9**

طسم

1. Tâ-Sîn-Mîm. [These letters are one of the miracles of the Qur'ân, and none but Allâh (Alone) knows their meanings.]

تِلْكَ ءَايَـٰتُ ٱلْكِتَـٰبِ ٱلْمُبِينِ

2. These are the Verses of the manifest Book ((this Qur'ân), which was promised by Allâh in the Taurât (Torah) and the Injeel (Gospel), makes things clear).

Chapter 26. Ash-Shu'araa (The Poets), Verses 001-227

لَعَلَّكَ بَـٰخِعٌ نَّفْسَكَ أَلَّا يَكُونُوا۟ مُؤْمِنِينَ ۝

3. It may be that you (O Muhammad (peace be upon him)) are going to kill yourself with grief, that they do not become believers (in your Risalah (Messengership) i.e. in your Message of Islâmic Monotheism).

إِن نَّشَأْ نُنَزِّلْ عَلَيْهِم مِّنَ ٱلسَّمَآءِ ءَايَةً فَظَلَّتْ أَعْنَـٰقُهُمْ لَهَا خَـٰضِعِينَ ۝

4. If We will, We could send down to them from the heaven a sign, to which they would bend their necks in humility.

وَمَا يَأْتِيهِم مِّن ذِكْرٍ مِّنَ ٱلرَّحْمَـٰنِ مُحْدَثٍ إِلَّا كَانُوا۟ عَنْهُ مُعْرِضِينَ ۝

5. And never comes there unto them a Reminder as a recent revelation from the Most Gracious (Allâh), but they turn away therefrom.

فَقَدْ كَذَّبُوا۟ فَسَيَأْتِيهِمْ أَنۢبَـٰٓؤُا۟ مَا كَانُوا۟ بِهِۦ يَسْتَهْزِءُونَ ۝

6. So they have indeed denied (the truth - this Qur'ân), then the news of what they mocked at will come to them.

أَوَلَمْ يَرَوْا۟ إِلَى ٱلْأَرْضِ كَمْ أَنۢبَتْنَا فِيهَا مِن كُلِّ زَوْجٍ كَرِيمٍ ۝

7. Do they not observe the earth, how much of every good kind We cause to grow therein?

إِنَّ فِى ذَٰلِكَ لَـَٔايَةً ۖ وَمَا كَانَ أَكْثَرُهُم مُّؤْمِنِينَ ۝

8. Verily, in this is an Ayâh (proof or sign), yet most of them (polytheists, pagans who do not believe in Resurrection) are not believers.

وَإِنَّ رَبَّكَ لَهُوَ ٱلْعَزِيزُ ٱلرَّحِيمُ ۝

9. And verily your Lord, He is truly the All-Mighty, the Most Merciful.

Transliteration

1. Ta-seen-meem 2. Tilka ayatu alkitabi almubeeni 3. LaAAallaka bakhiAAun nafsaka alla yakoonoo mu/mineena 4. In nasha/ nunazzil AAalayhim mina alssama-i ayatan fathallat aAAnaquhum laha khadiAAeena 5. Wama ya/teehim min thikrin mina alrrahmani muhdathin illa kanoo AAanhu muAArideena 6. Faqad kaththaboo fasaya/teehim anbao ma kanoo bihi yastahzi-oona 7. Awa lam yaraw ila al-ardi kam anbatna feeha min kulli zawjin kareemin 8. Inna fee thalika laayatan wama kana aktharuhum mu/mineena 9. Wa-inna rabbaka lahuwa alAAazeezu alrraheemu

Tafsir Ibn Kathir

The Qur'an and the Disbelievers turning away;

They could be compelled to believe if Allah so willed At the beginning of the explanation of Surat Al-Baqarah we discussed the letters which appear at the beginning of some Surahs. Allah's saying:

(These are the Ayat of the Book Mubin.) means, these are the verses of the Clear Qur'an, i.e. the clear and unambiguous Book which distinguishes between truth and falsehood, misguidance and guidance.

(It may be that you are going Bakhi` yourself,) means, destroy yourself -- because of your keenness that they should be guided and your grief for them.

(that they do not become believers.) Here Allah is consoling His Messenger for the lack of faith of those among the disbelievers who do not believe in him. This is like the Ayat:

(So destroy not yourself in sorrow for them) (35:8).

(Perhaps, you would Bakhi` yourself, over their footsteps, because they believe not in this narration) (18:6). Mujahid, `Ikrimah, Qatadah, `Atiyyah, Ad-Dahhak, Al-Hasan and others said that:

(It may be that you are going Bakhi` yourself,) means, `kill yourself.' Then Allah says:

(If We will, We could send down to them from the heaven a sign, to which they would bend their necks in humility.) meaning, `if We so willed, We could send down a sign that would force them to believe, but We will not do that because We do not want anyone to believe except by choice.' Allah says:

(And had your Lord willed, those on earth would have believed, all of them together. So, will you then compel mankind, until they become believers.) (10:99)

(And if your Lord had so willed, He could surely, have made mankind one Ummah...) (11:118) But Allah's will has acted, His decree has come to pass, and His proof has been conveyed to mankind by mission of Messengers and the revelation of Books to them. Then Allah says:

(And never comes there unto them a Reminder as a recent revelation from the Most Gracious, but they turn away therefrom.) meaning, every time a Scripture comes from heaven to them, most of the people turn away from it. As Allah says:

(And most of mankind will not believe even if you desire it eagerly.) (12:103)

(Alas for mankind! There never came a Messenger to them but they used to mock at him.) (36:30)

(Then We sent Our Messengers in succession. Every time there came to a nation their Messenger, they denied him...) (23:44). Allah says here:

Chapter 26. Ash-Shu'araa (The Poets), Verses 001-227

(So, they have indeed denied, then the news of what they mocked at will come to them.) meaning, they denied the truth that came to them, so they will come to know the news of the consequences of this denial after a while.

(And those who do wrong will come to know by what overturning they will be overturned) (26:227). Then Allah tells those who dared to oppose His Messenger and disbelieve in His Book, that He is the Subduer, the Almighty, the All-Powerful, Who created the earth and caused every good kind of crop, fruit and animal to grow therein. Sufyan Ath-Thawri narrated from a man from Ash-Sha`bi that people are a product of the earth. So whoever enters Paradise is good and noble, and whoever enters Hell is base and vile.

(Verily, in this is an Ayah,) meaning an evidence of the power of the Creator of all things. He spread out the earth and raised the canopy of the heavens, yet despite that the majority of people do not believe, rather they deny Him, His Messengers, and His Books, and they go against His commands doing the things He had prohibited. His saying:

(And verily your Lord, He is truly the All-Mighty,) means, the One Who has power over all things, to subdue and control them,

(the Most Merciful.) means, towards His creation, for He does not hasten to punish the one who sins, but He gives him time to repent, and if he does not, then He seizes him with a mighty punishment. Abu Al-`Aliyah, Qatadah, Ar-Rabi` bin Anas and Ibn Ishaq said: "He is Almighty in His punishment of those who went against His commands and worshipped others besides Him." Sa`id bin Jubayr said: "He is Most Merciful towards those who repent to Him and turn to Him."

Surah: 26 Ayah: 10, Ayah: 11, Ayah: 12, Ayah: 13, Ayah: 14, Ayah: 15, Ayah: 16, Ayah: 17, Ayah: 18, Ayah: 19, Ayah: 20, Ayah: 21 & Ayah: 22

وَإِذْ نَادَىٰ رَبُّكَ مُوسَىٰٓ أَنِ ٱئْتِ ٱلْقَوْمَ ٱلظَّٰلِمِينَ ﴿١٠﴾

10. And (remember) when your Lord called Mûsa (Moses) (saying): "Go to the people who are Zâlimûn (polytheists and wrong-doing)-

قَوْمَ فِرْعَوْنَ أَلَا يَتَّقُونَ ﴿١١﴾

11. The people of Fir'aun (Pharaoh): Will they not fear Allâh and become righteous?"

قَالَ رَبِّ إِنِّىٓ أَخَافُ أَن يُكَذِّبُونِ ﴿١٢﴾

12. He said: "My Lord! Verily, I fear that they will belie me,

وَيَضِيقُ صَدْرِى وَلَا يَنطَلِقُ لِسَانِى فَأَرْسِلْ إِلَىٰ هَـٰرُونَ ﴿١٣﴾

13. "And my breast straitens, and my tongue expresses not well. So send for Hârûn (Aaron) (to come along with me).

وَلَهُمْ عَلَىَّ ذَنبٌ فَأَخَافُ أَن يَقْتُلُونِ ﴿١٤﴾

14. "And they have a charge of crime against me, and I fear they will kill me."

قَالَ كَلَّا فَاذْهَبَا بِـَٔايَـٰتِنَآ إِنَّا مَعَكُم مُّسْتَمِعُونَ ﴿١٥﴾

15. Allâh said: "Nay! Go you both with Our Signs. Verily We shall be with you, listening.

فَأْتِيَا فِرْعَوْنَ فَقُولَآ إِنَّا رَسُولُ رَبِّ ٱلْعَـٰلَمِينَ ﴿١٦﴾

16. "And go both of you to Fir'aun (Pharaoh), and say: 'We are the Messengers of the Lord of the 'Alamîn (mankind, jinn and all that exists),

أَنْ أَرْسِلْ مَعَنَا بَنِىٓ إِسْرَٰٓءِيلَ ﴿١٧﴾

17. "So allow the Children of Israel to go with us.'"

قَالَ أَلَمْ نُرَبِّكَ فِينَا وَلِيدًا وَلَبِثْتَ فِينَا مِنْ عُمُرِكَ سِنِينَ ﴿١٨﴾

18. (Fir'aun (Pharaoh)) said (to Mûsa (Moses)) "Did we not bring you up among us as a child? And you did dwell many years of your life with us.

وَفَعَلْتَ فَعْلَتَكَ ٱلَّتِى فَعَلْتَ وَأَنتَ مِنَ ٱلْكَـٰفِرِينَ ﴿١٩﴾

19. "And you did your deed, which you did (i.e. the crime of killing a man). And you are one of the ingrates."

قَالَ فَعَلْتُهَآ إِذًا وَأَنَا۠ مِنَ ٱلضَّآلِّينَ ﴿٢٠﴾

20. Mûsa (Moses) said: "I did it then, when I was an ignorant (as regards my Lord and His Message).

فَفَرَرْتُ مِنكُمْ لَمَّا خِفْتُكُمْ فَوَهَبَ لِى رَبِّى حُكْمًا وَجَعَلَنِى مِنَ ٱلْمُرْسَلِينَ ﴿٢١﴾

21. "So I fled from you when I feared you. But my Lord has granted me Hukm (i.e. religious knowledge, right judgement of the affairs and Prophethood), and made me as one of the Messengers.

وَتِلْكَ نِعْمَةٌ تَمُنُّهَا عَلَىَّ أَنْ عَبَّدتَّ بَنِىٓ إِسْرَٰٓءِيلَ ﴿٢٢﴾

22. "And this is the past favor with which you reproach me: that you have enslaved the Children of Israel."

Transliteration

10. Wa-ith nada rabbuka moosa ani i/ti alqawma aththalimeena   11. Qawma firAAawna ala yattaqoona   12. Qala rabbi innee akhafu an yukaththibooni   13. Wayadeequ sadree wala yantaliqu lisanee faarsil ila haroona 14. Walahum AAalayya thanbun faakhafu an yaqtulooni 15. Qala kalla faithhaba bi-ayatina inna maAAakum mustamiAAoona 16. Fa/tiya firAAawna faqoola inna rasoolu rabbi alAAalameena   17. An arsil maAAana banee isra-eela   18. Qala alam nurabbika feena waleedan walabithta feena min AAumurika sineena 19. WafaAAalta faAAlataka allatee faAAalta waanta mina alkafireena   20. Qala faAAaltuha ithan waana mina alddalleena   21. Fafarartu minkum lamma khiftukum fawahaba lee rabbee hukman wajaAAalaneemina almursaleena 22. Watilka niAAmatun tamunnuha AAalayya an AAabbadta banee isra-eela

Tafsir Ibn Kathir

Between Musa and Fir`awn

Allah tells us what He commanded His servant, son of `Imran and Messenger Musa, peace be upon him, who spoke with Him, to do, when He called him from the right side of the mountain, and conversed with him, and chose him, sent him, and commanded him to go to Fir`awn and his people. Allah says:

(And when your Lord called Musa: "Go to the people who are wrongdoers. The people of Fir`awn. Will they not have Taqwa" He said: "My Lord! Verily, I fear that they will deny me, And my breast straitens, and my tongue expresses not well. So send for Harun. And they have a charge of crime against me, and I fear they will kill me.") So, Musa asked Allah to remove these difficulties for him, as he said in Surah Ta Ha:

(Musa said: "O my Lord! Open for me my chest. And ease my task for me.") (20:25-26) until:

(You are granted your request, O Musa!) (20:36)

(And they have a charge of crime against me, and I fear they will kill me.) because he had killed that Egyptian, which was the reason that he left the land of Egypt.

((Allah) said: "Nay!...") Allah told him: do not be afraid of anything like that. This is like the Ayah,

(Allah said: "We will strengthen your arm through your brother, and give you both power) meaning, proof;

(so they shall not be able to harm you, with Our signs, you two as well as those who follow you will be the victors) (28:35),

(Go you both with Our signs. Verily, We shall be with you, listening.) This is like the Ayah,

(I am with you both, hearing and seeing) (20:46). Meaning, `I will be with you by My protection, care, support and help.'

(And go both of you to Fir`awn, and say: `We are the Messengers of the Lord of the all that exists.') This is like the Ayah,

(Verily, we are both Messengers of your Lord) (20:47). which means, `both of us have been sent to you,'

(So allow the Children of Israel to go with us.) Meaning, `let them go, free them from your captivity, subjugation and torture, for they are the believing servants of Allah, devoted to Him, and with you they are in a position of humiliating torture.' When Musa said that to him, Fir`awn turned away and ignored him completely, regarding him with scorn and thinking little of him. Saying:

(Did we not bring you up among us as a child) meaning, we brought you up among us, in our home and on our bed, we nourished you and did favors for you for many years, and after all that you responded to our kindness in this manner: you killed one of our men and denied our favors to you.' So he said to him:

(While you were one of the ingrates.) meaning, one of those who deny favors. This was the view of Ibn `Abbas and `Abdur-Rahman bin Zayd bin Aslam, and was the view favored by Ibn Jarir.

((Musa) said: "I did it then...") meaning, at that time,

(when I was in error.) meaning, `before revelation was sent to me and before Allah made me a Prophet and sent me with this Message.'

(So, I fled from you when I feared you. But my Lord has granted me Hukm, and made me one of the Messengers.) means, `the first situation came to an end and another took its place. Now Allah has sent me to you, and if you obey Him, you will be safe, but if you oppose Him, you will be destroyed.' Then Musa said:

(And this is the past favor with which you reproach me, -- that you have enslaved the Children of Israel.) meaning, `whatever favors you did in bringing me up are offset by the evil you did by enslaving the Children of Israel and using them to do your hard labor. Is there any comparison between your favors to one man among them and the evil you have done to all of them What you have mentioned about me is nothing compared to what you have done to them.'

Surah: 26 Ayah: 23, Ayah: 24, Ayah: 25, Ayah: 26, Ayah: 27 & Ayah: 28

$$\text{قَالَ فِرْعَوْنُ وَمَا رَبُّ ٱلْعَٰلَمِينَ} \;⟨23⟩$$

23. Fir'aun (Pharaoh) said: "And what is the Lord of the 'Alamîn (mankind, jinn and all that exists)?"

$$\text{قَالَ رَبُّ ٱلسَّمَٰوَٰتِ وَٱلْأَرْضِ وَمَا بَيْنَهُمَآ ۖ إِن كُنتُم مُّوقِنِينَ} \;⟨24⟩$$

24. (Mûsa (Moses)) said: "The Lord of the heavens and the earth, and all that is between them, if you seek to be convinced with certainty."

$$\text{قَالَ لِمَنْ حَوْلَهُ أَلَا تَسْتَمِعُونَ}$$

25. (Fir'aun (Pharaoh)) said to those around: "Do you not hear (what he says)?"

$$\text{قَالَ رَبُّكُمْ وَرَبُّ ءَابَآئِكُمُ ٱلْأَوَّلِينَ}$$

26. (Mûsa (Moses)) said: "Your Lord and the Lord of your ancient fathers!"

$$\text{قَالَ إِنَّ رَسُولَكُمُ ٱلَّذِىٓ أُرْسِلَ إِلَيْكُمْ لَمَجْنُونٌ}$$

27. (Fir'aun (Pharaoh)) said: "Verily, your Messenger who has been sent to you is a madman!"

$$\text{قَالَ رَبُّ ٱلْمَشْرِقِ وَٱلْمَغْرِبِ وَمَا بَيْنَهُمَآ إِن كُنتُمْ تَعْقِلُونَ}$$

28. (Mûsa (Moses)) said: "Lord of the east and the west, and all that is between them, if you did but understand!"

Transliteration

23. Qala firAAawnu wama rabbu alAAalameena 24. Qala rabbu alssamawati waal-ardi wama baynahuma in kuntum mooqineena 25. Qala liman hawlahu ala tastamiAAoona 26. Qala rabbukum warabbu aba-ikumu al-awwaleena 27. Qala inna rasoolakumu allathee orsila ilaykum lamajnoonun 28. Qala rabbu almashriqi waalmaghribi wama baynahuma in kuntum taAAqiloona

Tafsir Ibn Kathir

Allah tells us about the disbelief, rebellion, oppression and denial of Fir`awn, as He says:

((Fir`awn said:) "And what is the Lord of the `Alamin") This is because he used to say to his people:

(I know not that you have a god other than me.) (28:28)

(Thus he fooled his people, and they obeyed him.) (43:54) They used to deny the Creator, may He be glorified, and they believed that they had no other lord than Fir`awn. When Musa said to them: "I am the Messenger of the Lord of the worlds," Fir`awn said to him, "Who is this who you are claiming is the Lord of Al-`Alamin other than me" This is how it was interpreted by the scholars of the Salaf and the Imams of later generations. As-Suddi said, "This Ayah is like the Ayah,

((Fir`awn) said: "Who then, O Musa, is the Lord of you two" He said: "Our Lord is He Who gave to each thing its form and nature, then guided it aright.") (20:49-50) Those among the philosophers and others who claimed that this was a question about the nature or substance (of Allah) are mistaken. Fir`awn did not believe in the Creator in the first place, so he was in no position to ask about the nature of the Creator; he denied that the Creator existed at all, as is apparent from the meaning, even though proof and evidence had been established against him. When Fir`awn asked him about the Lord of Al-`Alamin, Musa said:

((Musa) said: "The Lord of the heavens and the earth, and all that is between them...") meaning, the Creator, Sovereign and Controller of all that, their God Who has no partner or associate. He is the One Who has created all things. He knows the higher realms and the heavenly bodies that are in them, both those that are stationary and those that move and shine brightly. He knows the lower realms and what is in them; the oceans, continents, mountains, trees, animals, plants and fruits. He knows what is in between the two realms; the winds, birds, and whatever is in the air. All of them are servants to Him, submitting and humbling themselves before Him.

(if you seek to be convinced with certainty.) means, if you have believing hearts and clear insight. At this, Fir`awn turned to the chiefs and leaders of his state around him, and said to them -- mockingly expressing his disbelief in Musa:

("Do you not hear") meaning, `are you not amazed by what this man is claiming -- that you have another god other than me' Musa said to them:

(Your Lord and the Lord of your ancient fathers!) meaning, the One Who created you and your forefathers, those who came before Fir`awn and his time.

(He said) that is, Fir`awn said:

(Verily, your Messenger who has been sent to you is a madman!) meaning, there is no sense in his claim that there is any god other than me!'

((Musa) said) -- to those in whose hearts Fir`awn had planted doubts:

(Lord of the east and the west, and all that is between them, if you did but understand!) `He is the One Who made the east the place where the heavenly bodies rise, and made the west the place where they set; this is the system to which He has subjugated all the heavenly bodies, stationary and moving. If what Fir`awn claims is true, that he is your lord and your god, then let him turn things around so that the heavenly bodies set in the east and rise in the west.' This is similar to the Ayah,

(who disputed with Ibrahim about his Lord, because Allah had given him the kingdom When Ibrahim said: "My Lord is He Who gives life and causes death." He said, "I give life and cause death." Ibrahim said, "Verily, Allah brings the sun from the east. So cause it to rise from the west.") (2:258) So when Fir`awn was defeated in debate, he resorted to the use of his force and power, believing that this would be effective in dealing with Musa, peace be upon him, so he said, as Allah tells us:

Surah: 26 Ayah: 29, Ayah: 30, Ayah: 31, Ayah: 32, Ayah: 33, Ayah: 34, Ayah: 35, Ayah: 36 & Ayah: 37

قَالَ لَئِنِ ٱتَّخَذْتَ إِلَٰهًا غَيْرِى لَأَجْعَلَنَّكَ مِنَ ٱلْمَسْجُونِينَ ﴿٢٩﴾

29. (Fir'aun (Pharaoh)) said: "If you choose an ilâh (god) other than me, I will certainly put you among the prisoners."

قَالَ أَوَلَوْ جِئْتُكَ بِشَىْءٍ مُّبِينٍ ﴿٣٠﴾

30. (Mûsa (Moses)) said: "Even if I bring you something manifest (and convincing)?"

قَالَ فَأْتِ بِهِۦٓ إِن كُنتَ مِنَ ٱلصَّٰدِقِينَ ﴿٣١﴾

31. (Fir'aun (Pharaoh)) said: "Bring it forth then, if you are of the truthful!"

فَأَلْقَىٰ عَصَاهُ فَإِذَا هِىَ ثُعْبَانٌ مُّبِينٌ ﴿٣٢﴾

32. So (Mûsa (Moses)) threw his stick, and behold, it was a serpent, manifest.

وَنَزَعَ يَدَهُۥ فَإِذَا هِىَ بَيْضَآءُ لِلنَّٰظِرِينَ ﴿٣٣﴾

33. And he drew out his hand, and behold, it was white to all beholders!

قَالَ لِلْمَلَإِ حَوْلَهُۥٓ إِنَّ هَٰذَا لَسَٰحِرٌ عَلِيمٌ ﴿٣٤﴾

34. (Fir'aun (Pharaoh)) said to the chiefs around him: "Verily! This is indeed a well-versed sorcerer.

يُرِيدُ أَن يُخْرِجَكُم مِّنْ أَرْضِكُم بِسِحْرِهِۦ فَمَاذَا تَأْمُرُونَ ﴿٣٥﴾

35. "He wants to drive you out of your land by his sorcery, what is it then that you command?"

قَالُوٓاْ أَرْجِهْ وَأَخَاهُ وَٱبْعَثْ فِى ٱلْمَدَآئِنِ حَٰشِرِينَ ﴿٣٦﴾

36. They said: "Put him off and his brother (for a while), and send callers to the cities;

يَأْتُوكَ بِكُلِّ سَحَّارٍ عَلِيمٍ ﴿٣٧﴾

37. "To bring up to you every well-versed sorcerer."

Transliteration

29. Qala la-ini ittakhathta ilahan ghayree laajAAalannaka mina almasjooneena 30. Qala awa law ji/tuka bishay-in mubeenin 31. Qala fa/ti bihi in kunta mina alssadiqeena 32. Faalqa AAasahu fa-itha hiya thuAAbanun mubeenun 33. WanazaAAa

yadahu fa-itha hiya baydao lilnnathireena 34. Qala lilmala-i hawlahu inna hatha lasahirun Aaaleemun 35. Yureedu an yukhrijakum min ardikum bisihrihi famatha ta/muroona 36. Qaloo arjih waakhahu waibAAath fee almada-ini hashireena 37. Ya/tooka bikulli sahharin AAaleemin

Tafsir Ibn Kathir

After the Rational Proof, Fir`awn resorts to Force

When proof had been established against Fir`awn, clearly and rationally, he resorted to using force against Musa, thinking that after this there would no further room for discussion. So he said:

(If you choose a god other than me, I will certainly put you among the prisoners.) To this, Musa responded:

(Even if I bring you something manifest) meaning, clear and definitive proof.

(Fir`awn said: "Bring it forth then, if you are of the truthful!" So he threw his stick, and behold, it was a serpent, manifest.) meanig, it was very clear and obvious, with a huge body and a big mouth, terrifying in appearance.

(And he drew out his hand,) meaning, from his sleeve,

(and behold, it was white to all beholders!) It was shining like a piece of the moon. Since Fir`awn was already doomed, he hastened to stubborn denial, and said to the chiefs around him:

(Verily, this is indeed a well-versed sorcerer.) One who knows a great deal of magic or witchcraft. Fir`awn was trying to convince them that this was sorcery, not a miracle. Then he provoked them against Musa, trying to make them oppose him and disbelieve in him, and said:

(He wants to drive you out of your land by his sorcery...) meaning, `he wants to capture the people's hearts and win them over by doing this, so that they will support him, and help him and follow him, and he will defeat you in your own land and take the land from you. So advise me, what should I do with him'

(They said: "Put him off and his brother, and send callers to the cities; to bring up to you every well-versed sorcerer.") meaning, `delay him and his brother until you gather together all the sorcerers from every city and region of your kingdom so that they may confront him and produce something like he produces, then you will defeat him and have the victory.' So Fir`awn did as they suggested, which is what Allah decreed would happen to them, so that all the people would gather in one place and the signs and proof of Allah would be made manifest before them all in one day.

Chapter 26. Ash-Shu'araa (The Poets), Verses 001-227

Surah: 26 Ayah: 38, Ayah: 39, Ayah: 40, Ayah: 41, Ayah: 42, Ayah: 43, Ayah: 44, Ayah: 45, Ayah: 46, Ayah: 47 & Ayah: 48

فَجُمِعَ ٱلسَّحَرَةُ لِمِيقَٰتِ يَوْمٍ مَّعْلُومٍ ۝

38. So the sorcerers were assembled at a fixed time on a day appointed.

وَقِيلَ لِلنَّاسِ هَلْ أَنتُم مُّجْتَمِعُونَ ۝

39. And it was said to the people: "Are you (too) going to assemble?

لَعَلَّنَا نَتَّبِعُ ٱلسَّحَرَةَ إِن كَانُوا۟ هُمُ ٱلْغَٰلِبِينَ ۝

40. "That we may follow the sorcerers (who were on Fir'aun's (Pharaoh) religion of disbelief) if they are the winners."

فَلَمَّا جَاءَ ٱلسَّحَرَةُ قَالُوا۟ لِفِرْعَوْنَ أَئِنَّ لَنَا لَأَجْرًا إِن كُنَّا نَحْنُ ٱلْغَٰلِبِينَ ۝

41. So when the sorcerers arrived, they said to Fir'aun (Pharaoh): "Will there surely be a reward for us if we are the winners?"

قَالَ نَعَمْ وَإِنَّكُمْ إِذًا لَّمِنَ ٱلْمُقَرَّبِينَ ۝

42. He said: "Yes, and you shall then verily be of those brought near (to myself)."

قَالَ لَهُم مُّوسَىٰٓ أَلْقُوا۟ مَآ أَنتُم مُّلْقُونَ ۝

43. Mûsa (Moses) said to them: "Throw what you are going to throw!"

فَأَلْقَوْا۟ حِبَالَهُمْ وَعِصِيَّهُمْ وَقَالُوا۟ بِعِزَّةِ فِرْعَوْنَ إِنَّا لَنَحْنُ ٱلْغَٰلِبُونَ ۝

44. So they threw their ropes and their sticks, and said: "By the might of Fir'aun (Pharaoh), it is we who will certainly win!"

فَأَلْقَىٰ مُوسَىٰ عَصَاهُ فَإِذَا هِيَ تَلْقَفُ مَا يَأْفِكُونَ ۝

45. Then Mûsa (Moses) threw his stick, and behold, it swallowed up all that falsehoods they falsely showed!

فَأُلْقِيَ ٱلسَّحَرَةُ سَٰجِدِينَ ۝

46. And the sorcerers fell down prostrate.

قَالُوٓا۟ ءَامَنَّا بِرَبِّ ٱلْعَٰلَمِينَ ۝

47. Saying: "We believe in the Lord of the 'Alamîn (mankind, jinn and all that exists).

48. "The Lord of Mûsa (Moses) and Hârûn (Aaron)."

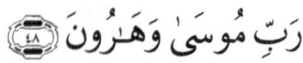

Transliteration

38. FajumiAAa alssaharatu limeeqati yawmin maAAloomin 39. Waqeela lilnnasi hal antum mujtamiAAoona 40. LaAAallana nattabiAAu alssaharata in kanoo humu alghalibeena 41. Falamma jaa alssaharatu qaloo lifirAAawna a-inna lana laajran in kunna nahnu alghalibeena 42. Qala naAAam wa-innakum ithan lamina almuqarrabeena 43. Qala lahum moosa alqoo ma antum mulqoona 44. Faalqaw hibalahum waAAisiyyahum waqaloo biAAizzati firAAawna inna lanahnu alghaliboona 45. Faalqa moosa AAasahu fa-itha hiya talqafu ma ya/fikoona 46. Faolqiya alssaharatu sajideena 47. Qaloo amanna birabbi alAAalameena 48. Rabbi moosa waharoona

Tafsir Ibn Kathir

Between Musa, peace be upon him, and the Sorcerers Allah describes the actual encounter between Musa, peace be upon him, and the Egyptians in Surat Al-A`raf, Surah Ta Ha, and in this Surah.

The Egyptians wanted to extinguish the Light of Allah with their words, but Allah insisted that His Light should prevail even though the disbelievers disliked that. This is the issue of disbelief and faith; they never confront one another but faith always prevails:

(Nay, We fling the truth against the falsehood, so it destroys it, and behold, it disappears. And woe to you for that which you ascribe.) (21:18)

(And say: "Truth has come and falsehood has vanished.") (17:81) The sorcerers of Egypt were the most skilled in the art of illusion, but when a huge group of them gathered from all corners of the land, and the people came together on that day whose exact numbers are known to Allah Alone, one of them said:

(That we may follow the sorcerers if they are the winners.) They did not say: `we will follow the truth, whether it rests with the sorcerers or with Musa;' the people were followers of the religion of their king.

(So, when the sorcerers arrived,) means, when they reached the court of Fir`awn, and a pavilion had been erected for him. There he gathered his servants, followers, administrators, and provincial leaders, and the soldiers of his kingdom. The sorcerers stood before Fir`awn, asking him to treat them well and bring them closer to him if they prevailed in this matter which he had brought them together for. They said:

("Will there surely be a reward for us if we are the winners" He said: "Yes, and you shall then verily be of those brought near.") meaning, `and you will be given more than what you are asking for; I will make you among those who are close to me, those who sit with me.' So they went back to their places:

(They said: "O Musa! Either you throw first or we be the first to throw" (Musa) said: "Nay, throw you (first)!") (20:65-66). Here the incident is described more briefly. Musa said to them:

("Throw what you are going to throw!" So, they threw their ropes and their sticks, and said: "By the might of Fir`awn, it is we who will certainly win!") This is what the ignorant masses say when they do something: `this is by the virtue of So-and-so!' In Surat Al-A`raf Allah mentioned that they:

(They bewitched the eyes of the people, and struck terror into them, and they displayed a great magic) (7:116). And in Surah Ta Ha He said:

(Then behold! their ropes and their sticks, by their magic, appeared to him as though they moved fast.) until Allah saying:

(and the magician will never be successful, whatever the amount (of skill) he may attain) (20:69). And here Allah says:

(Then Musa threw his stick, and behold, it swallowed up all that they falsely showed!) by snatching up and catching them from every corner and swallowing them up, and it did not leave any of them untouched. Allah says:

(Thus truth was confirmed, and all that they did was made of no effect.) until

(The Lord of Musa and Harun.) (7:118-122) This was a very serious matter, furnishing decisive proof leaving no room for any excuse. Fir`awn's supporters, who sought and hoped that they would prevail over Musa, were themselves defeated. At that moment they believed in Musa and prostrated to Allah, the Lord of Al-`Alamin Who sent Musa and Harun with the truth and an obvious miracle. Fir`awn was defeated in a manner the likes of which the world had never seen, but he remained arrogant and stubborn despite the clear evidence, may the curse of Allah and the angels and all of mankind be upon him. He resorted to arrogance and stubbornness and propagating falsehood. He began to issue threats against them, saying:

(Verily, he is your chief who has taught you magic) (20:71).

(Surely, this is a plot which you have plotted in the city) (7:123).

Surah: 26 Ayah: 49, Ayah: 50 & Ayah: 51

قَالَ ءَامَنتُمْ لَهُۥ قَبْلَ أَنْ ءَاذَنَ لَكُمْ ۖ إِنَّهُۥ لَكَبِيرُكُمُ ٱلَّذِى عَلَّمَكُمُ ٱلسِّحْرَ فَلَسَوْفَ تَعْلَمُونَ ۚ لَأُقَطِّعَنَّ أَيْدِيَكُمْ وَأَرْجُلَكُم مِّنْ خِلَٰفٍ وَلَأُصَلِّبَنَّكُمْ أَجْمَعِينَ ۝

49. (Fir'aun (Pharaoh)) said: "You have believed in him before I give you leave. Surely, he indeed is your chief, who has taught you magic! So verily, you shall come to know. Verily, I will cut off your hands and your feet on opposite sides, and I will crucify you all."

$$\text{قَالُوا۟ لَا ضَيْرَ ۖ إِنَّآ إِلَىٰ رَبِّنَا مُنقَلِبُونَ ﴿٥٠﴾}$$

50. They said: "No harm! Surely, to our Lord (Allâh) we are to return;

$$\text{إِنَّا نَطْمَعُ أَن يَغْفِرَ لَنَا رَبُّنَا خَطَـٰيَـٰنَآ أَن كُنَّآ أَوَّلَ ٱلْمُؤْمِنِينَ ﴿٥١﴾}$$

51. "Verily! We really hope that our Lord will forgive us our sins, as we are the first of the believers (in Mûsa (Moses) and in the Monotheism which he has brought from Allâh)."

Transliteration

49. Qala amantum lahu qabla an athana lakum innahu lakabeerukumu allathee AAallamakumu alssihra falasawfa taAAlamoona laoqattiAAanna aydiyakumwaarjulakum min khilafin walaosallibannakum ajmaAAeena 50. Qaloo la dayra inna ila rabbina munqaliboona 51. Inna natmaAAu an yaghfira lana rabbuna khatayana an kunna awwala almu/mineena

Tafsir Ibn Kathir

Between Fir`awn and the Sorcerers

His threats against them resulted only in an increase in their faith and submission to Allah, for the veil of disbelief had been lifted from their hearts and the truth became clear to them because they knew something that their people did not: that what Musa had done could not have been done by any human being unless Allah helped him, making it proof and an evidence of the truth of what he had brought from his Lord. Then Fir`awn said to them:

(You have believed in him before I give you leave.) meaning, `you should have asked my permission for what you did, and you did not consult with me; if I had given you permission you could have done it, and if I did not allow you, you should not have done it, for I am the ruler and the one to be obeyed.'

(Surely, he indeed is your chief, who has taught you magic!) This is stubborn talk, and anyone can see that it is nonsense, for they had never met Musa before that day, so how could he have been their chief who taught them how to do magic No rational person would say this. Then Fir`awn threatened to cut off their hands and feet, and crucify them. They said:

(No harm!) meaning, `no problem, that will not harm us and we do not care.'

(Surely, to our Lord we are to return.) means, `the return of us all is to Allah, may He be glorified, and He will never allow the reward of anyone who has done good to be lost. What you have done to us is not hidden from Him, and He will reward us in full for that.' So they said:

(Verily, we really hope that our Lord will forgive us our sins,) `the sins we have committed and the magic you forced us to do.'

(as we are the first of the believers,) means, because we are the first of our people, the Egyptians, to believe. So he killed them all.

Surah: 26 Ayah: 52, Ayah: 53, Ayah: 54, Ayah: 55, Ayah: 56, Ayah: 57, Ayah: 58 & Ayah: 59

$$\text{۞ وَأَوْحَيْنَا إِلَىٰ مُوسَىٰ أَنْ أَسْرِ بِعِبَادِي إِنَّكُم مُّتَّبَعُونَ ۝}$$

52. And We revealed to Mûsa (Moses), saying: " Depart by night with My slaves, verily you will be pursued."

$$\text{فَأَرْسَلَ فِرْعَوْنُ فِي ٱلْمَدَائِنِ حَاشِرِينَ ۝}$$

53. Then Fir'aun (Pharaoh) sent callers to (all) the cities.

$$\text{إِنَّ هَٰؤُلَاءِ لَشِرْذِمَةٌ قَلِيلُونَ ۝}$$

54. (Saying): "Verily! These indeed are but a small band.

$$\text{وَإِنَّهُمْ لَنَا لَغَائِظُونَ ۝}$$

55. "And verily, they have done what has enraged us.

$$\text{وَإِنَّا لَجَمِيعٌ حَاذِرُونَ ۝}$$

56. "But we are a host all assembled, amply fore-warned."

$$\text{فَأَخْرَجْنَاهُم مِّن جَنَّاتٍ وَعُيُونٍ ۝}$$

57. So, We expelled them from gardens and springs,

$$\text{وَكُنُوزٍ وَمَقَامٍ كَرِيمٍ ۝}$$

58. Treasures, and every kind of honorable place.

$$\text{كَذَٰلِكَ وَأَوْرَثْنَاهَا بَنِي إِسْرَائِيلَ ۝}$$

59. Thus (We turned them (Pharaoh's people) out) and We caused the Children of Israel to inherit them.

Transliteration

52. Waawhayna ila moosa an asri biAAibadee innakum muttabaAAoona 53. Faarsala firAAawnu fee almada-ini hashireena 54. Inna haola-i lashirthimatun qaleeloona 55. Wa-innahum lana lagha-ithoona 56. Wa-inna lajameeAAun hathiroona 57. Faakhrajnahum min jannatin waAAuyoonin 58. Wakunoozin wamaqamin kareemin 59. Kathalika waawrathnaha banee isra-eela

Tafsir Ibn Kathir

The Exodus of the Children of Israel from Egypt

After Musa stayed in Egypt for a long time, and the proof of Allah was established against Fir`awn and his chiefs, yet they were still arrogant and stubborn, then there was nothing left for them but punishment and vengeance. So Allah commanded Musa, peace be upon him, to take the Children of Israel out of Egypt by night, and take them wherever he would be commanded. So Musa, peace be upon him, did as he was commanded by his Lord, may He be glorified, and he led them forth after they had borrowed an abundance of jewelry from the people of Fir`awn. As more than one of the scholars of Tafsir have said, they left when the moon was rising, and Mujahid, may Allah have mercy on him, said that the moon was eclipsed that night. And Allah knows best. Musa asked about the grave of Yusuf (Prophet Joseph), peace be upon him, and an old woman from among the Children of Israel showed him where it was, so he took the remains with them, and it was said that they were among the things that were carried by Musa himself, may peace be upon them both. It was also said that Yusuf, peace be upon him, had left instructions in his will that if the Children of Israel ever left Egypt, they should take his remains with them. The following morning, when there was nobody to be found in the Israelite quarters, Fir`awn became angry and his anger intensified since Allah had decreed that he was to be destroyed. So he quickly sent his callers to all his cities, i.e., to mobilize his troops and bring them together, and he called out to them:

(Verily, these) meaning, the Children of Israel,

(indeed are but a small band.) meaning, a small group.

(And verily, they have done what has enraged us.) means, `every time we have heard anything about them, it has upset us and made us angry.'

(But we are a host all assembled, amply forewarned.) means, `we are constantly taking precautions lest they betray us.' Some of the Salaf read this with the meaning, "we are constantly forewarned and forearmed. And I want to destroy them to the last man, and destroy all their lands and property." So he and his troops were punished with the very things he sought to inflict upon the Children of Israel. Allah says:

(So, We expelled them from gardens and springs, treasures, and every kind of honorable place.) meaning, they were thrown out of those blessings and into Hell, and they left behind the honorable places, gardens and rivers, wealth, provision, position and power in this world:

(Thus and We caused the Children of Israel to inherit them.) This is like the Ayat:

(And We made the people who were considered weak to inherit the eastern parts of the land and the western parts thereof which We have blessed) (7: 137).

(And We wished to do a favor to those who were weak in the land, and to make them rulers and to make them the inheritors) The two Ayat thereafter: (28:5-6).

Chapter 26. Ash-Shu'araa (The Poets), Verses 001-227

Surah: 26 Ayah: 60, Ayah: 61, Ayah: 62, Ayah: 63, Ayah: 64, Ayah: 65, Ayah: 66, Ayah: 67 & Ayah: 68

فَأَتْبَعُوهُم مُّشْرِقِينَ ۝

60. So they pursued them at sunrise.

فَلَمَّا تَرَٰٓءَا ٱلْجَمْعَانِ قَالَ أَصْحَٰبُ مُوسَىٰٓ إِنَّا لَمُدْرَكُونَ ۝

61. And when the two hosts saw each other, the companions of Mûsa (Moses) said: "We are sure to be overtaken."

قَالَ كَلَّآ ۖ إِنَّ مَعِىَ رَبِّى سَيَهْدِينِ ۝

62. (Mûsa (Moses)) said: "Nay, verily! With me is my Lord, He will guide me."

فَأَوْحَيْنَآ إِلَىٰ مُوسَىٰٓ أَنِ ٱضْرِب بِّعَصَاكَ ٱلْبَحْرَ ۖ فَٱنفَلَقَ فَكَانَ كُلُّ فِرْقٍ كَٱلطَّوْدِ ٱلْعَظِيمِ ۝

63. Then We revealed to Mûsa (Moses) (saying): "Strike the sea with your stick." And it parted, and each separate part (of that sea water) became like huge mountain.

وَأَزْلَفْنَا ثَمَّ ٱلْءَاخَرِينَ ۝

64. Then We brought near the others (Fir'aun's (Pharaoh) party) to that place.

وَأَنجَيْنَا مُوسَىٰ وَمَن مَّعَهُۥٓ أَجْمَعِينَ ۝

65. And We saved Mûsa (Moses) and all those with him.

ثُمَّ أَغْرَقْنَا ٱلْءَاخَرِينَ ۝

66. Then We drowned the others.

إِنَّ فِى ذَٰلِكَ لَءَايَةً ۖ وَمَا كَانَ أَكْثَرُهُم مُّؤْمِنِينَ ۝

67. Verily in this is indeed a sign (or a proof), yet most of them are not believers.

وَإِنَّ رَبَّكَ لَهُوَ ٱلْعَزِيزُ ٱلرَّحِيمُ ۝

68. And verily your Lord, He is truly the All-Mighty, the Most Merciful.

Transliteration

60. FaatbaAAoohum mushriqeena 61. Falamma taraa aljamAAani qala as-habu moosa inna lamudrakoona 62. Qala kalla inna maAAiya rabbee sayahdeeni 63. Faawhayna ila moosa ani idrib biAAasaka albahra fainfalaqa fakana kullu firqin kaalttawdi

alAAatheemi   64. Waazlafna thamma al-akhareena 65. Waanjayna moosa waman maAAahu ajmaAAeena 66. Thumma aghraqna al-akhareena   67. Inna fee thalika laayatan wama kana aktharuhum mu/mineena   68. Wa-inna rabbaka lahuwa alAAazeezu alrraheemu

Tafsir Ibn Kathir

Fir`awn's Pursuit and Expulsion of the Children of Israel, and how He and His People were drowned

More than one of the scholars of Tafsir said that Fir`awn set out with a huge group, a group containing the leaders and entire government of Egypt at that time, i.e., the decision-makers and influential figures, princes, ministers, nobles, leaders and soldiers.

(So, they pursued them at sunrise.) means, they caught up with the Children of Israel at sunrise.

(And when the two hosts saw each other,) means, each group saw the other. At that point,

(the companions of Musa said: "We are sure to be overtaken.") This was because Fir`awn and his people caught up with them on the shores of the Red Sea, so the sea was ahead of them and Fir`awn and his troops were behind them. Hence they said:

("We are sure to be overtaken." (Musa) said: "Nay, verily with me is my Lord. He will guide me.") meaning, `nothing of what you fear will happen to you, for Allah is the One Who commanded me to bring you here, and He does not go back on His promise.' Harun, peace be upon him, was in the front, with Yusha` bin Nun and a believer from the family of Fir`awn, and Musa, peace be upon him, was in the rear. More than one of the scholars of Tafsir said that they stood there not knowing what to do, and Yusha` bin Nun or the believer from the family of Fir`awn said to Musa, peace be upon him, "O Prophet of Allah, is it here that your Lord commanded you to bring us" He said: "Yes." Then Fir`awn and his troops drew near and were very close indeed. At that point Allah commanded his Prophet Musa, peace be upon him, to strike the sea with his staff, so he struck it, and it parted, by the will of Allah. Allah says:

(And it parted, and each separate part became like huge mountain.) meaning, like mighty mountains. This was the view of Ibn Mas`ud, Ibn `Abbas, Muhammad bin Ka`b, Ad-Dahhak, Qatadah and others. `Ata' Al-Khurasani said, "It refers to a pass between two mountains." Ibn `Abbas said, "The sea divided into twelve paths, one for each of the tribes." As-Suddi added, "And in it there were windows through which they could see one another, and the water was erected like walls." Allah sent the wind to the sea bed to make it solid like the land. Allah says:

(and strike a dry path for them in the sea, fearing neither to be overtaken nor being afraid) (20:77). And here He says:

(Then We brought near the others to that place.) Ibn `Abbas, `Ata' Al-Khurasani, Qatadah and As-Suddi said:

(Then We brought near) means, "We brought Fir`awn and his troops near to the sea."

(And We saved Musa and all those with him. Then We drowned the others.) meaning: `We saved Musa and the Children of Israel and whoever followed their religion, and none of them were destroyed, but Fir`awn and his troops were drowned and not one of them remained alive, but was destroyed.' Then Allah says:

(Verily, in this is indeed a sign,) meaning, this story with its wonders and tales of aid to the believing servants of Allah is definitive proof and evidence of Allah's wisdom.

(yet most of them are not believers. And verily your Lord, He is truly the All-Mighty, the Most Merciful.) The explanation of this phrase has already been discussed above.

Surah: 26 Ayah: 69, Ayah: 70, Ayah: 71, Ayah: 72, Ayah: 73, Ayah: 74, Ayah: 75, Ayah: 76 & Ayah: 77

وَٱتْلُ عَلَيْهِمْ نَبَأَ إِبْرَٰهِيمَ ۝

69. And recite to them the story of Ibrâhim (Abraham).

إِذْ قَالَ لِأَبِيهِ وَقَوْمِهِۦ مَا تَعْبُدُونَ ۝

70. When he said to his father and his people: "What do you worship?"

قَالُوا۟ نَعْبُدُ أَصْنَامًا فَنَظَلُّ لَهَا عَٰكِفِينَ ۝

71. They said: "We worship idols, and to them we are ever devoted."

قَالَ هَلْ يَسْمَعُونَكُمْ إِذْ تَدْعُونَ ۝

72. He said: "Do they hear you, when you call (on them)?

أَوْ يَنفَعُونَكُمْ أَوْ يَضُرُّونَ ۝

73. "Or do they benefit you or do they harm (you)?"

قَالُوا۟ بَلْ وَجَدْنَآ ءَابَآءَنَا كَذَٰلِكَ يَفْعَلُونَ ۝

74. They said: "(Nay) but we found our fathers doing so."

قَالَ أَفَرَءَيْتُم مَّا كُنتُمْ تَعْبُدُونَ ۝

75. He said: "Do you observe that which you have been worshipping -

$$\text{أَنتُمْ وَءَابَاؤُكُمُ ٱلْأَقْدَمُونَ ۝}$$

76. "You and your ancient fathers?

$$\text{فَإِنَّهُمْ عَدُوٌّ لِّى إِلَّا رَبَّ ٱلْعَٰلَمِينَ ۝}$$

77. "Verily! They are enemies to me, save the Lord of the 'Alamîn (mankind, jinn and all that exists),

Transliteration

69. Waotlu AAalayhim nabaa ibraheema   70. Ith qala li-abeehi waqawmihi ma taAAbudoona 71. Qaloo naAAbudu asnaman fanathallu laha Aaakifeena 72. Qala hal yasmaAAoonakum ith tadAAoona 73. Aw yanfaAAoonakum aw yadurroona 74. Qaloo bal wajadna abaana kathalika yafAAaloona 75. Qala afaraaytum ma kuntum taAAbudoona 76. Antum waabaokumu al-aqdamoona 77. Fa-innahum AAaduwwun lee illa rabba alAAalameena

Tafsir Ibn Kathir

How the Close Friend of Allah, Ibrahim spoke out against Shirk

Here Allah tells us about His servant, Messenger and Close Friend, Ibrahim, upon him be peace, the leader of the pure monotheists. Allah commanded His Messenger Muhammad to recite this story to his Ummah so that they could follow this example of sincerity towards Allah, putting one's trust in Him, worshipping Him Alone with no partner or associate, and renouncing Shirk and its people. Allah granted guidance to Ibrahim before, i.e., from a very early age he had denounced his people's practice of worshipping idols with Allah, may He be exalted.

(When he said to his father and his people: "What do you worship") meaning: what are these statues to which you are so devoted

(They said: "We worship idols, and to them we are ever devoted.") meaning: we are devoted to worshipping them and praying to them.

(He said: "Do they hear you when you call Or do they benefit you or do they cause harm" They said: "(Nay) but we found our fathers doing so.") They knew that their idols could not do anything, but they had seen their fathers doing this, so they made haste to follow in their footsteps. So Ibrahim said to them:

(Do you observe that which you have been worshipping --you and your ancient fathers Verily, they are enemies to me, save the Lord of Al-`Alamin.) meaning, `if these idols mean anything and have any influence, then let them do me any kind of harm, for I am an enemy to them and I do not care about them or think anything of them.' This is akin to the way Allah described Nuh:

(So devise your plot, you and your partners) (10:71). And Hud, upon him be peace, said:

("I call Allah to witness and bear you witness that I am free from that which you ascribe as partners in worship. So plot against me, all of you, and give me no respite. I put my trust in Allah, my Lord and your Lord! There is not a moving creature but He has the grasp of its forelock. Verily, my Lord is on the straight path) (11:54-56). rSimilarly, Ibrahim denounced their gods and idols and said:

(And how should I fear those whom you associate in worship with Allah, while you fear not that you have joined in worship with Allah) (6:81). And Allah said:

(Indeed there has been an excellent example for you in Ibrahim) until His saying;

(until you believe in Allah Alone) (60:4).

(And (remember) when Ibrahim said to his father and his people: "Verily, I am innocent of what you worship, except Him Who created me; and verily, He will guide me." And he made it a Word lasting among his offspring, that they may turn back) (43:26-28). meaning: "La Ilaha Illallah."

Surah: 26 Ayah: 78, Ayah: 79, Ayah: 80, Ayah: 81 & Ayah: 82

ٱلَّذِى خَلَقَنِى فَهُوَ يَهْدِينِ ۝

78. "Who has created me, and it is He Who guides me.

وَٱلَّذِى هُوَ يُطْعِمُنِى وَيَسْقِينِ ۝

79. "And it is He Who feeds me and gives me to drink.

وَإِذَا مَرِضْتُ فَهُوَ يَشْفِينِ ۝

80. "And when I am ill, it is He who cures me.

وَٱلَّذِى يُمِيتُنِى ثُمَّ يُحْيِينِ ۝

81. "And Who will cause me to die, and then will bring me to life (again).

وَٱلَّذِى أَطْمَعُ أَن يَغْفِرَ لِى خَطِيئَتِى يَوْمَ ٱلدِّينِ ۝

82. "And Who, I hope will forgive me my faults on the Day of Recompense, (the Day of Resurrection)."

Transliteration

78. Allathee khalaqanee fahuwa yahdeeni   79. Waallathee huwa yutAAimunee wayasqeeni   80. Wa-itha maridtu fahuwa yashfeeni   81. Waallathee yumeetunee thumma yuhyeeni   82. Waallathee atmaAAu an yaghfira lee khatee-atee yawma alddeeni

Tafsir Ibn Kathir

Ibrahim mentions Allah's Kindness towards Him

Ibrahim said, "I will not worship any but the One Who does these things:

(Who has created me, and it is He Who guides me.) He is the Creator Who has decreed certain things to which He guides His creation, so each person follows the path which is decreed for him. Allah is the One Who guides whomsoever He wills and leaves astray whomsoever He wills.

(And it is He Who feeds me and gives me to drink.) He is my Creator Who provides for me from that which He has made available in the heavens and on earth. He drives the clouds and causes water to fall with which He revives the earth and brings forth its fruits as provision for mankind. He sends down the water fresh and sweet so that many of those whom He has created, animals and men alike, may drink from it.

(And when I am ill, it is He Who cures me.) Here he attributed sickness to himself, even though it is Allah Who decrees it, out of respect towards Allah. By the same token, Allah commands us to say in the prayer,

(Guide us to the straight way) (1:6) to the end of the Surah. Grace and guidance are attributed to Allah, may He be exalted, but the subject of the verb with reference to anger is omitted, and going astray is attributed to the people. This is like when the Jinn said:

(And we know not whether evil is intended for those on earth, or whether their Lord intends for them a right path) (72:10) Similarly, Ibrahim said:

(And when I am ill, it is He Who cures me.) meaning, `when I fall sick, no one is able to heal me but Him, Who heals me with the means that may lead to recovery'.

(And Who will cause me to die, and then will bring me to life.) He is the One Who gives life and causes death, and no one besides Him is able to do that, for He is the One Who originates and repeats.

(And Who, I hope, will forgive me my faults on the Day of Recompense.) means, no one is able to forgive sins in this world or the Hereafter except Him. Who can forgive sins except Allah For He is the One Who does whatever He wills.

Surah: 26 Ayah: 83, Ayah: 84, Ayah: 85, Ayah: 86, Ayah: 87, Ayah: 88 & Ayah: 89

رَبِّ هَبْ لِى حُكْمًا وَأَلْحِقْنِى بِالصَّالِحِينَ ۝

83. My Lord! Bestow Hukm (religious knowledge, right judgement of the affairs and Prophethood) on me, and join me with the righteous.

وَاجْعَل لِّى لِسَانَ صِدْقٍ فِى الْآخِرِينَ ۝

84. And grant me an honorable mention in later generations.

$$\text{وَاجْعَلْنِي مِن وَرَثَةِ جَنَّةِ ٱلنَّعِيمِ ۝}$$

85. And make me one of the inheritors of the Paradise of Delight.

$$\text{وَاغْفِرْ لِأَبِي إِنَّهُ كَانَ مِنَ ٱلضَّالِّينَ ۝}$$

86. And forgive my father, verily he is of the erring.

$$\text{وَلَا تُخْزِنِي يَوْمَ يُبْعَثُونَ ۝}$$

87. And disgrace me not on the Day when (all the creatures) will be resurrected.

$$\text{يَوْمَ لَا يَنفَعُ مَالٌ وَلَا بَنُونَ ۝}$$

88. The Day whereon neither wealth nor sons will avail,

$$\text{إِلَّا مَنْ أَتَى ٱللَّهَ بِقَلْبٍ سَلِيمٍ ۝}$$

89. Except him who brings to Allâh a clean heart (clean from Shirk (polytheism) and Nifâq (hypocrisy))

Transliteration

83. Rabbi hab lee hukman waalhiqnee bialssaliheena 84. WaijAAal lee lisana sidqin fee al-akhireena 85. WaijAAalnee min warathati jannati alnnaAAeemi 86. Waighfir li-abee innahu kana mina alddalleena 87. Wala tukhzinee yawma yubAAathoona 88. Yawma la yanfaAAu malun wala banoona 89. Illa man ata Allaha biqalbin saleemin

Tafsir Ibn Kathir

The Prayer of Ibrahim for Himself and for His Father

Here Ibrahim, upon him be peace, asks his Lord to give him Hukm. Ibn `Abbas said, "This is knowledge."

(and join me with the righteous.) means, `make me one of the righteous in this world and the Hereafter.' This is like the words the Prophet said three times when he was dying:

$$\text{«اللَّهُمَّ فِي الرَّفِيقِ الْأَعْلَى»}$$

(O Allah, with the Exalted Companion (of Paradise)).

(And grant me an honorable mention in later generations.) meaning, `cause me to be remembered in a good manner after my death, so that I will be spoken of and taken as a good example.' This is like the Ayah,

(And We left for him (a goodly remembrance) among the later generations: "Salam (peace) be upon Ibrahim. Thus indeed do we reward the good doers.) (37:108-110)

(And make me one of the inheritors of the Paradise of Delight.) meaning, `bless me in this world with honorable mention after I am gone, and in the Hereafter by making me one of the inheritors of the Paradise of Delight.'

(And forgive my father,) This is like the Ayah,

(My Lord! Forgive me, and my parents) (71:28). But this is something which Ibrahim, peace be upon him, later stopped doing, as Allah says:

(And Ibrahim's supplication for his father's forgiveness was only because of a promise he had made to him) (9:114) until:

(Verily, Ibrahim was Awwah and was forbearing) (9:114). Allah stopped Ibrahim from asking for forgiveness for his father, as He says:

(Indeed there has been an excellent example for you in Ibrahim and those with him), until His saying:

(but I have no power to do anything for you before Allah.) (60:4),

(And disgrace me not on the Day when they will be resurrected.) means, `protect me from shame on the Day of Resurrection and the Day when all creatures, the first and the last, will be raised.' Al-Bukhari recorded that Abu Hurayrah, may Allah be pleased with him, said that the Prophet said:

«إِنَّ إِبْرَاهِيمَ رَأَى أَبَاهُ يَوْمَ الْقِيَامَةِ عَلَيْهِ الْغَبَرَةُ وَالْقَتَرَة»

(Ibrahim will see his father on the Day of Resurrection, covered with dust and darkness.) According to another narration, also from Abu Hurayrah, may Allah be pleased with him, the Prophet said:

«يَلْقَى إِبْرَاهِيمُ أَبَاهُ فَيَقُولُ: يَا رَبِّ إِنَّكَ وَعَدْتَنِي أَنَّكَ لَا تُخْزِينِي يَوْمَ يُبْعَثُونَ، فَيَقُولُ اللهُ تَعَالَى: إِنِّي حَرَّمْتُ الْجَنَّةَ عَلَى الْكَافِرِين»

(Ibrahim will meet his father and will say: "O Lord, You promised me that You would not disgrace me on the Day when all creatures are resurrected." And Allah will say to him: "I have forbidden Paradise to the disbelievers.") He also recorded this in the Hadiths about the Prophets, upon them be peace, where the wording is:

«يَلْقَى إِبْرَاهِيمُ أَبَاهُ آزَرَ يَوْمَ الْقِيَامَةِ، وَعَلَى وَجْهِ آزَرَ قَتَرَةٌ وَغَبَرَةٌ، فَيَقُولُ لَهُ

Chapter 26. Ash-Shu'araa (The Poets), Verses 001-227

إِبْرَاهِيمُ: أَلَمْ أَقُلْ لَكَ لَا تَعْصِينِي، فَيَقُولُ أَبُوهُ: فَالْيَوْمَ لَا أَعْصِيكَ، فَيَقُولُ إِبْرَاهِيمُ: يَا رَبِّ إِنَّكَ وَعَدْتَنِي أَنْ لَا تُخْزِيَنِي يَوْمَ يُبْعَثُونَ، فَأَيُّ خِزْيٍ أَخْزَى مِنْ أَبِي الْأَبْعَدِ فَيَقُولُ اللهُ تَعَالَى: إِنِّي حَرَّمْتُ الْجَنَّةَ عَلَى الْكَافِرِينَ، ثُمَّ يُقَالُ: يَا إِبْرَاهِيمُ انْظُرْ تَحْتَ رِجْلِكَ، فَيَنْظُرَ، فَإِذَا هُوَ بِذِيخٍ مُتَلَطِّخٍ، فَيُؤْخَذُ بِقَوَائِمِهِ فَيُلْقَى فِي النَّارِ»

(Ibrahim will meet his father Azar on the Day of Resurrection, and there will be dust and darkness on Azar's face. Ibrahim will say to him, "Did I not tell you not to disobey me" His father will say to him: "Today I will not disobey you." Ibrahim will say: "O Lord, You promised me that You would not disgrace me on the Day when they are resurrected, but what disgrace can be greater than seeing my father in this state" Allah will say to him: "I have forbidden Paradise to the disbelievers." Then it will be said: "O Ibrahim! Look beneath your feet." So he will look and there he will see (that his father was changed into) a male hyena covered in dung, which will be caught by the legs and thrown in the Fire.) This was also recorded by Abu `Abdur-Rahman An-Nasa'i in the Tafsir of his Sunan Al-Kubra.

(The Day whereon neither wealth nor sons will avail,) means, a man's wealth will not protect him from the punishment of Allah, even if he were to pay a ransom equivalent to an earthful of gold.

(nor sons) means, `or if you were to pay a ransom of all the people on earth.' On that Day nothing will be of any avail except faith in Allah and sincere devotion to Him, and renunciation of Shirk and its people. Allah says:

(Except him who brings to Allah a clean heart.) meaning, free from any impurity or Shirk. Ibn Sirin said, "The clean heart knows that Allah is true, that the Hour will undoubtedly come and that Allah will resurrect those who are in the graves." Sa`id bin Al-Musayyib said, "The clean heart is the sound heart." This is the heart of the believer, for the heart of the disbeliever and the hypocrite is sick. Allah says:

(In their hearts is a disease) (2:10). Abu `Uthman An-Nisaburi said, "It is the heart that is free from innovation and is content with the Sunnah."

Surah: 26 Ayah: 90, Ayah: 91, Ayah: 92, Ayah: 93, Ayah: 94, Ayah: 95, Ayah: 96, Ayah: 97, Ayah: 98, Ayah: 99, Ayah: 100, Ayah: 101, Ayah: 102, Ayah: 103 & Ayah: 104

وَأُزْلِفَتِ ٱلْجَنَّةُ لِلْمُتَّقِينَ ۝

90. And Paradise will be brought near to the Muttaqûn (The pious and righteous persons. See V.2:2).

وَبُرِّزَتِ ٱلْجَحِيمُ لِلْغَاوِينَ ﴿٩١﴾

91. And the (Hell) Fire will be placed in full view of the erring.

وَقِيلَ لَهُمْ أَيْنَ مَا كُنتُمْ تَعْبُدُونَ ﴿٩٢﴾

92. And it will be said to them: "Where are those (the false gods whom you used to set up as rivals with Allâh) that you used to worship

مِن دُونِ ٱللَّهِ هَلْ يَنصُرُونَكُمْ أَوْ يَنتَصِرُونَ ﴿٩٣﴾

93. "Instead of Allâh? Can they help you or (even) help themselves?"

فَكُبْكِبُوا۟ فِيهَا هُمْ وَٱلْغَاوُۥنَ ﴿٩٤﴾

94. Then they will be thrown on their faces into the (Fire), they and the Ghâwûn (devils, and those who were in error).

وَجُنُودُ إِبْلِيسَ أَجْمَعُونَ ﴿٩٥﴾

95. And the whole hosts of Iblîs (Satan) together.

قَالُوا۟ وَهُمْ فِيهَا يَخْتَصِمُونَ ﴿٩٦﴾

96. They will say while contending therein,

تَٱللَّهِ إِن كُنَّا لَفِى ضَلَٰلٍ مُّبِينٍ ﴿٩٧﴾

97. By Allâh, we were truly in a manifest error,

إِذْ نُسَوِّيكُم بِرَبِّ ٱلْعَٰلَمِينَ ﴿٩٨﴾

98. When We held you (false gods) as equals (in worship) with the Lord of the 'Alamîn (mankind, jinn and all that exists);

وَمَا أَضَلَّنَا إِلَّا ٱلْمُجْرِمُونَ ﴿٩٩﴾

99. And none has brought us into error except the Mujrimûn (Iblîs (Satan) and those of human beings who commit crimes, murderers, polytheists, oppressors).

فَمَا لَنَا مِن شَٰفِعِينَ ﴿١٠٠﴾

100. Now we have no intercessors,

Chapter 26. Ash-Shu'araa (The Poets), Verses 001-227

وَلَا صَدِيقٍ حَمِيمٍ ﴿١١﴾

101. Nor a close friend (to help us).

فَلَوْ أَنَّ لَنَا كَرَّةً فَنَكُونَ مِنَ ٱلْمُؤْمِنِينَ ﴿١٢﴾

102. (Alas!) If we only had a chance to return (to the world), we shall truly be among the believers!

إِنَّ فِي ذَٰلِكَ لَآيَةً وَمَا كَانَ أَكْثَرُهُم مُّؤْمِنِينَ ﴿١٣﴾

103. Verily! In this is indeed a sign, yet most of them are not believers.

وَإِنَّ رَبَّكَ لَهُوَ ٱلْعَزِيزُ ٱلرَّحِيمُ ﴿١٤﴾

104. And verily, your Lord, He is truly the All-Mighty, the Most Merciful.

Transliteration

90. Waozlifati aljannatu lilmuttaqeena 91. Waburrizati aljaheemu lilghaweena 92. Waqeela lahum ayna ma kuntum taAAbudoona 93. Min dooni Allahi hal yansuroonakum aw yantasiroona 94. Fakubkiboo feeha hum waalghawoona 95. Wajunoodu ibleesa ajmaAAoona 96. Qaloo wahum feeha yakhtasimoona 97. TaAllahi in kunna lafee dalalin mubeenin 98. Ith nusawweekum birabbi alAAalameena 99. Wama adallana illa almujrimoona 100. Fama lana min shafiAAeena 101. Wala sadeeqin hameemin 102. Falaw anna lana karratan fanakoona mina almu/mineena 103. Inna fee thalika laayatan wama kana aktharuhum mu/mineena 104. Wa-inna rabbaka lahuwa alAAazeezu alrraheemu

Tafsir Ibn Kathir

Those Who have Taqwa and the Astray on the Day of Resurrection, and the Arguments and Sorrow of the Erring

(And Paradise will be brought near) means, it will be brought close to its people, adorned and decorated for them to behold it. Its people are the pious who preferred it to whatever was in this world, and strove for it in this world.

(And the (Hell) Fire will be placed in full view of the astray.) meaning, it will be shown to them and a neck will stretch forth from it, moaning and sighing, and their hearts will reach their throats. It will be said to its people by way of reproach and rebuke:

(Where are those that you used to worship instead of Allah Can they help you or help themselves) meaning, `the gods and idols whom you used to worship instead of Allah cannot help you today, and they cannot even protect themselves. You and they are fuel for Hell today, which you will surely enter.'

(Then they will be thrown on their faces into it (the Fire), they and the astray.) Mujahid said, "This means, they will be hurled into it." Others said: "They will be thrown on top of one another, the disbelievers and their leaders who called them to Shirk."

(And all of the hosts of Iblis together.) they will all be thrown into it.

(They will say while contending therein, "By Allah, we were truly in a manifest error, when we held you as equals with the Lord of all that exists.") The weak ones among them will say to their arrogant leaders: `Verily, we were following you; can you avail us anything from the Fire' Then they will realize that themselves are to blame and will say: a

(By Allah, we were truly in a manifest error, when we held you as equals with the Lord of all that exists.) meaning, `we obeyed your commands as we should have obeyed the commands of the Lord of the all that exits, and we worshipped you along with the Lord of all that exits.'

(And none has brought us into error except the criminals.) meaning, `nobody called us to do that except the evildoers.'

(Now we have no intercessors.) This is like the Ayah which tells us that they will say:

(...now are there any intercessors for us that they might intercede on our behalf Or could we be sent back so that we might do deeds other than those deeds which we used to do) (7:53). Similarly, in this Surah, Allah tells us that they will say:

(Now we have no intercessors, nor a close friend.)

((Alas!) If we only had a chance to return, we shall truly be among the believers!) They will wish that they could come back to this world so that they could do deeds of obedience to their Lord -- as they claim -- but Allah knows that if they were to come back to this world, they would only go back to doing forbidden things, and He knows that they are liars. Allah tells us in Surah Sad about how the people of Hell will argue with one another, as He says:

(Verily, that is the very truth -- the mutual dispute of the people of the Fire!) (38:64) Then He says:

(Verily, in this is indeed a sign, yet most of them are not believers.) meaning, in the dispute of Ibrahim with his people and his proof of Tawhid there is a sign, i.e., clear evidence that there is no God but Allah.

(yet most of them are not believers. And verily, your Lord, He is truly the All-Mighty, the Most Merciful.)

Surah: 26 Ayah: 105, Ayah: 106, Ayah: 107, Ayah: 108, Ayah: 109 & Ayah: 110

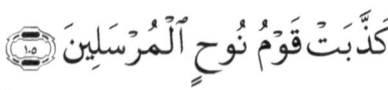

105. The people of Nûh (Noah) belied the Messengers.

إِذْ قَالَ لَهُمْ أَخُوهُمْ نُوحٌ أَلَا تَتَّقُونَ ۝

106. When their brother Nûh (Noah) said to them: "Will you not fear Allâh and obey Him?

إِنِّى لَكُمْ رَسُولٌ أَمِينٌ ۝

107. "I am a trustworthy Messenger to you.

فَاتَّقُوا۟ ٱللَّهَ وَأَطِيعُونِ ۝

108. "So fear Allâh, keep your duty to Him, and obey me.

وَمَا أَسْـَٔلُكُمْ عَلَيْهِ مِنْ أَجْرٍ إِنْ أَجْرِىَ إِلَّا عَلَىٰ رَبِّ ٱلْعَٰلَمِينَ ۝

109. "No reward do I ask of you for it (my Message of Islâmic Monotheism); my reward is only from the Lord of the 'Alamîn (mankind, jinn and all that exists).

فَاتَّقُوا۟ ٱللَّهَ وَأَطِيعُونِ ۝

110. "So keep your duty to Allâh, fear Him and obey me."

Transliteration

105. Kaththabat qawmu noohin almursaleena 106. Ith qala lahum akhoohum noohun ala tattaqoona 107. Innee lakum rasoolun ameenun 108. Faittaqoo Allaha waateeAAooni 109. Wama as-alukum AAalayhi min ajrin in ajriya illa AAala rabbi alAAalameena 110. Faittaqoo Allaha waateeAAooni

Tafsir Ibn Kathir

Nuh's preaching to His People, and Their Response

Here Allah tells us about His servant and Messenger Nuh, peace be upon him, who was the first Messenger sent by Allah to the people of earth after they started to worship idols. Allah sent him to forbid that and to warn people of the consequences of idol worship. But his people belied him and continued their evil practice of worshipping idols besides Allah. Allah revealed that their disbelieving in him was akin to disbelieving in all the Messengers, So Allah said:

(The people of Nuh belied the Messengers. When their brother Nuh said to them: "Will you not have Taqwa") meaning, `do you not fear Allah when you worship others instead of Him'

(I am a trustworthy Messenger to you.) means, `I am the Messenger of Allah to you, faithfully fulfilling the mission with which Allah has sent me. I convey the Messages of my Lord to you, and I do not add anything to them or take anything away from them.,

(So have Taqwa of Allah, and obey me. No reward do I ask of you for it;) means, `I do not want any payment for the advice I give you; I will save my reward for it with Allah.'

(So have Taqwa of Allah, and obey me.) `It is clear to you that I am telling the truth and that I am faithfully fulfilling the mission with which Allah has entrusted me.'

Surah: 26 Ayah: 111, Ayah: 112, Ayah: 113, Ayah: 114 & Ayah: 115

❊ قَالُوٓا۟ أَنُؤْمِنُ لَكَ وَٱتَّبَعَكَ ٱلْأَرْذَلُونَ ۝

111. They said: "Shall we believe in you, when the meanest (of the people) follow you?"

قَالَ وَمَا عِلْمِى بِمَا كَانُوا۟ يَعْمَلُونَ ۝

112. He said: "And what knowledge have I of what they used to do?

إِنْ حِسَابُهُمْ إِلَّا عَلَىٰ رَبِّى لَوْ تَشْعُرُونَ ۝

113. "Their account is only with my Lord, if you could (but) know.

وَمَآ أَنَا۠ بِطَارِدِ ٱلْمُؤْمِنِينَ ۝

114. "And I am not going to drive away the believers.

إِنْ أَنَا۠ إِلَّا نَذِيرٌ مُّبِينٌ ۝

115. I am only a plain warner."

Transliteration

111. Qaloo anu/minu laka waittabaAAaka al-arthaloona 112. Qala wama AAilmee bima kanoo yaAAmaloona 113. In hisabuhum illa AAala rabbee law tashAAuroona 114. Wama ana bitaridi almu/mineena 115. In ana illa natheerun mubeenun

Tafsir Ibn Kathir

The Demand of the People of Nuh and His Response

They said: "We do not believe in you, and we will not follow you and become equal to the meanest of the people, who follow you and believe in you, and they are the lowest among us."

(They said: "Shall we believe in you, when the inferior follow you" He said: "And what knowledge have I of what they used to do") meaning, `what does it have to do with me if they follow me No matter what they used to do before, I do not have to check on them and examine their background; all I have to do is accept it if they believe in me; whatever is in their hearts is for Allah to know.'

(Their account is only with my Lord, if you could (but) know. And I am not going to drive away the believers.) It seems that they asked him to drive these people away, then they would follow him, but he refused to do that, and said:

(And I am not going to drive away the believers. I am only a plain warner.) meaning, `I have been sent as a warner, and whoever obeys me and follows me and believes in me, then he belongs to me and I to him, whether he is noble or common, upper-class or lower-class.'

Surah: 26 Ayah: 116, Ayah: 117, Ayah: 118, Ayah: 119, Ayah: 120, Ayah: 121 & Ayah: 122

قَالُوا۟ لَئِن لَّمْ تَنتَهِ يَـٰنُوحُ لَتَكُونَنَّ مِنَ ٱلْمَرْجُومِينَ ﴿١١٦﴾

116. They said: "If you cease not, O Nûh (Noah) you will surely be among those stoned (to death)."

قَالَ رَبِّ إِنَّ قَوْمِى كَذَّبُونِ ﴿١١٧﴾

117. He said: "My Lord! Verily, my people have belied me.

فَٱفْتَحْ بَيْنِى وَبَيْنَهُمْ فَتْحًا وَنَجِّنِى وَمَن مَّعِىَ مِنَ ٱلْمُؤْمِنِينَ ﴿١١٨﴾

118. Therefore judge You between me and them, and save me and those of the believers who are with me."

فَأَنجَيْنَـٰهُ وَمَن مَّعَهُۥ فِى ٱلْفُلْكِ ٱلْمَشْحُونِ ﴿١١٩﴾

119. And We saved him and those with him in the laden ship.

ثُمَّ أَغْرَقْنَا بَعْدُ ٱلْبَاقِينَ ﴿١٢٠﴾

120. Then We drowned the rest (disbelievers) thereafter.

إِنَّ فِى ذَٰلِكَ لَـَٔايَةً ۖ وَمَا كَانَ أَكْثَرُهُم مُّؤْمِنِينَ ﴿١٢١﴾

121. Verily, in this is indeed a sign, yet most of them are not believers.

وَإِنَّ رَبَّكَ لَهُوَ ٱلْعَزِيزُ ٱلرَّحِيمُ ﴿١٢٢﴾

122. And verily your Lord, He is indeed the All-Mighty, the Most Merciful.

Transliteration

116. Qaloo la-in lam tantahi ya noohu latakoonanna mina almarjoomeena 117. Qala rabbi inna qawmee kaththabooni 118. Faiftah baynee wabaynahum fathan wanajjinee waman maAAiya mina almu/mineena 119. Faanjaynahu waman maAAahu fee alfulki almashhooni 120. Thumma aghraqna baAAdu albaqeena 121. Inna fee thalika

laayatan wama kana aktharuhum mu/mineena 122. Wa-inna rabbaka lahuwa alAAazeezu alrraheemu

Tafsir Ibn Kathir

His People's Threat, Nuh's Prayer against Them, and Their Destruction

Nuh stayed among his people for a long time, calling them to Allah night and day, in secret and openly. The more he repeated his call to them, the more determined were they to cling to their extreme disbelief and resist his call. In the end, they said:

(If you cease not, O Nuh you will surely be among those stoned.) meaning, `if you do not stop calling us to your religion,'

(you will surely be among those stoned.) meaning, `we will stone you.' At that point, he prayed against them, and Allah responded to his prayer. Nuh said:

(My Lord! Verily, my people have denied me. Therefore judge You between me and them.) This is like the Ayah:

(Then he invoked his Lord (saying): "I have been overcome, so help (me)!")(54:10) And Allah says here:

(And We saved him and those with him in the laden ship. Then We drowned the rest thereafter.) The "laden ship" is one that is filled with cargo and the couples, one pair from every species, that were carried in it. This Ayah means: `We saved Nuh and all of those who followed him, and We drowned those who disbelieved in him and went against his commands, all of them.'

(Verily, in this is indeed a sign, yet most of them are not believers. And verily your Lord, He is indeed the All-Mighty, the Most Merciful.)

> Surah: 26 Ayah: 123, Ayah: 124, Ayah: 125, Ayah: 126, Ayah: 127, Ayah: 128, Ayah: 129, Ayah: 130, Ayah: 131, Ayah: 132, Ayah: 133, Ayah: 134 & Ayah: 135

كَذَّبَتْ عَادٌ ٱلْمُرْسَلِينَ ۝

123. 'Ad (people) belied the Messengers.

إِذْ قَالَ لَهُمْ أَخُوهُمْ هُودٌ أَلَا تَتَّقُونَ ۝

124. When their brother Hûd said to them: "Will you not fear Allâh and obey Him?

إِنِّى لَكُمْ رَسُولٌ أَمِينٌ ۝

125. "Verily I am a trustworthy Messenger to you.

فَٱتَّقُوا۟ ٱللَّهَ وَأَطِيعُونِ ۝

126. "So fear Allâh, keep your duty to Him, and obey me.

وَمَآ أَسْـَٔلُكُمْ عَلَيْهِ مِنْ أَجْرٍ ۖ إِنْ أَجْرِىَ إِلَّا عَلَىٰ رَبِّ ٱلْعَـٰلَمِينَ ۝

127. "No reward do I ask of you for it (my Message of Islâmic Monotheism); my reward is only from the Lord of the 'Alamîn (mankind, jinn, and all that exists).

أَتَبْنُونَ بِكُلِّ رِيعٍ ءَايَةً تَعْبَثُونَ ۝

128. "Do you build high palaces on every high place, while you do not live in them?

وَتَتَّخِذُونَ مَصَانِعَ لَعَلَّكُمْ تَخْلُدُونَ ۝

129. "And do you get for yourselves palaces (fine buildings) as if you will live therein for ever.

وَإِذَا بَطَشْتُم بَطَشْتُمْ جَبَّارِينَ ۝

130. "And when you seize *somebody), seize you (him) as tyrants?

فَٱتَّقُوا۟ ٱللَّهَ وَأَطِيعُونِ ۝

131. "So fear Allâh, keep your duty to Him, and obey me.

وَٱتَّقُوا۟ ٱلَّذِىٓ أَمَدَّكُم بِمَا تَعْلَمُونَ ۝

132. "And keep your duty to Him, fear Him Who has aided you with all (good things) that you know.

أَمَدَّكُم بِأَنْعَـٰمٍ وَبَنِينَ ۝

133. "He has aided you with cattle and children.

وَجَنَّـٰتٍ وَعُيُونٍ ۝

134. "And gardens and springs.

إِنِّىٓ أَخَافُ عَلَيْكُمْ عَذَابَ يَوْمٍ عَظِيمٍ ۝

135. "Verily, I fear for you the torment of a Great Day."

Transliteration

123. Kaththabat AAadun almursaleena 124. Ith qala lahum akhoohum hoodun ala tattaqoona 125. Innee lakum rasoolun ameenun 126. Faittaqoo Allaha waateeAAooni 127. Wama as-alukum AAalayhi min ajrin in ajriya illa AAala rabbi alAAalameena 128.

Atabnoona bikulli reeAAin ayatan taAAbathoona 129. Watattakhithoona masaniAAa laAAallakum takhludoona 130. Wa-itha batashtum batashtum jabbareena 131. Faittaqoo Allaha waateeAAooni 132. Waittaqoo allathee amaddakum bima taAAlamoona 133. Amaddakum bi-anAAamin wabaneena 134. Wajannatin waAAuyoonin 135. Innee akhafu AAalaykum AAathaba yawmin AAatheemin

Tafsir Ibn Kathir

Hud's preaching to His People `Ad

Here Allah tells us about His servant and Messenger Hud, when he called his people `Ad. His people used to live in the Ahqaf, curved sand-hills near Hadramawt, on the borders of Yemen. They lived after the time of Nuh, as Allah says in Surat Al-A`raf:

(And remember that He made you successors after the people of Nuh and increased you amply in stature) (7:69). This refers to the fact that they were physically strong and well-built, and very violent, and very tall; they had also been given a great deal of provisions, wealth, gardens, rivers, sons, crops and fruits. Yet despite all of that, they worshipped others besides Allah. So Allah sent Hud, one of their own, as a Messenger bringing them good news and delivering warnings. He called them to worship Allah alone, and he warned them of Allah's wrath and punishment if they were to go against him and treating him harshly. He said to them, as Nuh had said to his people:

(Do you build on every Ri` an Ayah for your amusement) The scholars of Tafsir differed over the meaning of the word Ri`. In brief, they said that it refers to an elevated location at a well-known crossroads, where they would build a huge, dazzling, sturdy structure, this is why he said:

(Do you build on every Ri` an Ayah) i.e., a well-known landmark,

(for your amusement) meaning, `you are only doing that for the purpose of frivolity, not because you need it, but for fun and to show off your strength.' So their Prophet, peace be upon him, denounced them for doing that, because it was a waste of time and exhausted people's bodies for no purpose, and kept them busy with something that was of no benefit in this world or the next. He said:

(And do you get for yourselves Masani` as if you will live therein forever) Mujahid said, "This means fortresses built up strong and high and structures that are built to last."

(as if you will live therein forever) means, `so that you may stay there forever, but that is not going to happen, because they will eventually cease to be, just as happened in the case of those who came before you.'

(And when you seize (somebody), seize you (him) as tyrants) They are described as being strong, violent and tyrannical.

(So, have Taqwa of Allah, and obey me.) `Worship your Lord and obey your Messenger.' Then Hud began reminding them of the blessings that Allah had bestowed upon them. He said:

Chapter 26. Ash-Shu'araa (The Poets), Verses 001-227

(And have Taqwa of Him, Who has aided you with all that you know. He has aided you with cattle and children, and gardens and springs. Verily, I fear for you the torment of a Great Day.) meaning, `if you disbelieve and oppose (your Prophet).' So he called them to Allah with words of encouragement and words of warning, but it was to no avail.

Surah: 26 Ayah: 136, Ayah: 137, Ayah: 138, Ayah: 139 & Ayah: 140

$$\text{قَالُوا۟ سَوَآءٌ عَلَيْنَآ أَوَعَظْتَ أَمْ لَمْ تَكُن مِّنَ ٱلْوَٰعِظِينَ}$$

136. They said: "It is the same to us whether you preach or be not of those who preach.

$$\text{إِنْ هَٰذَآ إِلَّا خُلُقُ ٱلْأَوَّلِينَ}$$

137. "This is no other than the false-tales and religion of the ancients, (Tafsir At-Tabarî)

$$\text{وَمَا نَحْنُ بِمُعَذَّبِينَ}$$

138. "And we are not going to be punished."

$$\text{فَكَذَّبُوهُ فَأَهْلَكْنَٰهُمْ ۗ إِنَّ فِى ذَٰلِكَ لَءَايَةً ۖ وَمَا كَانَ أَكْثَرُهُم مُّؤْمِنِينَ}$$

139. So they belied him, and We destroyed them. Verily in this is indeed a sign, yet most of them are not believers.

$$\text{وَإِنَّ رَبَّكَ لَهُوَ ٱلْعَزِيزُ ٱلرَّحِيمُ}$$

140. And verily your Lord, He is indeed the All-Mighty, the Most Merciful.

Transliteration

136. Qaloo sawaon AAalayna awaAAathta am lam takun mina alwaAAitheena 137. In hatha illa khuluqu al-awwaleena 138. Wama nahnu bimuAAaththabeena 139. Fakaththaboohu faahlaknahum inna fee thalika laayatan wama kana aktharuhum mu/mineena 140. Wa-inna rabbaka lahuwa alAAazeezu alrraheemu

Tafsir Ibn Kathir

The Response of the People of Hud, and Their Punishment

Allah tells us how the people of Hud responded to him after he had warned them, encouraged them, and clearly explained the truth to them.

(They said: "It is the same to us whether you preach or be not of those who preach.") meaning, `we will not give up our ways.'

(And we shall not leave our gods for your (mere) saying! And we are not believers in you) (11:53). This is how it was, as Allah says:

(Verily, those who disbelieve, it is the same to them whether you warn them or do not warn them, they will not believe) (2:6).

(Truly, those, against whom the Word of your Lord has been justified, will not believe) (10:96-97). And they said:

(This is no other than Khuluq of the ancients.) Some scholars read this: "Khalq". According to Ibn Mas`ud and according to `Abdullah bin `Abbas -- as reported from Al-`Awfi -- and `Alqamah and Mujahid, they meant, "What you have brought to us is nothing but the tales (Akhlaq) of the ancients." This is like what the idolators of Quraysh said:

(And they say: "Tales of the ancients, which he has written down, and they are dictated to him morning and afternoon.") (25:5) And Allah said:

(Those who disbelieve say: "This is nothing but a lie that he has invented, and others have helped him in it. In fact, they have produced an injustice and a lie." And they say: "Tales of the ancients...") (25:4-5)

(And when it is said to them: "What is it that your Lord has sent down" They say: "Tales of the ancient!") (16:24). Some other scholars recited it,

(This is no other than Khuluq of the ancients,) "as Khuluq," meaning their religion. What they were following was the religion of the ancients, their fathers and grandfathers, as if they were saying: "We are following them, we will live as they lived and die as they died, and there will be no resurrection and no judgement." Hence they said:

(And we are not going to be punished.) Allah's saying;

(So they denied him, and We destroyed them.) meaning, they continued to disbelieve and stubbornly oppose Allah's Prophet Hud, so Allah destroyed them. The means of their destruction has been described in more than one place in the Qur'an: Allah sent against them a strong and furious wind, i.e., a fiercely blowing wind that was intensely cold. Thus the means of their destruction was suited to their nature, for they were the strongest and fiercest of people, so Allah overpowered them with something that was even stronger and fiercer than them, as Allah says:

(Have you not seen how your Lord dealt with `Ad of Iram Possessors of the pillars) (89:6-7). This refers to the former `Ad, as Allah says:

(And that it is He Who destroyed the former `Ad) (53:50). They were descendents of Iram bin Sam bin Nuh,

(Possesors of the pillars) They used to live among pillars. Those who claim that Iram was a city take this idea from Isra'iliyyat narrations, from the words of Ka`b and Wahb, but there is no real basis for that. Allah says:

(The like of which were not created in the land) (89:8). meaning, nothing like this tribe was created in terms of might, power and tyranny. If what was meant was a city, it would have said, "The like of which was not built in the land." And Allah says:

(As for `Ad, they were arrogant in the land without right, and they said: "Who is mightier than us in strength" See they not that Allah Who created them was mightier in strength than them. And they used to deny Our Ayat!) (41:15) And Allah says:

(And as for `Ad, they were destroyed by a furious violent wind!) until His saying:

(in succession) (69:6-7) meaning, consecutively (i.e., seven nights and eight days).

(so that you could see men lying overthrown (destroyed), as if they were hollow trunks of date palms!) (69:7) means, they were left as headless bodies, because the wind would come and carry one of them, then drop him on his head, so that his brains were spilled out, his head was broken and he was thrown aside, as if they were uprooted stems of date-palms. They used to build fortresses in the mountains and caves, and they dug ditches half as deep as a man is tall, but that did not help them against the command of Allah at all.

(Verily, the term given by Allah, when it comes, cannot be delayed) (71:4). Allah says here:

(So they denied him, and We destroyed them.)

Surah: 26 Ayah: 141, Ayah: 142, Ayah: 143, Ayah: 144 & Ayah: 145

كَذَّبَتْ ثَمُودُ ٱلْمُرْسَلِينَ ﴿١٤١﴾

141. Thamûd (people) belied the Messengers.

إِذْ قَالَ لَهُمْ أَخُوهُمْ صَٰلِحٌ أَلَا تَتَّقُونَ ﴿١٤٢﴾

142. When their brother Sâlih said to them: "Will you not fear Allâh and obey Him?

إِنِّى لَكُمْ رَسُولٌ أَمِينٌ ﴿١٤٣﴾

143. "I am a trustworthy Messenger to you.

فَٱتَّقُوا۟ ٱللَّهَ وَأَطِيعُونِ ﴿١٤٤﴾

144. "So fear Allâh, keep your duty to Him, and obey me.

وَمَآ أَسْـَٔلُكُمْ عَلَيْهِ مِنْ أَجْرٍ إِنْ أَجْرِىَ إِلَّا عَلَىٰ رَبِّ ٱلْعَٰلَمِينَ ﴿١٤٥﴾

145. "No reward do I ask of you for it (my Message of Islâmic Monotheism); my reward is only from the Lord of the 'Alamîn (mankind, jinn and all that exists).

Transliteration

141. Kaththabat thamoodu almursaleena 142. Ith qala lahum akhoohum salihun ala tattaqoona 143. Innee lakum rasoolun ameenun 144. Faittaqoo Allaha waateeAAooni 145. Wama as-alukum AAalayhi min ajrin in ajriya illa AAala rabbi alAAalameena

Tafsir Ibn Kathir

Salih and the People of Thamud

Here Allah tells us about His servant and Messenger Salih, whom He sent to his people Thamud. They were Arabs living in the city of Al-Hijr -- which is between Wadi Al-Qura and Greater Syria. Their location is well known. In our explanation of Surat Al-A`raf, we mentioned the Hadiths which tell how the Messenger of Allah passed by their dwelling place when he wanted to launch a raid on Syria. He went as far as Tabuk, then he went back to Al-Madinah to prepare himself for the campaign. Thamud came after `Ad and before Ibrahim, peace be upon him. Their Prophet Salih called them to Allah, to worship Him alone with no partner or associate, and to obey whatever commands were conveyed to them, but they refused, rejecting him and opposing him. He told them that he did not seek any reward from them for his call to them, but that he would seek the reward for that with Allah. Then he reminded them of the blessings of Allah.

Surah: 26 Ayah: 146, Ayah: 147, Ayah: 148, Ayah: 149, Ayah: 150, Ayah: 151 & Ayah: 152

أَتُتْرَكُونَ فِى مَا هَـٰهُنَآ ءَامِنِينَ ﴿١٤٦﴾

146. "Will you be left secure in that which you have here?

فِى جَنَّـٰتٍ وَعُيُونٍ ﴿١٤٧﴾

147. "In gardens and springs.

وَزُرُوعٍ وَنَخْلٍ طَلْعُهَا هَضِيمٌ ﴿١٤٨﴾

148. And green crops (fields) and date-palms with soft spadix.

وَتَنْحِتُونَ مِنَ ٱلْجِبَالِ بُيُوتًا فَـٰرِهِينَ ﴿١٤٩﴾

149. "And you hew out of in the mountains, houses with great skill.

فَٱتَّقُوا۟ ٱللَّهَ وَأَطِيعُونِ ﴿١٥٠﴾

150. "So fear Allâh, keep your duty to Him, and obey me.

وَلَا تُطِيعُوٓا۟ أَمْرَ ٱلْمُسْرِفِينَ ﴿١٥١﴾

151. "And follow not the command of Al-Musrifûn (i.e. their chiefs: leaders who were polytheists, criminals and sinners),

$$ ٱلَّذِينَ يُفْسِدُونَ فِى ٱلْأَرْضِ وَلَا يُصْلِحُونَ ﴿١٥٢﴾ $$

152. "Who make mischief in the land, and reform not."

Transliteration

146. Atutrakoona fee ma hahuna amineena 147. Fee jannatin waAAuyoonin 148. WazurooAAin wanakhlin talAAuha hadeemun 149. Watanhitoona mina aljibali buyootan fariheena 150. Faittaqoo Allaha waateeAAooni 151. Wala tuteeAAoo amra almusrifeena 152. Allatheena yufsidoona fee al-ardi wala yuslihoona

Tafsir Ibn Kathir

A Reminder to Them of their Circumstances and the Blessings

They enjoyed Salih preached to them, warning them that the punishment of Allah could overtake them and reminding them of the blessings that Allah had bestowed upon them, by giving them ample provision and making them safe from all kinds of dangers, giving them gardens and flowing springs, and bringing forth for them crops and fruits.

(and date palms with soft clusters.) Al-`Awfi narrated from Ibn `Abbas, "Ripe and rich." `Ali bin Abi Talhah narrated from Ibn `Abbas that this meant growing luxuriantly. Isma`il bin Abi Khalid narrated from `Amr bin Abi `Amr -- who met the Companions -- from Ibn `Abbas that this means, "When it becomes ripe and soft." This was narrated by Ibn Abi Hatim, then he said: "And something similar was narrated from Abu Salih."

(And you hew out in the mountains, houses with great skill.) Ibn `Abbas and others said, "With great skill." According to another report from him: "They were greedy and extravagant." This was the view of Mujahid and another group. There is no contradiction between the two views, because they built the houses which they carved in the mountains as a form of extravagant play, with no need for them as dwelling places. They were highly skilled in the arts of masonry and stone-carving, as is well known to anyone who has seen their structures. So, Salih said to them:

(So, have Taqwa of Allah, and obey me.) Pay attention to that which could benefit you in this world and the Hereafter; worshipping your Lord Who created you, who granted you provisions so that you could worship Him alone and glorify Him morning and evening.

(And follow not the command of the extravagant, who make mischief in the land, and reform not.) meaning, their chiefs and leaders, who called them to Shirk, disbelief and opposition to the truth.

Surah: 26 Ayah: 153, Ayah: 154, Ayah: 155, Ayah: 156, Ayah: 157, Ayah: 158 & Ayah: 159

قَالُوٓاْ إِنَّمَآ أَنتَ مِنَ ٱلْمُسَحَّرِينَ ۝

153. They said: "You are only of those bewitched!

مَآ أَنتَ إِلَّا بَشَرٌ مِّثْلُنَا فَأْتِ بِـَٔايَةٍ إِن كُنتَ مِنَ ٱلصَّـٰدِقِينَ ۝

154. "You are but a human being like us. Then bring us a sign if you are of the truthful."

قَالَ هَـٰذِهِۦ نَاقَةٌ لَّهَا شِرْبٌ وَلَكُمْ شِرْبُ يَوْمٍ مَّعْلُومٍ ۝

155. He said: "Here is a she-camel: it has a right to drink (water), and you have a right to drink (water) (each) on a day, known.

وَلَا تَمَسُّوهَا بِسُوٓءٍ فَيَأْخُذَكُمْ عَذَابُ يَوْمٍ عَظِيمٍ ۝

156. "And touch her not with harm, lest the torment of a Great Day should seize you."

فَعَقَرُوهَا فَأَصْبَحُواْ نَـٰدِمِينَ ۝

157. But they killed her, and then they became regretful.

فَأَخَذَهُمُ ٱلْعَذَابُ إِنَّ فِى ذَٰلِكَ لَـَٔايَةً وَمَا كَانَ أَكْثَرُهُم مُّؤْمِنِينَ ۝

158. So the torment overtook them. Verily, in this is indeed a sign, yet most of them are not believers.

وَإِنَّ رَبَّكَ لَهُوَ ٱلْعَزِيزُ ٱلرَّحِيمُ ۝

159. And verily your Lord, He is indeed the All-Mighty, the Most Merciful.

Transliteration

153. Qaloo innama anta mina almusahhareena 154. Ma anta illa basharun mithluna fa/ti bi-ayatin in kunta mina alssadiqeena 155. Qala hathihi naqatun laha shirbun walakum shirbu yawmin maAAloomin 156. Wala tamassooha bisoo-in faya/khuthakum AAathabu yawmin AAatheemin 157. FaAAaqarooha faasbahoo nadimeena 158. Faakhathahumu alAAathabu inna fee thalika laayatan wama kana aktharuhum mu/mineena 159. Wa-inna rabbaka lahuwa alAAazeezu alrraheemu

Tafsir Ibn Kathir

The Response of Thamud, Their Demand for a Sign, and Their Punishment

Allah tells us how Thamud responded to their Prophet Salih, upon him be peace, when he called them to worship their Lord, may He be glorified.

(They said: "You are only of those bewitched!") Mujahid said, "They meant he was one affected by witchcraft." Then they said:

(You are but a human being like us.) meaning, `how can you receive Revelation when we do not' This is like the Ayah where they are described as saying:

("Is it that the Reminder is sent to him alone from among us Nay, he is an insolent liar!" Tomorrow they will come to know who is the liar, the insolent one!) (54:26-27) Then they asked him for a sign to prove that what he brought to them from their Lord was the truth. A crowd of them gathered and demanded that he immediately bring forth from the rock a she-camel that was ten months pregnant, and they pointed to a certain rock in their midst. Allah's Prophet Salih made them promise that if he responded to their request, they would believe in him and follow him. So they agreed to that. The Prophet of Allah Salih, peace be upon him, stood and prayed, then he prayed to Allah to grant them their request. Then the rock to which they had pointed split open, revealing a she-camel that was ten months pregnant, excactly as they had requested. So some of them believed, but most of them disbelieved.

(He said: "Here is a she-camel: it has a right to drink (water), and you have a right to drink (water) (each) on a day, known.) meaning, `she will drink from your water one day, and on the next day you will drink from it.'

(And touch her not with harm, lest the torment of a Great Day should seize you.) He warned them of the punishment of Allah if they should do her any harm. The she-camel stayed among them for a while, drinking the water, eating leaves and grazing, and they benefitted from her milk which they took in sufficient quantities for every one to drink his fill. After this had gone on for a long time, and the time for their destruction drew near, they conspired to kill her:

(But they killed her, and then they became regretful. So, the torment overtook them.) Their land was shaken by a strong earthquake, and there came to them an overwhelming Sayhah (shout) which took their hearts from their places. They were overtaken by events which they were not expecting, so they were left (dead), lying prostrate in their homes.

(Verily, in this is indeed a sign, yet most of them are not believers. And verily your Lord, He is indeed the All-Mighty, the Most Merciful.)

Surah: 26 Ayah: 160, Ayah: 161, Ayah: 162, Ayah: 163 & Ayah: 164

كَذَّبَتْ قَوْمُ لُوطٍ ٱلْمُرْسَلِينَ ﴿١٦٠﴾

160. The propel of Lût (Lot) (-who dwelt in the town of Sodom in Palestine) belied the Messengers.

إِذْ قَالَ لَهُمْ أَخُوهُمْ لُوطٌ أَلَا تَتَّقُونَ ﴿١٦١﴾

161. When their brother Lût (Lot) said to them: "Will you not fear Allâh and obey Him?

$$إِنِّى لَكُمْ رَسُولٌ أَمِينٌ$$

162. "Verily I am a trustworthy Messenger to you.

$$فَاتَّقُوا اللَّهَ وَأَطِيعُونِ$$

163. "So fear Allâh, keep your duty to Him, and obey me.

$$وَمَا أَسْـَٔلُكُمْ عَلَيْهِ مِنْ أَجْرٍ إِنْ أَجْرِىَ إِلَّا عَلَىٰ رَبِّ الْعَـٰلَمِينَ$$

164. "No reward do I ask of you for it (my Message of Islâmic Monotheism); my reward is only from the Lord of the 'Alamîn (mankind, jinn and all that exists).

Transliteration

160. Kaththabat qawmu lootin almursaleena 161. Ith qala lahum akhoohum lootun ala tattaqoona 162. Innee lakum rasoolun ameenun 163. Faittaqoo Allaha waateeAAooni 164. Wama as-alukum AAalayhi min ajrin in ajriya illa AAala rabbi alAAalameena

Tafsir Ibn Kathir

Lut and His Call

Here Allah tells us about His servant and Messenger Lut, peace be upon him. He was Lut bin Haran bin Azar, the nephew of Ibrahim Al-Khalil, upon him be peace. Allah sent him to a mighty nation during the lifetime of Ibrahim, peace be upon them both. They lived in Sadum (Sodom) and its environs, where Allah destroyed them and turned the area into a putrid, stinking lake, which is well-known in the land of Al-Ghur (the Jordan Valley), bordering the mountains of Jerusalem, between the mountains and the land of Al-Karak and Ash-Shawbak. He called them to Allah, to worship Him alone with no partner or associate, and to obey the Messenger whom Allah sent to them. He forbade from disobeying Allah and committing the sin that they had invented which was unknown on earth before their time; intercourse with males instead of with females. Allah said:

Surah: 26 Ayah: 165, Ayah: 166, Ayah: 167, Ayah: 168, Ayah: 169, Ayah: 170, Ayah: 171, Ayah: 172, Ayah: 173, Ayah: 174 & Ayah: 175

$$أَتَأْتُونَ الذُّكْرَانَ مِنَ الْعَـٰلَمِينَ$$

165. "Go you in unto the males of the 'Alamîn (mankind),

$$وَتَذَرُونَ مَا خَلَقَ لَكُمْ رَبُّكُم مِّنْ أَزْوَٰجِكُم ۚ بَلْ أَنتُمْ قَوْمٌ عَادُونَ$$

166. "And leave those whom Allâh has created for you to be your wives? Nay, you are a trespassing people!"

قَالُوا لَئِن لَّمْ تَنتَهِ يَا لُوطُ لَتَكُونَنَّ مِنَ ٱلْمُخْرَجِينَ ۝

167. They said: "If you cease not O Lût (Lot)! Verily, you will be one of those who are driven out!"

قَالَ إِنِّي لِعَمَلِكُم مِّنَ ٱلْقَالِينَ ۝

168. He said: "I am, indeed, of those who disapprove with severe anger and fury your (this evil) action (of sodomy).

رَبِّ نَجِّنِي وَأَهْلِي مِمَّا يَعْمَلُونَ ۝

169. "My Lord! Save me and my family from what they do."

فَنَجَّيْنَاهُ وَأَهْلَهُ أَجْمَعِينَ ۝

170. So We saved him and his family, all,

إِلَّا عَجُوزًا فِي ٱلْغَابِرِينَ ۝

171. Except an old woman (his wife) among those who remained behind.

ثُمَّ دَمَّرْنَا ٱلْآخَرِينَ ۝

172. Then afterward We destroyed the others.

وَأَمْطَرْنَا عَلَيْهِم مَّطَرًا ۖ فَسَاءَ مَطَرُ ٱلْمُنذَرِينَ ۝

173. And We rained on them a rain (of torment). And how evil was the rain of those who had been warned.

إِنَّ فِي ذَٰلِكَ لَآيَةً ۖ وَمَا كَانَ أَكْثَرُهُم مُّؤْمِنِينَ ۝

174. Verily, in this is indeed a sign, yet most of them are not believers.

وَإِنَّ رَبَّكَ لَهُوَ ٱلْعَزِيزُ ٱلرَّحِيمُ ۝

175. And verily Your Lord, He is indeed the All-Mighty, the Most Merciful.

Transliteration

165. Ata/toona alththukrana mina alAAalameena 166. Watatharoona ma khalaqa lakum rabbukum min azwajikum bal antum qawmun AAadoona 167. Qaloo la-in lam tantahi ya lootu latakoonanna mina almukhrajeena 168. Qala innee liAAamalikum mina alqaleena 169. Rabbi najjinee waahlee mimma yaAAmaloona 170. Fanajjaynahu waahlahu ajmaAAeena 171. Illa AAajoozan fee alghabireena 172. Thumma dammarna al-akhareena 173. Waamtarna AAalayhim mataran fasaa mataru almunthareena 174.

Inna fee thalika laayatan wama kana aktharuhum mu/mineena 175. Wa-inna rabbaka lahuwa alAAazeezu alrraheemu

Tafsir Ibn Kathir

Lut's Denunciation of His People's Deeds, Their Response and Their Punishment

The Prophet of Allah forbade them from committing evil deeds and intercourse with males, and he taught them that they should have intercourse with their wives whom Allah had created for them. Their response was only to say:

(If you cease not, O Lut,) meaning, `if you do not give up what you have brought,'

(verily, you will be one of those who are driven out!) meaning, `we will expel you from among us.' This is like the Ayah,

(There was no other answer given by his people except that they said: "Drive out the family of Lut from your city. Verily, these are men who want to be clean and pure!") (27:56). When he saw that they would not give up their ways, and that they were persisting in their misguidance, he declared his innocence of them, saying:

(I am, indeed, of those who disapprove with severe anger and fury) `Of those who are outraged, I do not like it and I do not accept it, and I have nothing to do with you. ' Then he prayed to Allah against them and said:

(My Lord! Save me and my family from what they do.) Allah says:

(So, We saved him and his family, all. Except an old woman among those who remained behind.) This was his wife, who was a bad old woman. She stayed behind and was destroyed with whoever else was left. This is similar to what Allah says about them in Surat Al-A`raf and Surah Hud, and in Surat Al-Hijr, where Allah commanded him to take his family at night, except for his wife, and not to turn around when they heard the Sayhah as it came upon his people. So they patiently obeyed the command of Allah and persevered, and Allah sent upon the people a punishment which struck them all, and rained upon them stones of baked clay, piled up. Allah says:

(Then afterward We destroyed the others. And We rained on them a rain) until Allah's saying;

(And verily, your Lord, He is indeed the All-Mighty, the Most Merciful.)

Surah: 26 Ayah: 176, Ayah: 177, Ayah: 178, Ayah: 179 & Ayah: 180

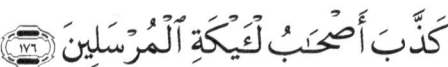

176. The dwellers of Al-Aiyka (near Madyan (Midian)) belied the Messengers.

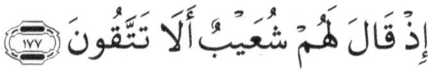

177. When Shu'âib said to them: "Will you not fear Allâh (and obey Him)?

إِنِّى لَكُمْ رَسُولٌ أَمِينٌ ﴿١٧٨﴾

178. "I am a trustworthy Messenger to you.

فَٱتَّقُوا۟ ٱللَّهَ وَأَطِيعُونِ ﴿١٧٩﴾

179. "So fear Allâh, keep your duty to Him, and obey me.

وَمَآ أَسْـَٔلُكُمْ عَلَيْهِ مِنْ أَجْرٍ إِنْ أَجْرِىَ إِلَّا عَلَىٰ رَبِّ ٱلْعَٰلَمِينَ ﴿١٨٠﴾

180. "No reward do I ask of you for it (my Message of Islâmic Monotheism); my reward is only from the Lord of the 'Alamîn (mankind, jinn and all that exists).

Transliteration

176. Kaththaba as-habu al-aykati almursaleena 177. Ith qala lahum shuAAaybun ala tattaqoona 178. Innee lakum rasoolun ameenun 179. Faittaqoo Allaha waateeAAooni 180. Wama as-alukum AAalayhi min ajrin in ajriya illa AAala rabbi alAAalameena

Tafsir Ibn Kathir

Shu`ayb and His Preaching to the Dwellers of Al-Aykah

The companions of Al-Aykah were the people of Madyan, according to the most correct view. The Prophet of Allah Shu`ayb was one of them, but it does not say here, their brother Shu`ayb, because they called themselves by a name denoting their deification of Al-Aykah, which was a tree which they used to worship; it was said that it was a group of trees which were tangled, like trees in a thicket. For this reason, when Allah said that the companions of Al-Aykah denied the Messengers, He did not say, "When their brother Shu`ayb said to them." Rather, He said:

(When Shu`ayb said to them) He is not described as belonging to them because of the meaning that was inherent in the name given to them even though he was their brother by blood. Some people did not notice this point, so they thought that the dwellers of Al-Aykah were different from the people of Madyan, and claimed that Shu`ayb was sent to two nations; some said that he was sent to three.

(The companions of Al-Aykah) were the people of Shu`ayb. This was the view of Ishaq bin Bishr. Someone besides Juwaybir said, "The dwellers of Al-Aykah and the people of Madyan are one and the same." And Allah knows best. Although there is another opinion that they were different nations with two identities, the correct view is that they were one nation, but they are described differently in different places. Shu`ayb preached to them and commanded them to be fair in their weights and measures, the same as is mentioned in the story of Madyan, which also indicates that they were the same nation.

Surah: 26 Ayah: 181, Ayah: 182, Ayah: 183 & Ayah: 184

۞ أَوْفُوا۟ ٱلْكَيْلَ وَلَا تَكُونُوا۟ مِنَ ٱلْمُخْسِرِينَ ﴿١٨١﴾

181. "Give full measure, and cause no loss (to others).

وَزِنُوا۟ بِٱلْقِسْطَاسِ ٱلْمُسْتَقِيمِ ﴿١٨٢﴾

182. "And weigh with the true and straight balance.

وَلَا تَبْخَسُوا۟ ٱلنَّاسَ أَشْيَآءَهُمْ وَلَا تَعْثَوْا۟ فِى ٱلْأَرْضِ مُفْسِدِينَ ﴿١٨٣﴾

183. "And defraud not people by reducing their things, nor do evil, making corruption and mischief in the land.

وَٱتَّقُوا۟ ٱلَّذِى خَلَقَكُمْ وَٱلْجِبِلَّةَ ٱلْأَوَّلِينَ ﴿١٨٤﴾

184. "And fear Him Who created you and the generations of the men of old."

Transliteration

181. Awfoo alkayla wala takoonoo mina almukhsireena 182. Wazinoo bialqistasi almustaqeemi 183. Wala tabkhasoo alnnasa ashyaahum wala taAAthaw fee al-ardi mufsideena 184. Waittaqoo allathee khalaqakum waaljibillata al-awwaleena

Tafsir Ibn Kathir

The Command to give Full Measure

Allah commanded them to give full measure, and forbade them to give short measure. He said:

(Give full measure, and cause no loss.) meaning, `when you give to people, give them full measure, and do not cause loss to them by giving them short measure, while taking full measure when you are the ones who are taking. Give as you take, and take as you give.'

(And weigh with the true and straight balance.) The balance is the scales.

(And defraud not people by reducing their things,) means, do not shortchange them.

(nor do evil, making corruption and mischief in the land.) means, by engaging in banditry. This is like the Ayah,

(And sit not on every road, threatening) (7:86).

(And have Taqwa of Him Who created you and the generations of the men of old.) Here he is frightening them with the punishment of Allah Who created them and created their forefathers. This is like when Musa, peace be upon him, said:

(Your Lord and the Lord of your ancient fathers!) (26:26). Ibn `Abbas, Mujahid, As-Suddi, Sufyan bin `Uyaynah and `Abdur-Rahman bin Zayd bin Aslam said:

(the generations of the men of old.) means, He created the early generations. And Ibn Zayd recited:

(And indeed he (Shaytan) did lead astray a great multitude of you) (36:62).

Surah: 26 Ayah: 185, Ayah: 186, Ayah: 187, Ayah: 188, Ayah: 189, Ayah: 190 & Ayah: 191

$$\text{قَالُوٓاْ إِنَّمَآ أَنتَ مِنَ ٱلْمُسَحَّرِينَ}$$

185. They said: "You are only one of those bewitched!

$$\text{وَمَآ أَنتَ إِلَّا بَشَرٌ مِّثْلُنَا وَإِن نَّظُنُّكَ لَمِنَ ٱلْكَٰذِبِينَ}$$

186. "You are but a human being like us and verily, we think that you are one of the liars!

$$\text{فَأَسْقِطْ عَلَيْنَا كِسَفًا مِّنَ ٱلسَّمَآءِ إِن كُنتَ مِنَ ٱلصَّٰدِقِينَ}$$

187. "So cause a piece of the heaven to fall on us, if you are of the truthful!"

$$\text{قَالَ رَبِّىٓ أَعْلَمُ بِمَا تَعْمَلُونَ}$$

188. He said: "My Lord is the Best Knower of what you do."

$$\text{فَكَذَّبُوهُ فَأَخَذَهُمْ عَذَابُ يَوْمِ ٱلظُّلَّةِ إِنَّهُۥ كَانَ عَذَابَ يَوْمٍ عَظِيمٍ}$$

189. But they belied him, so the torment of the day of shadow (a gloomy cloud) seized them. Indeed that was the torment of a Great Day.

$$\text{إِنَّ فِى ذَٰلِكَ لَءَايَةً وَمَا كَانَ أَكْثَرُهُم مُّؤْمِنِينَ}$$

190. Verily, in this is indeed a sign, yet most of them are not believers.

$$\text{وَإِنَّ رَبَّكَ لَهُوَ ٱلْعَزِيزُ ٱلرَّحِيمُ}$$

191. And verily! Your Lord, He is indeed the All-Mighty, the Most Merciful.

Transliteration

185. Qaloo innama anta mina almusahhareena 186. Wama anta illa basharun mithluna wa-in nathunnuka lamina alkathibeena 187. Faasqit AAalayna kisafan mina alssama-i in kunta mina alssadiqeena 188. Qala rabbee aAAlamu bima taAAmaloona 189. Fakaththaboohu faakhathahum AAathabu yawmi aiththullati innahu kana AAathaba yawmin AAatheemin 190. Inna fee thalika laayatan wama kana aktharuhum mu/mineena 191. Wa-inna rabbaka lahuwa alAAazeezu alrraheemu

Tafsir Ibn Kathir

The Response of Shu`ayb's People, Their Disbelief in Him and the coming of the Punishment upon Them

Allah tells us how his people responded, and how it was like the response of Thamud to their Messenger -- for they were of like mind -- when they said:

(You are only one of those bewitched!) meaning, `you are one of those who are affected by witchcraft.'

(You are but a human being like us and verily, we think that you are one of the liars!) means, `we think you are deliberately lying to us in what you say, and Allah has not sent you to us.'

(So cause a piece of the heaven to fall on us,) Ad-Dahhak said: "One side of the heavens." Qatadah said: "A piece of the heaven." As-Suddi said: "A punishment from heaven." This is like what the Quraysh said, as Allah tells us:

(And they say: "We shall not believe in you, until you cause a spring to gush forth from the earth for us) until:

(Or you cause the heaven to fall upon us in pieces, as you have pretended, or you bring Allah and the angels before (us) face to face.") (17:90-92)

(And (remember) when they said: "O Allah! If this is indeed the truth from You, then rain down stones on us from the sky....") (8:32). Similarly, these ignorant disbelievers said:

(So, cause a piece of the heaven to fall on us, if you are of the truthful!)

(He said: "My Lord is the Best Knower of what you do.") means, `Allah knows best about you, and if you deserve that, He will punish you therewith, and He will not treat you unjustly.' So this is what happened to them -- as they asked for -- an exact recompense. Allah says:

(But they denied him, so the torment of the Day of Shadow seized them. Indeed that was the torment of a Great Day.) This is what they asked for, when they asked for a part of the heaven to fall upon them. Allah made their punishment in the form of intense heat which overwhelmed them for seven days, and nothing could protect them from it. Then He sent a cloud to shade them, so they ran towards it to seek its shade from the heat. When all of them had gathered underneath it, Allah sent sparks of fire and flames and intense heat upon them, and caused the earth to convulse beneath them, and He sent against them a mighty Sayhah which destroyed their souls. Allah says:

(Indeed that was the torment of a Great Day.) Allah has mentioned how they were destroyed in three places in the Qur'an, in each of which it is described in a manner which fits the context. In Surat Al-A`raf He says that the earthquake seized them, and they lay (dead), prostrate in their homes. This was because they said:

Chapter 26. Ash-Shu'araa (The Poets), Verses 001-227

("We shall certainly drive you out, O Shu`ayb, and those who have believed with you from our town, or else you (all) shall return to our religion.") (7:88). They had sought to scare the Prophet of Allah and those who followed him, so they were seized by the earthquake. In Surah Hud, Allah says:

(And As-Sayhah seized the wrongdoers) (11:94). This was because they mocked the Allah's Prophet when they said:

("Does your Salah command that we give up what our fathers used to worship, or that we give up doing what we like with our property Verily, you are the forbearer, right-minded!") (11:87). They had said this in a mocking, sarcastic tone, so it was befitting that the Sayhah should come and silence them, as Allah says:

(So As-Saihah overtook them) (15:73).

(And As-Saihah seized the wrongdoers) (11:94). And here, they said:

(So, cause a piece of the heaven to fall on us,) in a stubborn and obstinate manner. So, it was fitting that something they never thought would happen should befall them:

(so the torment of the Day of Shadow seized them. Indeed that was the torment of a Great Day.) Muhammad bin Jarir narrated from Yazid Al-Bahili: "I asked Ibn `Abbas about this Ayah:

(so the torment of the Day of Shadow seized them.) He said: `Allah sent upon them thunder and intense heat, and it terrified them (so they entered their houses and it pursued them to the innermost parts of their houses and terrified them further), and they ran fleeing from their houses into the fields. Then Allah sent upon them clouds which shaded them from the sun, and they found it cool and pleasant, so they called out to one another until they had all gathered beneath the cloud, then Allah sent fire upon them.' Ibn `Abbas said, `That was the torment of the Day of Shadow, indeed that was the torment of a Great Day.'"

(Verily, in this is an Ayah, yet most of them are not believers. And verily, your Lord, He is truly, the All-Mighty, the Most Merciful.) (26:8-9) meaning, He is All-Mighty in His punishment of the disbelievers, and Most Merciful towards His believing servants.

Surah: 26 Ayah: 192, Ayah: 193, Ayah: 194 & Ayah: 195

وَإِنَّهُ لَتَنزِيلُ رَبِّ ٱلْعَٰلَمِينَ ۝

192. And truly, this (the Qur'ân) is a revelation from the Lord of the 'Alamîn (mankind, jinn and all that exists),

نَزَلَ بِهِ ٱلرُّوحُ ٱلْأَمِينُ ۝

193. Which the trustworthy Rûh (Jibrîl (Gabriel)) has brought down

194. Upon your heart (O Muhammad (peace be upon him)) that you may be (one) of the warners,

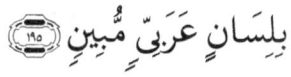

195. In the plain Arabic language.

Transliteration

192. Wa-innahu latanzeelu rabbi alAAalameena 193. Nazala bihi alrroohu al-ameenu 194. AAala qalbika litakoona mina almunthireena 195. Bilisanin AAarabiyyin mubeenin

Tafsir Ibn Kathir

The Qur'an was revealed by Allah

Here Allah tells us about the Book which He revealed to His servant and Messenger Muhammad.

(And truly, this) refers to the Qur'an, which at the beginning of the Surah was described as

(and never comes there unto them a Reminder as a recent revelation from the Most Gracious...) (26:5).

(is a revelation from the Lord of Al-`Alamin.) means, Allah has sent it down to you and revealed it to you.

(Which the trustworthy Ruh has brought down.) This refers to Jibril, peace be upon him. This was the view of more than one of the Salaf: Ibn `Abbas, Muhammad bin Ka`b, Qatadah, `Atiyyah Al-`Awfi, As-Suddi, Ad-Dahhak, Az-Zuhri and Ibn Jurayj. This is an issue concerning which there is no dispute. Az-Zuhri said, "This is like the Ayah:

(Say: "Whoever is an enemy to Jibril -- for indeed he has brought it down to your heart by Allah's permission, confirming what came before it...") (2:97).

(Upon your heart) `O Muhammad, free from any contamination, with nothing added or taken away.'

(that you may be of the warners,) means, `so that you may warn people with it of the punishment of Allah for those who go against it and disbelieve in it, and so that you may give glad tidings with it to the believers who follow it.'

(In the plain Arabic language.) meaning, `this Qur'an which We have revealed to you, We have revealed in perfect and eloquent Arabic, so that it may be quite clear, leaving no room for excuses and establishing clear proof, showing the straight path.'

Surah: 26 Ayah: 196, Ayah: 197, Ayah: 198 & Ayah: 199

196. And verily, it (the Qur'ân, and its revelation to Prophet Muhammad (peace be upon him)) is (announced) in the Scriptures (i.e. the Taurât (Torah) and the Injeel (Gospel)) of former people.

أَوَلَمْ يَكُن لَّهُمْ ءَايَةً أَن يَعْلَمَهُ عُلَمَٰٓؤُاْ بَنِىٓ إِسْرَٰٓءِيلَ ۝

197. Is it not a sign to them that the learned scholars (like 'Abdullâh bin Salâm (may Allah be pleased with him) who embraced Islâm) of the Children of Israel knew it (as true)?

وَلَوْ نَزَّلْنَٰهُ عَلَىٰ بَعْضِ ٱلْأَعْجَمِينَ ۝

198. And if We had revealed it (this Qur'ân) unto any of the non-Arabs,

فَقَرَأَهُۥ عَلَيْهِم مَّا كَانُواْ بِهِۦ مُؤْمِنِينَ ۝

199. And he had recited it unto them, they would not have believed in it.

Transliteration

196. Wa-innahu lafee zuburi al-awwaleena 197. Awa lam yakun lahum ayatan an yaAAlamahu AAulamao banee isra-eela 198. Walaw nazzalnahu AAala baAAdi al-aAAjameena 199. Faqaraahu AAalayhim ma kanoo bihi mu/mineena

Tafsir Ibn Kathir

The Qur'an was mentioned in the Previous Scriptures

Allah says: this Qur'an was mentioned and referred to in the previous Scriptures that were left behind by their Prophets who foretold it in ancient times and more recently. Allah took a covenant from them that they would follow it, and the last of them stood and addressed his people with the good news of Ahmad:

(And (remember) when `Isa, son of Maryam, said: "O Children of Israel! I am the Messenger of Allah unto you, confirming the Tawrah before me, and giving glad tidings of a Messenger to come after me, whose name shall be Ahmad.) (61:6) Zubur here refers to Books; Zubur is the plural of Az-Zabur, which is also the name used to refer to the Book given to Dawud. Allah says:

(And everything they have done is noted in the Az-Zubur.) (54:52), meaning, it is recorded against them in the books of the angels. Then Allah says:

(Is it not a sign to them that the learned scholars of the Children of Israel knew it) meaning, is it not sufficient witness to the truth for them that the scholars of the Children of Israel found this Qur'an mentioned in the Scriptures which they study The meaning is: the fair-minded among them admitted that the attributes of Muhammad and his mission and his Ummah were mentioned in their Books, as was stated by those among them who believed, such as `Abdullah bin Salam, Salman Al-Farisi and others who met the Prophet . Allah said:

(Those who follow the Messenger, the Prophet who can neither read nor write ...) (7:157)

The Intense Disbelief of Quraysh

Then Allah tells us how intense the disbelief of Quraysh was, and how stubbornly they resisted the Qur'an. If this Book with all its eloquence had been revealed to a non-Arab who did not know one word of Arabic, they still would not have believed in him. Allah says:

(And if We had revealed it unto any of the non-Arabs, And he had recited it unto them, they would not have believed in it.) And Allah says:

(And even if We opened to them a gate from the heaven and they were to keep on ascending thereto. They would surely say: "Our eyes have been dazzled...") (15:14-15)

(And even if We had sent down unto them angels, and the dead had spoken unto them...) (6:111)

(Truly, those, against whom the Word of your Lord has been justified, will not believe.) (10:96)

Surah: 26 Ayah: 200, Ayah: 201, Ayah: 202, Ayah: 203, Ayah: 204, Ayah: 205, Ayah: 206, Ayah: 207, Ayah: 208 & Ayah: 209

كَذَٰلِكَ سَلَكْنَٰهُ فِى قُلُوبِ ٱلْمُجْرِمِينَ ۞

200. Thus have We caused it (the denial of the Qur'ân) to enter the hearts of the Mûjrimûn (criminals, polytheists, sinners).

لَا يُؤْمِنُونَ بِهِۦ حَتَّىٰ يَرَوُاْ ٱلْعَذَابَ ٱلْأَلِيمَ ۞

201. They will not believe in it until they see the painful torment.

فَيَأْتِيَهُم بَغْتَةً وَهُمْ لَا يَشْعُرُونَ ۞

202. It shall come to them of a sudden, while they perceive it not.

فَيَقُولُواْ هَلْ نَحْنُ مُنظَرُونَ ۞

203. Then they will say: "Can we be respited?"

أَفَبِعَذَابِنَا يَسْتَعْجِلُونَ ۞

204. Would they then wish for Our Torment to be hastened on?

أَفَرَءَيْتَ إِن مَّتَّعْنَٰهُمْ سِنِينَ ۞

205. Tell Me,(even) if We do let them enjoy for years,

﴿ثُمَّ جَآءَهُم مَّا كَانُواْ يُوعَدُونَ﴾

206. And afterwards comes to them that (punishment) which they had been promised,

﴿مَآ أَغْنَىٰ عَنْهُم مَّا كَانُواْ يُمَتَّعُونَ﴾

207. All that with which they used to enjoy shall not avail them.

﴿وَمَآ أَهْلَكْنَا مِن قَرْيَةٍ إِلَّا لَهَا مُنذِرُونَ﴾

208. And never did We destroy a township but it had its warners

﴿ذِكْرَىٰ وَمَا كُنَّا ظَٰلِمِينَ﴾

209. By way of reminder, and We have never been unjust.

Transliteration

200. Kathalika salaknahu fee quloobi almujrimeena 201. La yu/minoona bihi hatta yarawoo alAAathaba al-aleema 202. Faya/tiyahum baghtatan wahum la yashAAuroona 203. Fayaqooloo hal nahnu muntharoona 204. AfabiAAathabina yastaAAjiloona 205. Afaraayta in mattaAAnahum sineena 206. Thumma jaahum ma kanoo yooAAadoona 207. Ma aghna AAanhum ma kanoo yumattaAAoona 208. Wama ahlakna min qaryatin illa laha munthiroona 209. Thikra wama kunna thalimeena

Tafsir Ibn Kathir

The Deniers will never believe until They see the Torment

Allah says: `thus We caused denial, disbelief, rejection and stubbornness to enter the hearts of the sinners.'

(They will not believe in it), i.e., the truth,

(until they see the painful torment.) means, when their excuses will be of no avail, and the curse will be upon them, and theirs will be an evil abode.

(It shall come to them of a sudden,) means, the punishment of Allah will come upon them suddenly,

(while they perceive it not. Then they will say: "Can we be respited") means, when they see the punishment, then they will wish they had a little more time so that they can obey Allah -- or so they claim. This is like the Ayah:

(And warn mankind of the Day when the torment will come unto them) until:

(that you would not leave) (14: 44). When every sinner and evildoer sees his punishment, he will feel intense regret. Such was the case of Fir`awn, when Musa prayed against him:

(Our Lord! "You have indeed bestowed on Fir`awn and his chiefs splendor and wealth in the life of this world) until:

((Allah) said: "Verily, the invocation of you both is accepted.") (10:88-89). This supplication had an effect on Fir`awn: he did not believe until he saw the painful torment:

(till when drowning overtook him, he said: "I believe that none has the right to be worshipped but He in Whom the Children of Israel believe.") until:

(and you were one of the mischief-makers) (10:90-91). And Allah says:

(so when they saw Our punishment, they said: "We believe in Allah Alone...") (40:84-85).

(Would they then wish for Our torment to be hastened on) This is a denunciation and a threat, because they used to say to the Messenger, by way of denial, thinking it unlikely ever to happen:

(Bring Allah's torment upon us) (29:29). This is as Allah said:

(And they ask you to hasten on the torment...) (29:53-55). Then Allah says:

(Think, if We do let them enjoy for years, and afterwards comes to them that which they had been promised, all that with which they used to enjoy shall not avail them.) meaning, `even if We delay the matter and give them respite for a short while or for a long time, then the punishment of Allah comes upon them, what good will their life of luxury do them then'

(The Day they see it, (it will be) as if they had not tarried (in this world) except an afternoon or a morning) (79:46). And Allah says:

(Everyone of them wishes that he could be given a life of a thousand years. But the grant of such life will not save him even a little from punishment) (2:96).

(And what will his wealth avail him when he goes down) (92:11) Allah says here:

(All that with which they used to enjoy shall not avail them.) According to an authentic Hadith:

«يُؤْتَى بِالْكَافِرِ فَيُغْمَسُ فِي النَّارِ غَمْسَةً ثُمَّ يُقَالُ لَهُ: هَلْ رَأَيْتَ خَيْرًا قَطُّ؟ هَلْ رَأَيْتَ نَعِيمًا قَطُّ؟ فَيَقُولُ: لَا وَاللهِ يَا رَبِّ، وَيُؤْتَى بِأَشَدِّ النَّاسِ بُؤْسًا كَانَ فِي

الدُّنْيَا، فَيُصْبَغُ فِي الْجَنَّةِ صَبْغَةً، ثُمَّ يُقَالُ لَهُ::هَلْ رَأَيْتَ بُؤْسًا قَطُّ؟ فَيَقُولُ: لَا وَاللَّهِ يَا رَبِّ»

(The disbelievers will be brought and once dipped into the Fire, then it will be said to him: "Did you ever see anything good Did you ever see anything good" He will say, "No, O Lord!" Then the most miserable person who ever lived on earth will be brought, and he will be put in Paradise for a brief spell, then it will be said to him, "Did you ever see anything bad" He will say, "No, O Lord.") meaning: as if nothing ever happened. Then Allah tells us of His justice towards His creation, in that He does not destroy any nation until after He has left them with no excuse, by warning them, sending Messengers to them and establishing proof against them. He says:

(And never did We destroy a township but it had its warners by way of reminder, and We have never been unjust.) This is like the Ayat:

(And We never punish until We have sent a Messenger) (17:15).

(And never will your Lord destroy the towns until He sends to their mother town a Messenger reciting to them Our Ayat.) until;

(the people thereof are wrongdoers) (28:59).

Surah: 26 Ayah: 210, Ayah: 211 & Ayah: 212

تَنَزَّلَتْ بِهِ ٱلشَّيَٰطِينُ ﴿٢١٠﴾

210. And it is not the Shayâtin (devils) who have brought it (this Qur'ân) down.

وَمَا يَنۢبَغِى لَهُمْ وَمَا يَسْتَطِيعُونَ ﴿٢١١﴾

211. Neither would it suit them, nor they can (produce it).

إِنَّهُمْ عَنِ ٱلسَّمْعِ لَمَعْزُولُونَ ﴿٢١٢﴾

212. Verily, they have been removed far from hearing it.

Transliteration

210. Wama tanazzalat bihi alshshayateenu 211. Wama yanbaghee lahum wama yastateeAAoona 212. Innahum AAani alssamAAi lamaAAzooloona

Tafsir Ibn Kathir

The Qur'an was brought down by Jibril, not Shaytan

Allah tells us about His Book, which falsehood cannot approach from before or behind it, sent down by the All-Wise, Worthy of all praise. He states that it has been brought down by the trustworthy Ruh (i.e., Jibril) who is helped by Allah,

(And it is not the Shayatin who have brought it down.) Then He tells us that it could not be the case for three reasons that the Shayatin brought it down. One is that it would not suit them, i.e., they have no desire to do so and they do not want to, because their nature is to corrupt and misguide people, but this contains words enjoining what is right and forbidding what is evil, and light, guidance and mighty proofs. There is a big difference between this and the Shayatin, Allah says:

(Neither would it suit them)

(nor are they able.) meaning, even if they wanted to, they could not do it. Allah says:

(Had We sent down this Qur'an on a mountain, you would surely have seen it humbling itself and rent asunder by the fear of Allah) (59:21). Then Allah explains that even if they wanted to and were able to bear it and convey it, they still would not be able to achieve that, because they were prevented from hearing the Qur'an when it was brought down, for the heavens were filled with guardians and shooting stars at the time when the Qur'an was being revealed to the Messenger of Allah , so none of the Shayatin could hear even one letter of it, lest there be any confusion in the matter. This is a part of Allah's mercy towards His servants, protection of His Laws, and support for His Book and His Messenger . Allah says:

(Verily, they have been removed far from hearing it.) This is like what Allah tells us about the Jinn:

(And we have sought to reach the heaven; but found it filled with stern guards and flaming fires. And verily, we used to sit there in stations, to (steal) a hearing, but any who listens now will find a flaming fire watching him in ambush.) until;

(or whether their Lord intends for them a right path) (72:8-10).

Surah: 26 Ayah: 213, Ayah: 214, Ayah: 215, Ayah: 216, Ayah: 217, Ayah: 218, Ayah: 219 & Ayah: 220

فَلَا تَدْعُ مَعَ ٱللَّهِ إِلَٰهًا ءَاخَرَ فَتَكُونَ مِنَ ٱلْمُعَذَّبِينَ ﴿٢١٣﴾

213. So invoke not with Allâh another ilâh (god) lest you be among those who receive punishment.

وَأَنذِرْ عَشِيرَتَكَ ٱلْأَقْرَبِينَ ﴿٢١٤﴾

214. And warn your tribe (O Muhammad (peace be upon him)) of near kindred.

وَٱخْفِضْ جَنَاحَكَ لِمَنِ ٱتَّبَعَكَ مِنَ ٱلْمُؤْمِنِينَ ﴿٢١٥﴾

215. And be kind and humble to the believers who follow you.

فَإِنْ عَصَوْكَ فَقُلْ إِنِّي بَرِىٓءٌ مِّمَّا تَعْمَلُونَ ﴿٢١٦﴾

216. Then if they disobey you, say: "I am innocent of what you do."

Chapter 26. Ash-Shu'araa (The Poets), Verses 001-227

وَتَوَكَّلْ عَلَى ٱلْعَزِيزِ ٱلرَّحِيمِ ﴿٢١٧﴾

217. And put your trust in the All-Mighty, the Most Merciful,

ٱلَّذِى يَرَىٰكَ حِينَ تَقُومُ ﴿٢١٨﴾

218. Who sees you (O Muhammad (peace be upon him)) when you stand up (alone at night for Tahajjud prayers).

وَتَقَلُّبَكَ فِى ٱلسَّٰجِدِينَ ﴿٢١٩﴾

219. And your movements among those who fall prostrate (to Allâh in the five compulsory congregational prayers).

إِنَّهُۥ هُوَ ٱلسَّمِيعُ ٱلْعَلِيمُ ﴿٢٢٠﴾

220. Verily He, only He, is the All-Hearer, the All-Knower.

Transliteration

213. Fala tadAAu maAAa Allahi ilahan akhara fatakoona mina almuAAaththabeena 214. Waanthir AAasheerataka al-aqrabeena   215. Waikhfid janahaka limani ittabaAAaka mina almu/mineena 216. Fa-in AAasawka faqul innee baree-on mimma taAAmaloona 217. Watawakkal AAala alAAazeezi alrraheemi   218. Allathee yaraka heena taqoomu 219. Wataqallubaka fee alssajideena 220. Innahu huwa alssameeAAu alAAaleemu

Tafsir Ibn Kathir

The Command to warn His Tribe of near Kindred

Here Allah commands (His Prophet) to worship Him alone, with no partner or associate, and tells him that whoever associates others in worship with Him, He will punish them. Then Allah commands His Messenger to warn his tribe of near kindred, i.e., those who were most closely related to him, and to tell them that nothing could save any of them except for faith in Allah. Allah also commanded him to be kind and gentle with the believing servants of Allah who followed him, and to disown those who disobeyed him, no matter who they were. Allah said:

(Then if they disobey you, say: "I am innocent of what you do.") This specific warning does not contradict the general warning; indeed it is a part of it, as Allah says elsewhere:

(In order that you may warn a people whose forefathers were not warned, so they are heedless.) (36:6),

(that you may warn the Mother of the Towns and all around it) (42:7),

(And warn therewith those who fear that they will be gathered before their Lord) (6:51), (that you may give glad tidings to those who have Taqwa, and warn with it the most quarrelsome people.) (19:97),

(that I may therewith warn you and whomsoever it may reach) (6:19), and

(but those of the sects that reject it, the Fire will be their promised meeting place) (11:17). According to Sahih Muslim, (the Prophet said:)

«وَالَّذِي نَفْسِي بِيَدِهِ، لَا يَسْمَعُ بِي أَحَدٌ مِنْ هَذِهِ الْأُمَّةِ يَهُودِيٌّ وَلَا نَصْرَانِيٌّ، ثُمَّ لَا يُؤْمِنُ بِي إِلَّا دَخَلَ النَّارَ»

(By the One in Whose Hand is my soul, no one from these nations -- Jewish or Christian -- hears of me then does not believe in me, but he will enter Hell.) Many Hadiths have been narrated concerning the revelation of this Ayah, some of which we will quote below: Imam Ahmad, may Allah have mercy on him, recorded that Ibn `Abbas, may Allah be pleased with him, said: "When Allah revealed the Ayah,

(And warn your tribe of near kindred.), the Prophet went to As-Safa', climbed up and called out,

«يَا صَبَاحَاه»

(O people!) The people gathered around him, some coming of their own accord and others sending people on their behalf to find out what was happening. The Messenger of Allah said:

«يَا بَنِي عَبْدِالْمُطَّلِبِ، يَا بَنِي فِهْرٍ، يَاأَبَنِي لُؤَيَ، أَرَأَيْتُمْ لَوْ أَخْبَرْتُكُمْ أَنَّ خَيْلًا بِسَفْحِ هَذَا الْجَبَلِ تُرِيدُ أَنْ تُغِيرَ عَلَيْكُمْ صَدَّقْتُمُونِي؟»

(O Bani `Abd Al-Muttalib, O Bani Fihr, O Bani Lu'ayy! What do you think, if I told you that there was a cavalry at the foot of this mountain coming to attack you -- would you believe me) They said, "Yes." He said:

«فَإِنِّي نَذِيرٌ لَكُمْ بَيْنَ يَدَي عَذَابٍ شَدِيدٍ»

(Then I warn you of a great punishment that is close at hand.) Abu Lahab said, "May you perish for the rest of the day! You only called us to tell us this" Then Allah revealed:

(Perish the two hands of Abu Lahab and perish he!) (111:1) This was also recorded by Al-Bukhari, Muslim, At-Tirmidhi and An-Nasa'i. Imam Ahmad recorded that `A'ishah, may Allah be pleased with her said: "When the Ayah:

(And warn your tribe of near kindred) was revealed, the Messenger of Allah stood up and said:

«يَا فَاطِمَةُ ابْنَةَ مُحَمَّدٍ، يَا صَفِيَّةُ ابْنَةَ عَبْدِالْمُطَّلِبِ، يَا بَنِي عَبْدِالْمُطَّلِبِ، لَا أَمْلِكُ لَكُمْ مِنَ اللهِ شَيْئًا سَلُونِي مِنْ مَالِي مَا شِئْتُم»

(O Fatimah daughter of Muhammad, O Safiyyah daughter of `Abd Al-Muttalib, O Bani `Abd Al-Muttalib, I cannot help you before Allah. Ask me for whatever you want of my wealth.) This was recorded by Muslim. Imam Ahmad recorded that Qabisah bin Mukhariq and Zuhayr bin `Amr said: "When the Ayah:

(And warn your tribe of near kindred.) was revealed, the Messenger of Allah climbed on top of a rock on the side of a mountain and started to call out:

«يَا بَنِي عَبْدِ مَنَافٍ، إِنَّمَا أَنَا نَذِيرٌ، وَإِنَّمَا مَثَلِي وَمَثَلُكُمْ كَرَجُلٍ رَأَى الْعَدُوَّ فَذَهَبَ يَرْبَأُ أَهْلَهُ يَخْشَى أَنْ يَسْبِقُوهُ، فَجَعَلَ يُنَادِي وَيَهْتِفُ: يَا صَبَاحَاه»

(O Bani `Abd Manaf, I am indeed a warner, and the parable of me and you is that of a man who sees the enemy so he goes to save his family, fearing that the enemy may reach them before he does.) And he started to call out, (O people!) It was also recorded by Muslim and An-Nasa'i. Allah's saying:

(And put your trust in the All-Mighty, the Most Merciful,) means, `in all your affairs, for He is your Helper, Protector and Supporter, and He is the One Who will cause you to prevail and will make your word supreme.'

(Who sees you when you stand up.) means, He is taking care of you. This is like the Ayah,

(So wait patiently for the decision of your Lord, for verily, you are under Our Eyes) (52:48) Ibn `Abbas said that the Ayah,

(Who sees you when you stand up.) means, "To pray." `Ikrimah said: "He sees him when he stands and bows and prostrates." Al-Hasan said:

(Who sees you when you stand up.) "When you pray alone." Ad-Dahhak said:

(Who sees you when you stand up.) "When you are lying in bed and when you are sitting." Qatadah said:

(Who sees you) "When you are standing, when you are sitting, and in all other situations."

(And your movements among those who fall prostrate.) Qatadah said:

(Who sees you when you stand up. And your movements among those who fall prostrate.) "When you pray, He sees you when you pray alone and when you pray in congregation." This was also the view of `Ikrimah, `Ata' Al-Khurasani and Al-Hasan Al-Basri.

(Verily, He, only He, is the All-Hearer, the All-Knower.) He hears all that His servants say and He knows all their movements, as He says:

(Neither you do any deed nor recite any portion of the Qur'an, nor you do any deed, but We are Witness thereof, when you are doing it) (10:61).

Surah: 26 Ayah: 221, Ayah: 222, Ayah: 223, Ayah: 224, Ayah: 225, Ayah: 226 & Ayah: 227

هَلْ أُنَبِّئُكُمْ عَلَىٰ مَن تَنَزَّلُ ٱلشَّيَـٰطِينُ ﴿٢٢١﴾

221. Shall I inform you (O people!) upon whom the Shayâtin (devils) descend?

تَنَزَّلُ عَلَىٰ كُلِّ أَفَّاكٍ أَثِيمٍ ﴿٢٢٢﴾

222. They descend on every lying, sinful person.

يُلْقُونَ ٱلسَّمْعَ وَأَكْثَرُهُمْ كَـٰذِبُونَ ﴿٢٢٣﴾

223. Who gives ear (to the devils and they pour what they may have heard of the Unseen from the angels), and most of them are liars.

وَٱلشُّعَرَآءُ يَتَّبِعُهُمُ ٱلْغَاوُۥنَ ﴿٢٢٤﴾

224. As for the poets, the erring ones follow them,

أَلَمْ تَرَ أَنَّهُمْ فِى كُلِّ وَادٍ يَهِيمُونَ ﴿٢٢٥﴾

225. See you not that they speak about every subject (praising people - right or wrong) in their poetry?

وَأَنَّهُمْ يَقُولُونَ مَا لَا يَفْعَلُونَ ﴿٢٢٦﴾

226. And that they say what they do not do.

إِلَّا ٱلَّذِينَ ءَامَنُوا۟ وَعَمِلُوا۟ ٱلصَّٰلِحَٰتِ وَذَكَرُوا۟ ٱللَّهَ كَثِيرًا وَٱنتَصَرُوا۟ مِنۢ بَعْدِ مَا ظُلِمُوا۟ ۗ وَسَيَعْلَمُ ٱلَّذِينَ ظَلَمُوٓا۟ أَىَّ مُنقَلَبٍ يَنقَلِبُونَ ۝

227. Except those who believe (in the Oneness of Allâh - Islâmic Monotheism), and do righteous deeds, and remember Allâh much, and vindicate themselves after they have been wronged (by replying back in poetry to the unjust poetry (which the pagan poets utter against the Muslims). And those who do wrong will come to know by what overturning they will be overturned.

Transliteration

221. Hal onabbi-okum AAala man tanazzalu alshshayateenu 222. Tanazzalu AAala kulli affakin atheemin 223. Yulqoona alssamAAa waaktharuhum kathiboona 224. WaalshshuAAarao yattabiAAuhumu alghawoona 225. Alam tara annahum fee kulli wadin yaheemoona 226. Waannahum yaqooloona ma la yafAAaloona 227. Illa allatheena amanoo waAAamiloo alssalihati wathakaroo Allaha katheeran waintasaroo min baAAdi ma thulimoo wasayaAAlamu allatheena thalamoo ayyamunqalabin yanqaliboona

Tafsir Ibn Kathir

Refutation of the Fabrications of the Idolators

Here Allah addresses those idolators who claimed that what was brought by the Messenger was not the truth but was merely something that he had made up by himself, or that it came to him in visions from the Jinn. Allah stated that His Messenger was above their claims and fabrications, and that what he had brought did indeed come from Allah, and that it was a revelation and inspiration, brought down by a noble, trustworthy and mighty angel. It did not come from the Shayatin, because they have no desire for anything like this Noble Qur'an -- they descend upon those who are like them, the lying fortune-tellers. Allah says:

(Shall I inform you) meaning, shall I tell you,

(upon whom the Shayatin descend They descend on every lying, sinful person (Athim)) meaning, one whose speech is lies and fabrication.

(Athim) means, whose deeds are immoral. This is the person upon whom the Shayatin descend, fortune-tellers and other sinful liars. The Shayatin are also sinful liars.

(Who gives ear,) means, they try to overhear what is said in the heavens, and they try to hear something of the Unseen, then they add to it a hundred lies and tell it to their human comrades, who then tell it to others. Then the people believe everything they say because they were right about the one thing which was heard from the heavens. This was stated in an authentic Hadith recorded by Al-Bukhari from `A'ishah, may Allah be pleased with her, who said, "The people asked the Prophet about fortune-tellers, and he said:

«إِنَّهُمْ لَيْسُوا بِشَيْءٍ»

(They are nothing.) They said: "O Messenger of Allah, they say things that come true." The Prophet said:

«تِلْكَ الْكَلِمَةُ مِنَ الْحَقِّ يَخْطَفُهَا الْجِنِّيُّ فَيُقَرْقِرُهَا فِي أُذُنِ وَلِيِّهِ كَقَرْقَرَةِ الدَّجَاجِ، فَيَخْلِطُونَ مَعَهَا أَكْثَرَ مِنْ مِائَةِ كَذْبَةٍ»

(That is a word of truth which the Jinn snatches, then he gabbles it like the clucking of a chicken into the ear of his friend, but he mixes it with more than one hundred lies.) Al-Bukhari also recorded that Abu Hurayrah said, "The Prophet said:

«إِذَا قَضَى اللهُ الْأَمْرَ فِي السَّمَاءِ ضَرَبَتِ الْمَلَائِكَةُ بِأَجْنِحَتِهَا خُضْعَانًا لِقَوْلِهِ، كَأَنَّهَا سِلْسِلَةٌ عَلَى صَفْوَانٍ، فَإِذَا فُزِّعَ عَنْ قُلُوبِهِمْ قَالُوا: مَاذَا قَالَ رَبُّكُمْ؟ قَالُوا (لِلَّذِي قَالَ): الْحَقَّ، وَهُوَ الْعَلِيُّ الْكَبِيرُ، فَيَسْمَعُهَا مُسْتَرِقُو السَّمْعِ، وَمُسْتَرِقُو السَّمْعِ هَكَذَا بَعْضُهُمْ فَوْقَ بَعْضٍ وَصَفَ سُفْيَانُ بِيَدِهِ، فَحَرَّفَهَا وَبَدَّدَ بَيْنَ أَصَابِعِهِ فَيَسْمَعُ الْكَلِمَةَ فَيُلْقِيهَا إِلَى مَنْ تَحْتَهُ، ثُمَّ يُلْقِيهَا الْآخَرُ إِلَى مَنْ تَحْتَهُ، حَتَّى يُلْقِيَهَا عَلَى لِسَانِ السَّاحِرِ أَوِ الْكَاهِنِ، فَرُبَّمَا أَدْرَكَهُ الشِّهَابُ قَبْلَ أَنْ يُلْقِيَهَا، وَرُبَّمَا أَلْقَاهَا قَبْلَ أَنْ يُدْرِكَهُ، فَيَكْذِبُ مَعَهَا مِائَةَ كَذْبَةٍ، فَيُقَالُ: أَلَيْسَ قَدْ قَالَ لَنَا يَوْمَ كَذَا وَكَذَا: كَذَا وَكَذَا؟ فَيُصَدَّقُ بِتِلْكَ الْكَلِمَةِ الَّتِي سُمِعَتْ مِنَ السَّمَاءِ»

(When Allah decrees a matter in heaven, the angels beat their wings in submission to His decree, a chain beating on a rock. And when the fear in their hearts subsides, they say: "What is it that your Lord has said" They say: "The truth. And He is the Most High, the Most Great." Then when the Jinn who are listening out, one above the other) -- and Sufyan illustrated this with a gesture, holding his hand vertically with his fingers outspread -- (when they hear this, they throw it down from one to another, until it is passed to the fortune-teller or soothsayer. The shooting star may strike the Jinn before he passes it on, or he may pass it on before he is struck, and he adds to it one hundred lies, thus it is said: "Did he not tell us that on such and such a day, such and such would happen" So they believe him because of that one thing which was heard from the heavens.) This was recorded by Al-Bukhari. Al-Bukhari recorded from `A'ishah, may Allah be pleased with her, that the Prophet said:

«إِنَّ الْمَلَائِكَةَ تَحَدَّثُ فِي الْعَنَانِ وَالْعَنَانُ: الْغَمَامُ بِالْأَمْرِ (يَكُونُ) فِي الْأَرْضِ، فَتَسْمَعُ الشَّيَاطِينُ الْكَلِمَةَ، فَتَقُرُّهَا فِي أُذُنِ الْكَاهِنِ كَمَا تُقَرُّ الْقَارُورَةُ، فَيَزِيدُونَ مَعَهَا مِائَةَ كَذْبَةٍ»

(The angels speak in the clouds about some matter on earth, and the Shayatin overhear what they say, so they tell it to the fortune-teller, gurgling into his ear like (a liquid poured) from a glass bottle, and he adds to it one hundred lies.)

Refutation of the Claim that the Prophet was a Poet

(As for the poets, the astray ones follow them.) `Ali bin Abi Talhah reported from Ibn `Abbas that this means: "The disbelievers follow the misguided among mankind and the Jinn." This was also the view of Mujahid, `Abdur-Rahman bin Zayd bin Aslam, and others. `Ikrimah said, "Two poets would ridicule one another in verse, with one group of people supporting one and another group supporting the other. Hence Allah revealed the Ayah,

(As for the poets, the erring ones follow them.)

(See you not that they speak about every subject in their poetry) `Ali bin Abi Talhah reported from Ibn `Abbas that this means: "They indulge in every kind of nonsense." Ad-Dahhak reported that Ibn `Abbas said, "They engage in every kind of verbal art." This was also the view of Mujahid and others.

(And that they say what they do not do.) Al-`Awfi reported that Ibn `Abbas said that at the time of the Messenger of Allah , two men, one from among the Ansar and one from another tribe, were ridiculing one another in verse, and each one of them was supported by a group of his own people, who were the foolish ones, and Allah said:

(As for the poets, the erring ones follow them. See you not that they speak about every subject in their poetry And that they say what they do not do.) What is meant here is that the Messenger , to whom this Qur'an was revealed, was not a soothsayer or a poet, because his situation was quite obviously different to theirs, as Allah says:

(And We have not taught him poetry, nor is it suitable for him. This is only a Reminder and a plain Qur'an.) (36:69),

(That this is verily, the word of an honored Messenger. It is not the word of a poet, little is that you believe! Nor is it the word of a soothsayer, little is that you remember! This is the Revelation sent down from the Lord of all that exits.) (69:40-43)

The Exception of the Poets of Islam

(Except those who believe and do righteous deeds,) Muhammad bin Ishaq narrated from Yazid bin `Abdullah bin Qusayt, that Abu Al-Hasan Salim Al-Barrad, the freed servant of Tamim Ad-Dari said: "When the Ayah --

(As for the poets, the erring ones follow them.) was revealed, Hassan bin Thabit, `Abdullah bin Rawahah and Ka`b bin Malik came to the Messenger of Allah , weeping, and said: "Allah knew when He revealed this Ayah that we are poets. The Prophet recited to them the Ayah,

(Except those who believe and do righteous deeds,) and said:

《أَنتُمْ》

((This means) you.)

(and remember Allah much). He said:

《أَنتُمْ》

((This means) you.)

(and vindicate themselves after they have been wronged.) He said:

《أَنتُمْ》

((This means) you.) This was recorded by Ibn Abi Hatim and Ibn Jarir from the narration of Ibn Ishaq. But this Surah was revealed in Makkah, so how could the reason for its revelation be the poets of the Ansar This is something worth thinking about. The reports that have been narrated about this are all Mursal and cannot be relied on. And Allah knows best. But this exception could include the poets of the Ansar and others. It even includes those poets of the Jahiliyyah who indulged in condemning Islam and its followers, then repented and turned to Allah, and gave up what they used to do and started to do righteous deeds and remember Allah much, to make up for the bad things that they had previously said, for good deeds wipe out bad deeds. So they praised Islam and its followers in order to make up for their insults, as (the poet) `Abdullah bin Az-Zab`ari said when he became Muslim: "O Messenger of Allah, indeed my tongue will try to make up for things it said when I was bad -- When I went along with the Shaytan during the years of misguidance, and whoever inclines towards his way is in a state of loss." Similarly, Abu Sufyan bin Al-Harith bin `Abd Al-Muttalib was one of the most hostile people towards the Prophet , even though he was his cousin, and he was the one who used to mock him the most. But when he became Muslim, there was no one more beloved to him than the Messenger of Allah . He began to praise the Messenger of Allah where he had mocked him, and take him as a close friend where he had regarded him as an enemy.

(and vindicate themselves after they have been wronged.) Ibn `Abbas said, "They responded in kind to the disbelievers who used to ridicule the believers in verse." This was also the view of Mujahid, Qatadah and several others. It was also recorded in the Sahih that the Messenger of Allah said to Hassan:

》اهْجُهُم《

(Ridicule them in verse.) Or he said:

》هَاجِهِمْ وَجِبْرِيلُ مَعَك《

(Ridicule them in verse, and Jibril is with you.) Imam Ahmad recorded that Ka`b bin Malik said to the Prophet , "Allah has revealed what He revealed about the poets. The Messenger of Allah said:

》إِنَّ الْمُؤْمِنَ يُجَاهِدُ بِسَيْفِهِ وَلِسَانِهِ، وَالَّذِي نَفْسِي بِيَدِهِ لَكَأَنَّ مَا تَرْمُونَهُمْ بِهِ نَضْحُ النَّبْلِ《

(The believer wages Jihad with his sword and with his tongue, By the One in Whose Hand is my soul, it is as if you are attacking them with arrows.)

(And those who do wrong will come to know by what overturning they will be overturned.) This is like the Ayah,

(The Day when their excuses will be of no profit to wrongdoers) (40: 52). According to the Sahih, the Messenger of Allah said:

》إِيَّاكُمْ وَالظُّلْمَ، فَإِنَّ الظُّلْمَ ظُلُمَاتٌ يَوْمَ الْقِيَامَةِ《

(Beware of wrongdoing, for wrongdoing will be darkness on the Day of Resurrection.) Qatadah bin Di`amah said concerning the Ayah --

(And those who do wrong will come to know by what overturning they will be overturned.) this refers to the poets and others. This is the end of the Tafsir Surat Ash-Shu`ara'. Praise be to Allah, Lord of the worlds.

CHAPTER (SURAH) 27: AN-NAML (THE ANT, THE ANTS), VERSES 001–055

(بِسْمِ اللَّهِ الرَّحْمَـنِ الرَّحِيمِ)

In the Name of Allah, the Most Gracious, the Most Merciful.

Surah: 27 Ayah: 1, Ayah: 2, Ayah: 3, Ayah: 4, Ayah: 5 & Ayah: 6

$$\text{طسٓ ۚ تِلْكَ ءَايَـٰتُ ٱلْقُرْءَانِ وَكِتَابٍ مُّبِينٍ ۝}$$

1. Tâ-Sîn. [These letters are one of the miracles of the Qur'ân, and none but Allâh (Alone) knows their meanings]. These are the Verses of the Qur'ân, and (it is) a Book (that makes things) clear;

$$\text{هُدًى وَبُشْرَىٰ لِلْمُؤْمِنِينَ ۝}$$

2. A guide (to the Right Path) and glad tidings for the believers (who believe in the Oneness of Allâh (i.e. Islâmic Monotheism))

$$\text{ٱلَّذِينَ يُقِيمُونَ ٱلصَّلَوٰةَ وَيُؤْتُونَ ٱلزَّكَوٰةَ وَهُم بِٱلْءَاخِرَةِ هُمْ يُوقِنُونَ ۝}$$

3. Those who perform As-Salât (Iqâmat-as-Salât) and give Zakât and they believe with certainty in the Hereafter (resurrection, recompense of their good and bad deeds, Paradise and Hell).

$$\text{إِنَّ ٱلَّذِينَ لَا يُؤْمِنُونَ بِٱلْءَاخِرَةِ زَيَّنَّا لَهُمْ أَعْمَـٰلَهُمْ فَهُمْ يَعْمَهُونَ ۝}$$

4. Verily, those who believe not in the Hereafter, We have made their deeds fair-seeming to them, so they wander about blindly.

$$\text{أُو۟لَـٰٓئِكَ ٱلَّذِينَ لَهُمْ سُوٓءُ ٱلْعَذَابِ وَهُمْ فِى ٱلْءَاخِرَةِ هُمُ ٱلْأَخْسَرُونَ ۝}$$

5. They are those for whom there will be an evil torment (in this world). And in the Hereafter they will be the greatest losers.

$$\text{وَإِنَّكَ لَتُلَقَّى ٱلْقُرْءَانَ مِن لَّدُنْ حَكِيمٍ عَلِيمٍ ۝}$$

6. And verily, you (O Muhammad (peace be upon him)) are being taught the Qur'ân from the One, All-Wise, All-Knowing.

Transliteration

1. Ta-seen tilka ayatu alqur-ani wakitabin mubeenin 2. Hudan wabushra lilmu/mineena 3. Allatheena yuqeemoona alssalata wayu/toona alzzakata wahum bial-akhirati hum yooqinoona 4. Inna allatheena la yu/minoona bial-akhirati zayyanna lahum aAAmalahum fahum yaAAmahoona 5. Ola-ika allatheena lahum soo-o alAAathabi wahum fee al-akhirati humu alakhsaroona 6. Wa-innaka latulaqqa alqur-ana min ladun hakeemin AAaleemin

Tafsir Ibn Kathir

The Qur'an is Guidance and Glad Tidings for the Believers, a Warning to the Disbelievers, and it is from Allah

In (the comments on) Surat Al-Baqarah, we discussed the letters which appear at the beginning of some Surahs.

(These are the Ayat of the Qur'an, and (it is) a Book (that is) clear.) It is plain and evident.

(A guide and glad tidings for the believers.) meaning, guidance and good news may be attained from the Qur'an for those who believe in it, follow it and put it into practice. They establish obligatory prayers, pay Zakah and believe with certain faith in the Hereafter, the resurrection after death, reward and punishment for all deeds, good and bad, and Paradise and Hell. This is like the Ayat:

(Say: "It is for those who believe, a guide and a healing. And as for those who disbelieve, there is heaviness (deafness) in their ears...") (41:44).

(that you may give glad tidings to those who have Taqwa, and warn with it the Ludd (most quarrelsome) people) (19: 97). Allah says here:

(Verily, those who believe not in the Hereafter,) meaning, those who deny it and think that it will never happen,

(We have made their deeds fair seeming to them, so that they wander about blindly.) means, `We have made what they are doing seem good to them, and We have left them to continue in their misguidance, so they are lost and confused.' This is their recompense for their disbelief in the Hereafter, as Allah says:

(And We shall turn their hearts and their eyes away, as they refused to believe therein for the first time) (6:110).

(They are those for whom there will be an evil torment.) in this world and the Hereafter.

(And in the Hereafter they will be the greatest losers.) means, no one but they, among all the people who will be gathered, will lose their souls and their wealth.

(And verily, you are being taught the Qur'an from One, All-Wise, All-Knowing.)

(And verily, you) O Muhammad. Qatadah said:

(are being taught) "Are receiving."

(the Qur'an from One, All-Wise, All-Knowing.) from One Who is Wise in His commands and prohibitions, and Who knows all things, major and minor. Whatever He says is absolute Truth, and His rulings are entirely fair and just, as Allah says:

(And the Word of your Lord has been fulfilled in truth and in justice) (6:115).

Surah: 27 Ayah: 7, Ayah: 8, Ayah: 9, Ayah: 10, Ayah: 11, Ayah: 12, Ayah: 13 & Ayah: 14

إِذْ قَالَ مُوسَىٰ لِأَهْلِهِ إِنِّي ءَانَسْتُ نَارًا سَـَٔاتِيكُم مِّنْهَا بِخَبَرٍ أَوْ ءَاتِيكُم بِشِهَابٍ قَبَسٍ لَّعَلَّكُمْ تَصْطَلُونَ ۞

7. (Remember) when Mûsâ (Moses) said to his household: "Verily I have seen a fire; I will bring you from there some information, or I will bring you a burning brand, that you may warm yourselves."

فَلَمَّا جَآءَهَا نُودِيَ أَنْ بُورِكَ مَن فِي ٱلنَّارِ وَمَنْ حَوْلَهَا وَسُبْحَـٰنَ ٱللَّهِ رَبِّ ٱلْعَـٰلَمِينَ ۞

8. But when he came to it, he was called: "Blessed is whosoever is in the fire, and whosoever is round about it! And glorified is Allâh, the Lord of the 'Alamîn (mankind, jinn and all that exists).

يَـٰمُوسَىٰٓ إِنَّهُۥٓ أَنَا ٱللَّهُ ٱلْعَزِيزُ ٱلْحَكِيمُ ۞

9. "O Mûsâ (Moses)! Verily! It is I, Allâh, the All-Mighty, the All-Wise.

وَأَلْقِ عَصَاكَ ۚ فَلَمَّا رَءَاهَا تَهْتَزُّ كَأَنَّهَا جَآنٌّ وَلَّىٰ مُدْبِرًا وَلَمْ يُعَقِّبْ ۚ يَـٰمُوسَىٰ لَا تَخَفْ إِنِّي لَا يَخَافُ لَدَىَّ ٱلْمُرْسَلُونَ ۞

10. "And throw down your stick!" But when he saw it moving as if it were a snake, he turned in flight, and did not look back. (It was said): "O Mûsâ (Moses)! Fear not: verily! The Messengers fear not in front of Me.

إِلَّا مَن ظَلَمَ ثُمَّ بَدَّلَ حُسْنًا بَعْدَ سُوٓءٍ فَإِنِّي غَفُورٌ رَّحِيمٌ ۞

11. "Except him who has done wrong and afterwards has changed evil for good; then surely, I am Oft-Forgiving, Most Merciful.

وَأَدْخِلْ يَدَكَ فِي جَيْبِكَ تَخْرُجْ بَيْضَآءَ مِنْ غَيْرِ سُوٓءٍ ۖ فِي تِسْعِ ءَايَـٰتٍ إِلَىٰ فِرْعَوْنَ وَقَوْمِهِۦٓ ۚ إِنَّهُمْ كَانُوا۟ قَوْمًا فَـٰسِقِينَ ۞

12. "And put your hand into your bosom, it will come forth white without hurt. (These are) among the nine signs (you will take) to Fir'aun (Pharaoh) and his people. Verily they are a people who are the Fâsiqûn (rebellious, disobedient to Allâh).

فَلَمَّا جَآءَتْهُمْ ءَايَـٰتُنَا مُبْصِرَةً قَالُوا۟ هَـٰذَا سِحْرٌ مُّبِينٌ ۞

13. But when Our Ayât (proofs, evidences, verses, lessons, signs, revelations, etc.) came to them, clear to see, they said: "This is a manifest magic."

وَجَحَدُواْ بِهَا وَٱسْتَيْقَنَتْهَآ أَنفُسُهُمْ ظُلْمًا وَعُلُوًّا ۚ فَٱنظُرْ كَيْفَ كَانَ عَـٰقِبَةُ ٱلْمُفْسِدِينَ ۞

14. And they belied them (those Ayât) wrongfully and arrogantly, though their own selves were convinced thereof (i.e. those (Ayât) are from Allâh, and Mûsâ (Moses) is the Messenger of Allâh in truth, but they disliked to obey Mûsâ (Moses), and hated to believe in his Message of Monotheism). So see what was the end of the Mufsidûn (disbelievers, disobedient to Allâh, evil-doers and liars.).

Transliteration

7. Ith qala moosa li-ahlihi innee anastu naran saateekum minha bikhabarin aw ateekum bishihabin qabasin laAAallakum tastaloona 8. Falamma jaaha noodiya an boorika man fee alnnari waman hawlaha wasubhana Allahi rabbi alAAalameena 9. Ya moosa innahu ana Allahu alAAazeezu alhakeemu 10. Waalqi AAasaka falamma raaha tahtazzu kaannaha jannun walla mudbiran walam yuAAaqqib ya moosa la takhaf innee la yakhafu ladayya almursaloona 11. Illa man thalama thumma baddala husnan baAAda soo-in fa-innee ghafoorun raheemun 12. Waadkhil yadaka fee jaybika takhruj baydaa min ghayri soo-in fee tisAAi ayatin ila firAAawna waqawmihi innahum kanoo qawman fasiqeena 13. Falamma jaat-hum ayatuna mubsiratan qaloo hatha sihrun mubeenun 14. Wajahadoo biha waistayqanat-ha anfusuhum thulman waAAuluwwan faonthur kayfa kana AAaqibatu almufsideena

Tafsir Ibn Kathir

The Story of Musa and the End of Fir`awn

Here Allah tells His Messenger Muhammad about what happened to Musa, peace be upon him, how Allah chose him, spoke with him and gave him mighty, dazzling signs and overwhelming proof, and sent him to Fir`awn and his people, but they denied the proof, disbelieved in him and arrogantly refused to follow him. Allah says:

(when Musa said to his household), meaning, remember when Musa was traveling with his family and lost his way. This was at night, in the dark. Musa had seen a fire beside the mountain, i.e., he had noticed a fire burning brightly, and said,

(to his household: "Verily, I have seen a fire; I will bring you from there some information...") meaning, `about the way we should take.'

(or I will bring you a burning ember, that you may warm yourselves.) meaning, so that they could keep warm. And it was as he said: "He came back with great news, and a great light." Allah says:

(But when he came to it, he was called: "Blessed is whosoever is in the fire, and whosoever is round about it!") meaning, when he came to it, he saw a great and terrifying sight: the fire was burning in a green bush, and the fire was burning ever brighter while the bush was growing ever more green and beautiful. Then he raised his head, and saw that its light was connected to the clouds of the sky. Ibn `Abbas and others said, "It was not a fire, rather it was shining light." According to one report narrated from Ibn `Abbas, it was the Light of the Lord of the worlds. Musa stood amazed by what he was seeing, and

(he was called: "Blessed is whosoever is in the fire...") Ibn `Abbas said, "This means, Holy is (whosoever is in the fire)."

(and whosoever is round about it) means, of the angels. This was the view of Ibn `Abbas, `Ikrimah, Sa`id bin Jubayr, Al-Hasan and Qatadah.

(And glorified be Allah, the Lord of all that exists), Who does whatever He wills and there is nothing like Him among His creation. Nothing He has made can encompass Him, and He is the Exalted, the Almighty, Who is utterly unlike all that He has created. Heaven and earth cannot contain Him, but He is the One, the Self-Sufficient Master, Who is far above any comparison with His creation.

(O Musa! Verily, it is I, Allah, the All-Mighty, the All-Wise.) Allah told him that the One Who was addressing him was his Lord Allah, the All-Mighty, Who has subjugated and subdued all things, the One Who is Wise in all His words and deeds. Then He commanded him to throw down the stick that was in his hand, so that He might show him clear proof that He is the One Who is able to do all things, whatever He wills. When Musa threw that stick down, it changed into the form of a huge and terrifying snake, moving quickly despite its size. Allah says:

(But when he saw it moving as if it were a Jann (snake).) Jann refers to a type of snake that is the fastest-moving and most agile. When Musa saw that with his own eyes,

(he turned in flight, and did not look back.) meaning, he did not turn around, because he was so afraid. Allah's saying:

(O Musa! Fear not: verily, the Messengers fear not in front of Me.) means, `do not be afraid of what you see, for I want to choose you as a Messenger and make you a great Prophet.'

(Except him who has done wrong and afterwards has changed evil for good; then surely, I am Oft-Forgiving, Most Merciful.) This is an exception of the exclusionary type. This is good news for mankind, for whoever does an evil deed then gives it up and repents and turns to Allah, Allah will accept his repentance, as He says:

(And verily, I am indeed forgiving to him who repents, believes and does righteous good deeds, and then Ahtada.) (20:82)

(And whoever does evil or wrongs himself...) (4:110). And there are many other Ayat which say the same.

(And put your hand into the opening of your garment, it will come forth white without hurt.) This is another sign, further brilliant proof of the ability of Allah to do whatever

He wills. It is also confirmation of the truth of the one to whom the miracle was given. Allah commanded him to put his hand into the opening of his garment, and when he put his hand in and took it out again, it came out white and shining as if it were a piece of the moon or a flash of dazzling lightning.

(among the nine signs) means, `these are two of the nine signs which you will be supported with and which will serve as proof for you. '

(to Fir`awn and his people. Verily, they are a people who are rebellious.) These were the nine signs of which Allah said:

(And indeed We gave Musa nine clear signs) (17:101) -- as we have stated there.

(But when Our Ayat came to them, clear to see,), i.e., clear and obvious,

(they said: "This is a manifest magic".) They wanted to oppose it with their own magic, but they were defeated and were returned disgraced.

(And they belied them) means, verbally,

(though they themselves were convinced thereof.) means, they knew deep down that this was truth from Allah, but they denied it and were stubborn and arrogant.

(wrongfully and arrogantly) means, wronging themselves because this was the despicable manner to which they were accustomed, and they were arrogant because they were too proud to follow the truth. Allah said:

(So, see what was the end of the mischief-makers.) meaning, `see, O Muhammad, what were the consequences of their actions when Allah destroyed them and drowned every last one of them in a single morning.' The point of this story is: beware, `O you who disbelieve in Muhammad and deny the Message that he has brought from his Lord, lest the same thing that befell them befall you also.' But what is worse, is that Muhammad is nobler and greater than Musa, and his proof is stronger than that of Musa, for the signs that Allah has given him are combined with his presence and his character, in addition to the fact that previous Prophets foretold his coming and took a covenant from the people that they would follow him if they should see him, may the best of blessings and peace from his Lord be upon him.

Surah: 27 Ayah: 15, Ayah: 16, Ayah: 17, Ayah: 18 & Ayah: 19

وَلَقَدْ ءَاتَيْنَا دَاوُۥدَ وَسُلَيْمَٰنَ عِلْمًا ۖ وَقَالَا ٱلْحَمْدُ لِلَّهِ ٱلَّذِى فَضَّلَنَا عَلَىٰ كَثِيرٍ مِّنْ عِبَادِهِ ٱلْمُؤْمِنِينَ ۝

15. And indeed We gave knowledge to Dâwûd (David) and Sulaimân (Solomon), and they both said: "All the praises and thanks be to Allâh, Who has preferred us above many of His believing slaves!"

$$\text{وَوَرِثَ سُلَيْمَـٰنُ دَاوُۥدَ ۖ وَقَالَ يَـٰٓأَيُّهَا ٱلنَّاسُ عُلِّمْنَا مَنطِقَ ٱلطَّيْرِ وَأُوتِينَا مِن كُلِّ شَىْءٍ ۖ إِنَّ هَـٰذَا لَهُوَ ٱلْفَضْلُ ٱلْمُبِينُ ﴿١٦﴾}$$

16. And Sulaimân (Solomon) inherited (the knowledge of) Dâwûd (David). He said: "O mankind! We have been taught the language of birds, and on us have been bestowed all things. This, verily, is an evident grace (from Allâh)."

$$\text{وَحُشِرَ لِسُلَيْمَـٰنَ جُنُودُهُۥ مِنَ ٱلْجِنِّ وَٱلْإِنسِ وَٱلطَّيْرِ فَهُمْ يُوزَعُونَ ﴿١٧﴾}$$

17. And there were gathered before Sulaimân (Solomon) his hosts of jinn and men, and birds, and they all were set in battle order (marching forwards).

$$\text{حَتَّىٰٓ إِذَآ أَتَوْا۟ عَلَىٰ وَادِ ٱلنَّمْلِ قَالَتْ نَمْلَةٌ يَـٰٓأَيُّهَا ٱلنَّمْلُ ٱدْخُلُوا۟ مَسَـٰكِنَكُمْ لَا يَحْطِمَنَّكُمْ سُلَيْمَـٰنُ وَجُنُودُهُۥ وَهُمْ لَا يَشْعُرُونَ ﴿١٨﴾}$$

18. Till, when they came to the valley of the ants, one of the ants said: "O ants! Enter your dwellings, lest Sulaimân (Solomon) and his hosts crush you, while they perceive not."

$$\text{فَتَبَسَّمَ ضَاحِكًا مِّن قَوْلِهَا وَقَالَ رَبِّ أَوْزِعْنِىٓ أَنْ أَشْكُرَ نِعْمَتَكَ ٱلَّتِىٓ أَنْعَمْتَ عَلَىَّ وَعَلَىٰ وَٰلِدَىَّ وَأَنْ أَعْمَلَ صَـٰلِحًا تَرْضَـٰهُ وَأَدْخِلْنِى بِرَحْمَتِكَ فِى عِبَادِكَ ٱلصَّـٰلِحِينَ ﴿١٩﴾}$$

19. So he (Sulaimân (Solomon)) smiled, amused at her speech and said: "My Lord! Inspire me and bestow upon me the power and ability that I may be grateful for Your Favors which You have bestowed on me and on my parents, and that I may do righteous good deeds that will please You, and admit me by Your Mercy among Your righteous slaves."

Transliteration

15. Walaqad atayna dawooda wasulaymana AAilman waqala alhamdu lillahi allathee faddalana AAala katheerin min AAibadihi almu/mineena 16. Wawaritha sulaymanu dawooda waqala ya ayyuha alnnasu AAullimna mantiqa alttayri waooteena min kulli shay-in inna hatha lahuwa alfadlu almubeenu 17. Wahushira lisulaymana junooduhu mina aljinni waal-insi waalttayri fahumyoozaAAoona 18. Hatta itha ataw AAala wadi alnnamli qalat namlatun ya ayyuha alnnamlu odkhuloo masakinakum la yahtimannakum sulaymanu wajunooduhu wahum la yashAAuroona 19. Fatabassama dahikan min qawliha waqala rabbi awziAAnee an ashkura niAAmataka allatee anAAamta AAalayya waAAala walidayya waan aAAmala salihan tardahu waadkhilnee birahmatika fee AAibadika alssaliheena

Tafsir Ibn Kathir

Dawud and Sulayman (peace be upon them), the organization of Sulayman's Troops and His passage through the Valley of the Ants

Here Allah tells us about the great blessings and favors which He bestowed upon two of His servants and Prophets, Dawud (David) and his son Sulayman (Solomon), peace be upon them both, and how they enjoyed happiness in this world and the Hereafter, power and authority in this world, and the position of being Prophets and Messengers. Allah says:

(And indeed We gave knowledge to Dawud and Sulayman, and they both said: "All the praises and thanks be to Allah, Who has preferred us above many of His believing servants!")

(And Sulayman inherited from Dawud.) means, in kingship and prophethood. What is meant here is not wealth, because if that were the case, Sulayman would not have been singled out from among the sons of Dawud, as Dawud had one hundred wives. Rather what is meant is the inheritance of kingship and prophethood, for the wealth of the Prophets cannot be inherited, as the Messenger of Allah said:

《نَحْنُ مَعَاشِرَ الْأَنْبِيَاءِ لَا نُورَثُ، مَا تَرَكْنَاهُ فَهُوَ صَدَقَة》

(We Prophets cannot be inherited from; whatever we leave behind is charity.) And Sulayman said:

(O mankind! We have been taught the language of birds, and we have been given from everything.) Here Sulayman was speaking of the blessings that Allah bestowed upon him, by giving him complete authority and power, whereby mankind, the Jinn and the birds were subjugated to him. He also knew the language of the birds and animals, which is something that had never been given to any other human being -- as far as we know from what Allah and His Messenger told us. Allah enabled Sulayman to understand what the birds said to one another as they flew through the air, and what the different kinds of animals said. Sulayman said:

(We have been taught the language of birds, and we have been given from everything.) i.e., all things that a king needs.

(This, verily, is an evident grace.) means, `this is clearly the blessings of Allah upon us.'

(And there were gathered before Sulayman his hosts of Jinn and men, and birds, and they all were set in battle order.) means, all of Sulayman's troops of Jinn, men and birds were gathered together, and he rode with them in a display of might and glory, with people marching behind him, followed by the Jinn, and the birds flying above his head. When it was hot, they would shade him with their wings.

(and they all were set in battle order.) The first and the last of them were brought together, so that none of them would step out of place. Mujahid said: "Officials were appointed to keep each group in order, and to keep the first and the last together so that no one would step out of line -- just as kings do nowadays."

(Till, when they came to the valley of the ants,) meaning, when Sulayman, the soldiers and the army with him crossed the valley of the ants,

(one of the ants said: "O ants! Enter your dwellings, lest Sulayman and his armies should crush you, while they perceive not.") Sulayman, peace be upon him, understood what the ant said,

(So he smiled, amused at her speech and said: "My Lord! Grant me the power and ability that I may be grateful for Your favors which You have bestowed on me and on my parents, and that I may do righteous good deeds that will please You,) meaning: `inspire me to give thanks for the blessings that You have bestowed upon me by teaching me to understand what the birds and animals say, and the blessings that You have bestowed upon my parents by making them Muslims who believe in You.'

(and that I may do righteous good deeds that will please You,) means, `deeds that You love which will earn Your pleasure.'

(and admit me by Your mercy among Your righteous servants.) means, `when You cause me to die, then join me with the righteous among Your servants, and the Higher Companion among Your close friends.'

Surah: 27 Ayah: 20 & Ayah: 21

وَتَفَقَّدَ ٱلطَّيْرَ فَقَالَ مَا لِيَ لَآ أَرَى ٱلْهُدْهُدَ أَمْ كَانَ مِنَ ٱلْغَآئِبِينَ ﴿٢٠﴾

20. He inspected the birds, and said: "What is the matter that I see not the hoopoe? Or is he among the absentees?

لَأُعَذِّبَنَّهُۥ عَذَابًا شَدِيدًا أَوْ لَأَاْذْبَحَنَّهُۥٓ أَوْ لَيَأْتِيَنِّى بِسُلْطَٰنٍ مُّبِينٍ ﴿٢١﴾

21. "I will surely punish him with a severe torment, or slaughter him, unless he brings me a clear reason."

Transliteration

20. Watafaqqada alttayra faqala ma liya la ara alhudhuda am kana mina algha-ibeena
21. LaoAAaththibannahu AAathaban shadeedan aw laathbahannahu aw laya/tiyannee bisultanin mubeenin

Tafsir Ibn Kathir

The Absence of the Hoopoe

Mujahid, Sa`id bin Jubayr and others narrated from Ibn `Abbas and others that the hoopoe was an expert who used to show Sulayman where water was if he was out in open land and needed water. The hoopoe would look for water for him in the various strata of the earth, just as a man looks at things on the surface of the earth, and he would know just how far below the surface the water was. When the hoopoe showed him where the water was, Sulayman would command the Jinn to dig in that place until they brought water from the depths of the earth. One day Sulayman went to some open land and checked on the birds, but he could not see the hoopoe.

(and (Sulayman) said: "What is the matter that I see not the hoopoe Or is he among the absentees") One day `Abdullah bin `Abbas told a similar story, and among the people was a man from the Khawarij whose name was Nafi` bin Al-Azraq, who often used to raise objections to Ibn `Abbas. He said to him, "Stop, O Ibn `Abbas; you will be defeated (in argument) today!" Ibn `Abbas said: "Why" Nafi` said: "You are telling us that the hoopoe can see water beneath the ground, but any boy can put seed in a trap and cover the trap with dirt, and the hoopoe will come and take the seed, so the boy can catch him in the trap." Ibn `Abbas said, "If it was not for the fact that this man would go and tell others that he had defeated Ibn `Abbas in argument, I would not even answer." Then he said to Nafi`: "Woe to you! When the decree strikes a person, his eyes become blind and he loses all caution." Nafi` said: "By Allah I will never dispute with you concerning anything in the Qur'an. "

(I will surely punish him with a severe torment) Al-A`mash said, narrating from Al-Minhal bin `Amr from Sa`id that Ibn `Abbas said: "He meant, by plucking his feathers." `Abdullah bin Shaddad said: "By plucking his feathers and exposing him to the sun." This was also the view of more than one of the Salaf, that it means plucking his feathers and leaving him exposed to be eaten by ants.

(or slaughter him,) means, killing him.

(unless he brings me a clear reason.) i.e., a valid excuse. Sufyan bin `Uyaynah and `Abdullah bin Shaddad said: "When the hoopoe came back, the other birds said to him: "What kept you Sulayman has vowed to shed your blood." The hoopoe said: "Did he make any exception (did he say `unless')" They said, "Yes, he said:

(I will surely punish him with a severe torment or slaughter him, unless he brings me a clear reason.) The hoopoe said, "Then I am saved."

Surah: 27 Ayah: 22, Ayah: 23, Ayah: 24, Ayah: 25 & Ayah: 26

فَمَكَثَ غَيْرَ بَعِيدٍ فَقَالَ أَحَطتُ بِمَا لَمْ تُحِطْ بِهِ وَجِئْتُكَ مِن سَبَإٍ بِنَبَإٍ يَقِينٍ

22. But the hoopoe stayed not long: he (came up and) said: "I have grasped (the knowledge of a thing) which you have not grasped and I have come to you from Saba' (Sheba) with true news.

إِنِّي وَجَدتُّ امْرَأَةً تَمْلِكُهُمْ وَأُوتِيَتْ مِن كُلِّ شَيْءٍ وَلَهَا عَرْشٌ عَظِيمٌ

23. "I found a woman ruling over them: she has been given all things that could be possessed by any ruler of the earth, and she has a great throne.

$$وَجَدتُّهَا وَقَوْمَهَا يَسْجُدُونَ لِلشَّمْسِ مِن دُونِ ٱللَّهِ وَزَيَّنَ لَهُمُ ٱلشَّيْطَانُ أَعْمَالَهُمْ فَصَدَّهُمْ عَنِ ٱلسَّبِيلِ فَهُمْ لَا يَهْتَدُونَ ﴿٢٤﴾$$

24. "I found her and her people worshipping the sun instead of Allâh, and Shaitân (Satan) has made their deeds fair-seeming to them, and has barred them from (Allâh's) Way: so they have no guidance."

$$أَلَّا يَسْجُدُوا۟ لِلَّهِ ٱلَّذِى يُخْرِجُ ٱلْخَبْءَ فِى ٱلسَّمَـٰوَٰتِ وَٱلْأَرْضِ وَيَعْلَمُ مَا تُخْفُونَ وَمَا تُعْلِنُونَ ﴿٢٥﴾$$

25. (as Shaitân (Satan) has barred them from Allâh's Way) so they do not worship (prostrate themselves before) Allâh, Who brings to light what is hidden in the heavens and the earth, and knows what you conceal and what you reveal. (Tafsir At-Tabarî)

$$ٱللَّهُ لَآ إِلَـٰهَ إِلَّا هُوَ رَبُّ ٱلْعَرْشِ ٱلْعَظِيمِ ﴿٢٦﴾$$

26. Allâh, Lâ ilâha illa Huwa (none has the right to be worshipped but He), the Lord of the Supreme Throne!

Transliteration

22. Famakatha ghayra baAAeedin faqala ahattu bima lam tuhit bihi waji/tuka min sabain binaba-in yaqeenin 23. Innee wajadtu imraatan tamlikuhum waootiyat min kulli shay-in walaha AAarshun AAatheemun 24. Wajadtuha waqawmaha yasjudoona lilshshamsi min dooni Allahi wazayyanalahumu alshshaytanu aAAmalahum fasaddahum AAani alssabeeli fahum la yahtadoona 25. Alla yasjudoo lillahi allathee yukhriju alkhabaa fee alssamawati waal-ardi wayaAAlamu ma tukhfoona wama tuAAlinoona 26. Allahu la ilaha illa huwa rabbu alAAarshi alAAatheemi

Tafsir Ibn Kathir

How the Hoopoe came before Sulayman and told Him about Saba'

Allah says:

(But (the hoopoe) stayed not long,) meaning, he was absent for only a short time. Then he came and said to Sulayman:

(I have grasped which you have not grasped) meaning, `I have come to know something that you and your troops do not know.'

(and I have come to you from Saba' with true news.) meaning, with true and certain news. Saba' (Sheba) refers to Himyar, they were a dynasty in Yemen. Then the hoopoe said:

(I found a woman ruling over them,) Al-Hasan Al-Basri said, "This is Bilqis bint Sharahil, the queen of Saba'." Allah's saying:

(she has been given all things,) means, all the conveniences of this world that a powerful monarch could need.

(and she has a great throne.) meaning, a tremendous chair adorned with gold and different kinds of jewels and pearls. The historians said, "This throne was in a great, strong palace which was high and firmly constructed. In it there were three hundred and sixty windows on the east side, and a similar number on the west, and it was constructed in such a way that each day when the sun rose it would shine through one window, and when it set it would shine through the opposite window. And the people used to prostrate to the sun morning and evening. This is why the hoopoe said:

(I found her and her people worshipping the sun instead of Allah, and Shaytan has made their deeds fair seeming to them, and has prevented them from the way,) meaning, from the way of truth,

(so they have no guidance.) Allah's saying:

(and Shaytan has made their deeds fair seeming to them, and has prevented them from the way, so they have no guidance, so they do not prostrate themselves before Allah.) They do not know the way of truth, prostrating only before Allah alone and not before anything that He has created, whether heavenly bodies or anything else. This is like the Ayah:

(And from among His signs are the night and the day, and the sun and the moon. Prostrate yourselves not to the sun nor to the moon, but prostrate yourselves to Allah Who created them, if you indeed worship Him.) (41:37)

(Who brings to light what is hidden in the heavens and the earth,) `Ali bin Abi Talhah reported that Ibn `Abbas said: "He knows everything that is hidden in the heavens and on earth." This was also the view of `Ikrimah, Mujahid, Sa`id bin Jubayr, Qatadah and others. His saying:

(and knows what you conceal and what you reveal.) means, He knows what His servants say and do in secret, and what they say and do openly. This is like the Ayah:

(It is the same whether any of you conceals his speech or declares it openly, whether he be hid by night or goes forth freely by day) (13:10). His saying:

(Allah, La ilaha illa Huwa, the Lord of the Supreme Throne!) means, He is the One to be called upon, Allah, He is the One other than Whom there is no god, the Lord of the Supreme Throne, and there is none greater than Him in all of creation. Since the hoopoe was calling to what is good, and for people to worship and prostrate to Allah alone, it would have been forbidden to kill him. Imam Ahmad, Abu Dawud and Ibn Majah recorded that Abu Hurayrah, may Allah be pleased with him, said that the Prophet forbade killing four kinds of animals: ants, bees, hoopoes and the sparrow hawks. Its chain of narration is Sahih.

Surah: 27 Ayah: 27, Ayah: 28, Ayah: 29, Ayah: 30 & Ayah: 31

﴿ قَالَ سَنَنظُرُ أَصَدَقْتَ أَمْ كُنتَ مِنَ ٱلْكَـٰذِبِينَ ۝ ﴾

27. (Sulaimân (Solomon)) said: "We shall see whether you speak the truth or you are (one) of the liars.

﴿ ٱذْهَب بِّكِتَـٰبِى هَـٰذَا فَأَلْقِهْ إِلَيْهِمْ ثُمَّ تَوَلَّ عَنْهُمْ فَٱنظُرْ مَاذَا يَرْجِعُونَ ۝ ﴾

28. "Go you with this letter of mine, and deliver it to them, then draw back from them, and see what (answer) they return."

﴿ قَالَتْ يَـٰأَيُّهَا ٱلْمَلَؤُاْ إِنِّى أُلْقِىَ إِلَىَّ كِتَـٰبٌ كَرِيمٌ ۝ ﴾

29. She said: "O chiefs! Verily! Here is delivered to me a noble letter,

﴿ إِنَّهُ مِن سُلَيْمَـٰنَ وَإِنَّهُ بِسْمِ ٱللَّهِ ٱلرَّحْمَـٰنِ ٱلرَّحِيمِ ۝ ﴾

30. "Verily it is from Sulaimân (Solomon), and verily, it (reads): In the Name of Allâh, the Most Gracious, the Most Merciful:

﴿ أَلَّا تَعْلُواْ عَلَىَّ وَأْتُونِى مُسْلِمِينَ ۝ ﴾

31. "Be you not exalted against me, but come to me as Muslims (true believers who submit to Allâh with full submission).' "

Transliteration

27. Qala sananthuru asadaqta am kunta mina alkathibeena 28. Ithhab bikitabee hatha faalqih ilayhim thumma tawalla AAanhum faonthur matha yarjiAAoona 29. Qalat ya ayyuha almalao innee olqiya ilayya kitabun kareemun 30. Innahu min sulaymana wa-innahu bismi Allahi alrrahmani alrraheemi 31. Alla taAAloo AAalayya wa/toonee muslimeena

Tafsir Ibn Kathir

Sulayman's Letter to Bilqis

Allah tells us what Sulayman said to the hoopoe when he told him about the people of Saba' and their queen:

((Sulayman) said: "We shall see whether you speak the truth or you are (one) of the liars.") meaning, `are you telling the truth'

(or you are (one) of the liars.) meaning, `or are you telling a lie in order to save yourself from the threat I made against you'

(Go you with this letter of mine and deliver it to them then draw back from them and see what they return.) Sulayman wrote a letter to Bilqis and her people and gave it to the hoopoe to deliver. It was said that he carried it on his wings, as is the way with birds, or that he carried it in his beak. He went to their land and found the palace of Bilqis, then he went to her private chambers and threw the letter through a small window, then he stepped to one side out of good manners. Bilqis was amazed and confused when she saw that, then she went and picked up the letter, opened its seal and read it. The letter said:

(it is from Sulayman, and it (reads): `In the Name of Allah, the Most Gracious, the Most Merciful; Be you not exalted against me, but come to me submitting (as Muslims).') So she gathered her commanders and ministers and the leaders of her land, and said to them:

("O chiefs! Verily, here is delivered to me a noble letter.") She described it as such because of the wondrous things she had seen, that it was delivered by a bird who threw it to her, then stood aside out of good manners. This was something that no king could do. Then she read the letter to them:

(Verily, it is from Sulayman, and it (reads): `In the Name of Allah, the Most Gracious, the Most Merciful; Be you not exalted against me, but come to me submitting (as Muslims).') Thus they knew that it was from Allah's Prophet Sulayman, upon him be peace, and that they could not match him. This letter was the utmost in brevity and eloquence, coming straight to the point.

(Be you not exalted against me,) Qatadah said: "Do not be arrogant with me.

(but come to me submitting (as Muslims).)" `Abdur-Rahman bin Zayd bin Aslam said: "Do not refuse or be too arrogant to come to me

(but come to me submitting (as Muslims).)"

Surah: 27 Ayah: 32, Ayah: 33, Ayah: 34 & Ayah: 35

قَالَتْ يَٰٓأَيُّهَا ٱلْمَلَؤُاْ أَفْتُونِى فِىٓ أَمْرِى مَا كُنتُ قَاطِعَةً أَمْرًا حَتَّىٰ تَشْهَدُونِ ﴿٣٢﴾

32. She said: "O chiefs! Advise me in (this) case of mine. I decide no case till you are present with me (and give me your opinions)."

قَالُواْ نَحْنُ أُوْلُواْ قُوَّةٍ وَأُوْلُواْ بَأْسٍ شَدِيدٍ وَٱلْأَمْرُ إِلَيْكِ فَٱنظُرِى مَاذَا تَأْمُرِينَ ﴿٣٣﴾

33. They said: "We have great strength, and great ability for war, but it is for you to command: so think over what you will command."

قَالَتْ إِنَّ ٱلْمُلُوكَ إِذَا دَخَلُواْ قَرْيَةً أَفْسَدُوهَا وَجَعَلُوٓاْ أَعِزَّةَ أَهْلِهَآ أَذِلَّةً وَكَذَٰلِكَ يَفْعَلُونَ ﴿٣٤﴾

34. She said: "Verily kings, when they enter a town (country), they despoil it, and make the most honorable amongst its people the lowest. And thus they do.

$$\text{وَإِنِّى مُرْسِلَةٌ إِلَيْهِم بِهَدِيَّةٍ فَنَاظِرَةٌ بِمَ يَرْجِعُ ٱلْمُرْسَلُونَ}$$ ﴿٣٥﴾

35. "But verily! I am going to send him a present, and see with what (answer) the messengers return."

Transliteration

32. Qalat ya ayyuha almalao aftoonee fee amree ma kuntu qatiAAatan amran hatta tashhadoona 33. Qaloo nahnu oloo quwwatin waoloo ba/sin shadeedin waal-amru ilayki faonthuree matha ta/mureena 34. Qalat inna almulooka itha dakhaloo qaryatan afsadooha wajaAAaloo aAAizzataahliha athillatan wakathalika yafAAaloona 35. Wa-innee mursilatun ilayhim bihadiyyatin fanathiratun bima yarjiAAu almursaloona

Tafsir Ibn Kathir

Bilqis consults with Her Chiefs

When she read Sulayman's letter to them and consulted with them about this news, she said:

("O chiefs! Advise me in (this) case of mine. I decide no case till you are present with me.") meaning, `until you come together and offer me your advice.'

(They said: "We have great strength, and great ability for war...") They reminded her of their great numbers, preparedness and strength, then they referred the matter to her and said:

(but it is for you to command; so think over what you will command.) meaning, `we have the power and strength, if you want to go to him and fight him.' The matter is yours to decide, so instruct us as you see fit and we will obey. Ibn `Abbas said: "Bilqis said:

(Verily, kings, when they enter a town, they destroy it and make the most honorable amongst its people the lowest.) And Allah said:

(And thus they do.) Then she resorted to peaceful means, seeking a truce and trying to placate Sulayman, and said:

(But verily, I am going to send him a present, and see with what the messengers return.) meaning, `I will send him a gift befitting for one of his status, and will wait and see what his response will be. Perhaps he will accept that and leave us alone, or he will impose a tax which we can pay him every year, so that he will not fight us and wage war against us.' Qatadah said: "May Allah have mercy on her and be pleased with her -- how wise she was as a Muslim and (before that) as an idolator! She understood how gift-giving has a good effect on people." Ibn `Abbas and others said: "She said to her people, if he accepts the gift, he is a king, so fight him; but if he does not accept it, he is a Prophet, so follow him."

Chapter 27: An-Naml (The Ant, The Ants), Verses 001-055

Surah: 27 Ayah: 36 & Ayah: 37

فَلَمَّا جَآءَ سُلَيْمَـٰنَ قَالَ أَتُمِدُّونَنِ بِمَالٍ فَمَآ ءَاتَىٰنِۦَ ٱللَّهُ خَيْرٌ مِّمَّآ ءَاتَىٰكُم بَلْ أَنتُم بِهَدِيَّتِكُمْ تَفْرَحُونَ ۝

36. So when (the messengers with the present) came to Sulaimân (Solomon), he said: "Will you help me in wealth? What Allâh has given me is better than that which He has given you! Nay, you rejoice in your gift!"

ٱرْجِعْ إِلَيْهِمْ فَلَنَأْتِيَنَّهُم بِجُنُودٍ لَّا قِبَلَ لَهُم بِهَا وَلَنُخْرِجَنَّهُم مِّنْهَآ أَذِلَّةً وَهُمْ صَـٰغِرُونَ ۝

37. (Then Sulaimân (Solomon) said to the chief of her messengers who brought the present): "Go back to them. We verily shall come to them with hosts that they cannot resist, and we shall drive them out from there in disgrace, and they will be abased."

Transliteration

36. Falamma jaa sulaymana qala atumiddoonani bimalin fama ataniya Allahu khayrunmimma atakum bal antum bihadiyyatikum tafrahoona 37. IrjiAA ilayhim falana/tiyannahum bijunoodin la qibala lahum biha walanukhrijannahum minha athillatan wahum saghiroona

Tafsir Ibn Kathir

The Gift and the Response of Sulayman

More than one of the scholars of Tafsir among the Salaf and others stated that she sent him a huge gift of gold, jewels, pearls and other things. It is apparent that Sulayman, peace be upon him, did not even look at what they brought at all and did not pay any attention to it, but he turned away and said, rebuking them:

("Will you help me in wealth") meaning, `are you trying to flatter me with wealth so that I will leave you alone with your Shirk and your kingdom'

(What Allah has given me is better than that which He has given you!) means, `what Allah has given to me of power, wealth and troops, is better than that which you have.'

(Nay, you rejoice in your gift!) means, `you are the ones who are influenced by gifts and presents; we will accept nothing from you except Islam or the sword.'

(Go back to them) means, with their gift,

(We verily, shall come to them with armies that they cannot resist,) they have no power to match them or resist them.

(and we shall drive them out from there in disgrace,) `we shall drive them out in disgrace from their land.'

(and they will be abased.) means, humiliated and expelled. When her messengers came back to her with her undelivered gift, and told her what Sulayman said, she and her people paid heed and obeyed him. She came to him with her troops in submission and humility, honoring Sulayman and intending to follow him in Islam. When Sulayman, peace be upon him, realized that they were coming to him, he rejoiced greatly.

Surah: 27 Ayah: 38, Ayah: 39 & Ayah: 40

قَالَ يَٰٓأَيُّهَا ٱلْمَلَؤُاْ أَيُّكُمْ يَأْتِينِى بِعَرْشِهَا قَبْلَ أَن يَأْتُونِى مُسْلِمِينَ ۝

38. He said: "O chiefs! Which of you can bring me her throne before they come to me surrendering themselves in obedience?"

قَالَ عِفْرِيتٌ مِّنَ ٱلْجِنِّ أَنَا۠ ءَاتِيكَ بِهِۦ قَبْلَ أَن تَقُومَ مِن مَّقَامِكَ وَإِنِّى عَلَيْهِ لَقَوِىٌّ أَمِينٌ ۝

39. An Ifrît (strong one) from the jinn said: "I will bring it to you before you rise from your place (council). And verily, I am indeed strong, and trustworthy for such work."

قَالَ ٱلَّذِى عِندَهُۥ عِلْمٌ مِّنَ ٱلْكِتَٰبِ أَنَا۠ ءَاتِيكَ بِهِۦ قَبْلَ أَن يَرْتَدَّ إِلَيْكَ طَرْفُكَ فَلَمَّا رَءَاهُ مُسْتَقِرًّا عِندَهُۥ قَالَ هَٰذَا مِن فَضْلِ رَبِّى لِيَبْلُوَنِى ءَأَشْكُرُ أَمْ أَكْفُرُ وَمَن شَكَرَ فَإِنَّمَا يَشْكُرُ لِنَفْسِهِۦ وَمَن كَفَرَ فَإِنَّ رَبِّى غَنِىٌّ كَرِيمٌ ۝

40. One with whom was knowledge of the Scripture said: "I will bring it to you within the twinkling of an eye!" then when (Sulaimân (Solomon)) saw it placed before him, he said: "This is by the Grace of my Lord - to test me whether I am grateful or ungrateful! And whoever is grateful, truly, his gratitude is for (the good of) his own self; and whoever is ungrateful, (he is ungrateful only for the loss of his own self). Certainly my Lord is Rich (Free of all needs), Bountiful."

Transliteration

38. Qala ya ayyuha almalao ayyukum ya/teenee biAAarshiha qabla an ya/toonee muslimeena 39. Qala AAifreetun mina aljinni ana ateeka bihi qabla an taqooma min maqamika wainne AAalayhi laqawiyyun ameenun 40. Qala allathee AAindahu AAilmun mina alkitabi ana ateeka bihi qabla an yartadda ilayka tarfuka falamma raahu mustaqirran AAindahu qala hatha min fadli rabbee liyabluwanee aashkuru am akfuru waman shakara fa-innama yashkuru linafsihi wamankafara fa-inna rabbee ghaniyyun kareemun

Tafsir Ibn Kathir

How the Throne of Bilqis was brought in an Instant

Muhammad bin Ishaq reported from Yazid bin Ruman: "When the messengers returned with word of what Sulayman said, she said: `By Allah, I knew he was more than a king, and that we have no power to match him, and that we can gain nothing by being stubborn with him. So, she sent word to him saying: "I am coming to you with the leaders of my people to see what you will instruct us to do and what you are calling us to of your religion." Then she issued commands that her throne, which was made of gold and inlaid with rubies, chrysolite and pearls, should be placed in the innermost of seven rooms, one within the other, and all the doors should be locked. Then she told her deputy whom she was leaving in charge, "Take care of my people and my throne, and do not let anyone approach it or see it until I come back to you." Then she set off to meet Sulayman with twelve thousand of her commanders from the leaders of Yemen, under each of whose command were many thousands of men. Sulayman sent the Jinn to bring him news of her progress and route every day and night, then when she drew near, he gathered together the Jinns and humans who were under his control and said:

(O chiefs! Which of you can bring me her throne before they come to me surrendering themselves in obedience (as Muslims))."

(An `Ifrit from the Jinn said:) Mujahid said, "A giant Jinn." Abu Salih said, "It was as if he was a mountain."

(I will bring it to you before you rise from your place.) Ibn `Abbas, may Allah be pleased with him, said, "Before you get up from where you are sitting." As-Suddi and others said: "He used to sit to pass judgements and rulings over the people, and to eat, from the beginning of the day until noon."

(And verily, I am indeed strong and trustworthy for such work.) Ibn `Abbas said: "Strong enough to carry it and trustworthy with the jewels it contains. Sulayman, upon him be peace, said, "I want it faster than that." From this it seems that Sulayman wanted to bring this throne as a demonstration of the greatness of the power and authority that Allah had bestowed upon him and the troops that He had subjugated to him. Power such as had never been given to anyone else, before or since, so that this would furnish proof of his prophethood before Bilqis and her people, because this would be a great and wondrous thing, if he brought her throne as if he were in her country, before they could come to it, although it was hidden and protected by so many locked doors. When Sulayman said, "I want it faster than that,

(One with whom was knowledge of the Scripture said:) Ibn `Abbas said, "This was Asif, the scribe of Sulayman." It was also narrated by Muhammad bin Ishaq from Yazid bin Ruman that he was Asif bin Barkhiya' and he was a truthful believer who knew the Greatest Name of Allah. Qatadah said: "He was a believer among the humans, and his name was Asif."

(I will bring it to you within the twinkling of an eye!) Meaning, lift your gaze and look as far as you can, and before you get tired and blink, you will find it before you. Then he got up, performed ablution and prayed to Allah, may He be exalted. Mujahid said: "He said, O Owner of majesty and honor." When Sulayman and his chiefs saw it before them,

(he said: "This is by the grace of my Lord...") meaning, `this is one of the blessings which Allah has bestowed upon me.'

(to test whether I am grateful or ungrateful! And whoever is grateful, truly, his gratitude is for himself;) This is like the Ayat:

(Whosoever does righteous good deed, it is for himself; and whosoever does evil, it is against himself.) (41:46)

(and whosoever does righteous good deed, then such will prepare a good place for themselves.) (30:44).

(and whoever is ungrateful, certainly my Lord is Rich, Bountiful.) He has no need of His servants or their worship.

(Bountiful) He is Bountiful in and of Himself, even if no one were to worship Him. His greatness does not depend on anyone. This is like what Musa said:

(If you disbelieve, you and all on earth together, then verily, Allah is Rich, Owner of all praise.) (14:8). It is recorded in Sahih Muslim:

«يَقُولُ اللهُ تَعَالَى: يَا عِبَادِي لَوْ أَنَّ أَوَّلَكُمْ وَآخِرَكُمْ وَإِنْسَكُمْ وَجِنَّكُمْ كَانُوا عَلَى أَتْقَى قَلْبِ رَجُلٍ مِنْكُمْ مَا زَادَ ذَلِكَ فِي مُلْكِي شَيْئًا. يَا عِبَادِي لَوْ أَنَّ أَوَّلَكُمْ وَآخِرَكُمْ وَإِنْسَكُمْ وَجِنَّكُمْ كَانُوا عَلَى أَفْجَرِ قَلْبِ رَجُلٍ مِنْكُمْ مَا نَقَصَ ذَلِكَ مِنْ مُلْكِي شَيْئًا. يَا عِبَادِي إِنَّمَا هِيَ أَعْمَالُكُمْ أُحْصِيهَا لَكُمْ ثُمَّ أُوَفِّيكُمْ إِيَّاهَا فَمَنْ وَجَدَ خَيْرًا فَلْيَحْمَدِ اللهَ، وَمَنْ وَجَدَ غَيْرَ ذَلِكَ فَلَا يَلُومَنَّ إِلَّا نَفْسَه»

(Allah, may He be exalted, says: "O My servants, if the first of you and the last of you, mankind and Jinn alike, were all to be as pious as the most pious among you, that would not add to My dominion in the slightest. O My servants, if the first of you and the last of you, mankind and Jinn alike, were all to be as evil as the most evil one among you, that would not detract from My dominion in the slightest. O My servants, these are deeds which I am recording for you, and I will judge you according to them, so whoever finds something good, let him praise Allah, and whoever finds otherwise, let him blame no one but himself.")

Surah: 27 Ayah: 41, Ayah: 42, Ayah: 43 & Ayah: 44

قَالَ نَكِّرُوا۟ لَهَا عَرْشَهَا نَنظُرْ أَتَهْتَدِىٓ أَمْ تَكُونُ مِنَ ٱلَّذِينَ لَا يَهْتَدُونَ ۝

41. He said: "Disguise her throne for her that we may see whether she will be guided (to recognize her throne), or she will be one of those not guided."

فَلَمَّا جَآءَتْ قِيلَ أَهَٰكَذَا عَرْشُكِ ۖ قَالَتْ كَأَنَّهُۥ هُوَ ۚ وَأُوتِينَا ٱلْعِلْمَ مِن قَبْلِهَا وَكُنَّا مُسْلِمِينَ ۝

42. So when she came, it was said (to her): "Is your throne like this?" She said: "(It is) as though it were the very same." And (Sulaimân (Solomon) said): "Knowledge was bestowed on us before her, and we were submitted to Allâh (in Islâm as Muslims before her)."

وَصَدَّهَا مَا كَانَت تَّعْبُدُ مِن دُونِ ٱللَّهِ ۖ إِنَّهَا كَانَتْ مِن قَوْمٍ كَٰفِرِينَ ۝

43. And that which she used to worship besides Allâh has prevented her (from Islâm), for she was of a disbelieving people.

قِيلَ لَهَا ٱدْخُلِى ٱلصَّرْحَ ۖ فَلَمَّا رَأَتْهُ حَسِبَتْهُ لُجَّةً وَكَشَفَتْ عَن سَاقَيْهَا ۚ قَالَ إِنَّهُۥ صَرْحٌ مُّمَرَّدٌ مِّن قَوَارِيرَ ۗ قَالَتْ رَبِّ إِنِّى ظَلَمْتُ نَفْسِى وَأَسْلَمْتُ مَعَ سُلَيْمَٰنَ لِلَّهِ رَبِّ ٱلْعَٰلَمِينَ ۝

44. It was said to her: "Enter As-Sarh" (a glass surface with water underneath it or a palace): but when she saw it, she thought it was a pool, and she (tucked up her clothes) uncovering her legs. (Sulaimân (Solomon)) said: "Verily, it is Sarh (a glass surface with water underneath it or a palace)." She said: "My Lord! Verily, I have wronged myself, and I submit (in Islâm, together with Sulaimân (Solomon)) to Allâh, the Lord of the 'Alamîn (mankind, jinn and all that exists)."

Transliteration

41. Qala nakkiroo laha AAarshaha nanthur atahtadee am takoonu mina allatheena la yahtadoona   42. Falamma jaat qeela ahakatha AAarshuki qalat kaannahu huwa waooteena alAAilma min qabliha wakunna muslimeena   43. Wasaddaha ma kanat taAAbudu min dooni Allahi innaha kanat min qawmin kafireena   44. Qeela laha odkhulee alssarha falamma raat-hu hasibat-hu lujjatan wakashafat AAan saqayha qala innahu sarhun mumarradun min qawareera qalat rabbi innee thalamtu nafsee waaslamtu maAAa sulaymana lillahi rabbi alAAalameena

Tafsir Ibn Kathir

The Test of Bilqis

When Sulayman brought the throne of Bilqis before she and her people arrived, he issued orders that some of its features should be altered, so that he could test her and see whether she recognized it and how composed she would be when she saw it. Would she hasten to say either that it was her throne or that it was not So he said:

(Disguise her throne for her that we may see whether she will be guided, or she will be one of those not guided.) Ibn `Abbas said: "Remove some of its adornments and parts." Mujahid said: "He issued orders that it should be changed, so whatever was red should be made yellow and vice versa, and whatever was green should be made red, so everything was altered." `Ikrimah said, "They added some things and took some things away." Qatadah said, "It was turned upside down and back to front, and some things were added and some things were taken away."

(So when she came, it was said: "Is your throne like this") Her throne, which had been altered and disguised, with some things added and others taken away, was shown to her. She was wise and steadfast, intelligent and strong-willed. She did not hasten to say that this was her throne, because it was far away from her. Neither did she hasten to say that it was not her throne, when she saw that some things had been altered and changed. She said,

((It is) as though it were the very same.) This is the ultimate in intelligence and strong resolve.

(Knowledge was bestowed on us before her, and we had submitted to Allah.) Mujahid said, "This was spoken by Sulayman."

(And Saddaha that which she used to worship besides Allah has prevented her, for she was of a disbelieving people.) This is a continuation of the words of Sulayman -- according to the opinion of Mujahid and Sa`id bin Jubayr, may Allah be pleased with them both -- i.e., Sulayman said:

(Knowledge was bestowed on us before her, and we had submitted to Allah.) and what stopped her from worshipping Allah alone was

(that which she used to worship besides Allah, for she was of a disbelieving people.) What Mujahid and Sa`id said is good; it was also the view of Ibn Jarir. Then Ibn Jarir said, "It could be that the subject of the verb.

(And Saddaha) refers to Sulayman or to Allah, so that the phrase now means:

(She would not worship anything over than Allah.)

(for she was of a disbelieving people.) I say: the opinion of Mujahid is supported by the fact that she declared her Islam after she entered the Sarh, as we shall see below.

(It was said to her: "Enter As-Sarh" but when she saw it, she thought it was a pool, and she (tucked up her clothes) uncovering her legs.) Sulayman had commanded the

Shayatin to build for her a huge palace of glass beneath which water was flowing. Anyone who did not know the nature of the building would think that it was water, but in fact there was a layer of glass between a person walking and the water.

Verily, it is a Sarh Mumarrad of Qawarir Sarh means a palace or any lofty construction.

Allah says of Fir`awn -- may Allah curse him -- that he said to his minister Haman:

(Build me a Sarh that I may arrive at the ways.) (40:36-37) Sarh is also used to refer to the high constructed palaces in Yemen. Mumarrad means sturdily constructed and smooth.

(of Qawarir) means, made of glass, i.e., it was built with smooth surfaces. Marid is a fortress in Dawmat Al-Jandal. What is meant here is that Sulayman built a huge, lofty palace of glass for this queen, in order to show her the greatness of his authority and power. When she saw for herself what Allah had given him and how majestic his position was, she submitted to the command of Allah and acknowledged that he was a noble Prophet, so she submitted to Allah and said:

(My Lord! Verily, I have wronged myself,) meaning, by her previous disbelief and Shirk and by the fact that she and her people had worshipped the sun instead of Allah.

(and I submit, together with Sulayman to Allah, the Lord of all that exists.) meaning, following the religion of Sulayman, worshipping Allah alone with no partner or associate, Who created everything and measured it exactly according to its due measurements.

Surah: 27 Ayah: 45, Ayah: 46 & Ayah: 47

وَلَقَدْ أَرْسَلْنَآ إِلَىٰ ثَمُودَ أَخَاهُمْ صَٰلِحًا أَنِ ٱعْبُدُوا۟ ٱللَّهَ فَإِذَا هُمْ فَرِيقَانِ يَخْتَصِمُونَ ۝

45. And indeed We sent to Thamûd their brother Sâlih (Saleh), saying: "Worship Allâh (Alone and none else). Then look! They became two parties (believers and disbelievers) quarreling with each other."

قَالَ يَٰقَوْمِ لِمَ تَسْتَعْجِلُونَ بِٱلسَّيِّئَةِ قَبْلَ ٱلْحَسَنَةِ ۖ لَوْلَا تَسْتَغْفِرُونَ ٱللَّهَ لَعَلَّكُمْ تُرْحَمُونَ ۝

46. He said: "O my people! Why do you seek to hasten the evil (torment) before the good (Allâh's Mercy)? Why seek you not the Forgiveness of Allâh, that you may receive mercy?"

قَالُوا۟ ٱطَّيَّرْنَا بِكَ وَبِمَن مَّعَكَ ۚ قَالَ طَٰٓئِرُكُمْ عِندَ ٱللَّهِ ۖ بَلْ أَنتُمْ قَوْمٌ تُفْتَنُونَ ۝

47. They said: "We augur ill omen from you and those with you." He said: "Your ill omen is with Allâh; nay, but you are a people that are being tested."

Transliteration

45. Walaqad arsalna ila thamooda akhahum salihan ani oAAbudoo Allaha fa-itha hum fareeqani yakhtasimoona 46. Qala ya qawmi lima tastaAAjiloona bialssayyi-ati qabla alhasanati lawla tastaghfiroona Allaha laAAallakum turhamoona 47. Qaloo ittayyarna bika wabiman maAAaka qala ta-irukum AAinda Allahi bal antum qawmun tuftanoona

Tafsir Ibn Kathir

Salih and Thamud

Allah tells us about Thamud and how they responded to their Prophet Salih, when Allah sent him to call them to worship Allah alone, with no partner or associate.

(Then look! They became two parties quarrelling with each other.) Mujahid said, "These were believers and disbelievers." This is like the Ayah,

(The leaders of those who were arrogant among his people said to those who were counted weak -- to such of them as believed: "Know you that Salih is one sent from his Lord." They said: "We indeed believe in that with which he has been sent." Those who were arrogant said: "Verily, we disbelieve in that which you believe in.") (7:75-76)

(He said: "O my people! Why do you seek to hasten the evil before the good") meaning, `why are you praying for the punishment to come, and not asking Allah for His mercy' Then he said:

("Why seek you not the forgiveness of Allah, that you may receive mercy" They said: "We augur an omen from you and those with you.") This means: "We do not see any good in your face and the faces of those who are following you." Since they were doomed, whenever anything bad happened to any of them they would say, "This is because of Salih and his companions." Mujahid said, "They regarded them as bad omens." This is similar to what Allah said about the people of Fir`awn:

(But whenever good came to them, they said: "Ours is this." And if evil afflicted them, they saw it as an omen about Musa and those with him) (7:131). And Allah says:

(And if some good reaches them, they say, "This is from Allah," but if some evil befalls them, they say, "This is from you." Say: "All things are from Allah.") (4:78) i.e., by virtue of His will and decree. And Allah tells us about the dwellers of the town, when the Messengers came to them:

(They (people) said: "For us, we see an omen from you; if you cease not, we will surely stone you, and a painful torment will touch you from us." They (Messengers) said: "Your omens are with yourselves!) (36:18) And these people (Thamud) said:

("We augur an omen from you and those with you." He said: "Your omen is of Allah;) meaning, Allah will punish you for that.

(nay, but you are a people that are being tested.) Qatadah said: "You are being tested to see whether you will obey or disobey." The apparent meaning of the phrase

(are being tested) is: you will be left to get carried away in your state of misguidance.

Surah: 27 Ayah: 48, Ayah: 49, Ayah: 50, Ayah: 51, Ayah: 52 & Ayah: 53

وَكَانَ فِي ٱلْمَدِينَةِ تِسْعَةُ رَهْطٍ يُفْسِدُونَ فِي ٱلْأَرْضِ وَلَا يُصْلِحُونَ ۝

48. And there were in the city nine men (from the sons of their chiefs), who made mischief in the land, and would not reform.

قَالُوا۟ تَقَاسَمُوا۟ بِٱللَّهِ لَنُبَيِّتَنَّهُۥ وَأَهْلَهُۥ ثُمَّ لَنَقُولَنَّ لِوَلِيِّهِۦ مَا شَهِدْنَا مَهْلِكَ أَهْلِهِۦ وَإِنَّا لَصَـٰدِقُونَ ۝

49. They said: "Swear one to another by Allâh that we shall make a secret night attack on him and his household, and thereafter we will surely say to his near relatives: 'We witnessed not the destruction of his household, and verily we are telling the truth.'"

وَمَكَرُوا۟ مَكْرًا وَمَكَرْنَا مَكْرًا وَهُمْ لَا يَشْعُرُونَ ۝

50. So they plotted a plot, and We planned a plan, while they perceived not.

فَٱنظُرْ كَيْفَ كَانَ عَـٰقِبَةُ مَكْرِهِمْ أَنَّا دَمَّرْنَـٰهُمْ وَقَوْمَهُمْ أَجْمَعِينَ ۝

51. Then see how was the end of their plot! Verily! We destroyed them and their nation, all together.

فَتِلْكَ بُيُوتُهُمْ خَاوِيَةًۢ بِمَا ظَلَمُوٓا۟ إِنَّ فِى ذَٰلِكَ لَـَٔايَةً لِّقَوْمٍ يَعْلَمُونَ ۝

52. These are their houses in utter ruin, for they did wrong. Verily, in this is indeed an Ayâh (a lesson or a sign) for people who know.

وَأَنجَيْنَا ٱلَّذِينَ ءَامَنُوا۟ وَكَانُوا۟ يَتَّقُونَ ۝

53. And We saved those who believed, and used to fear Allâh, and keep their duty to Him.

Transliteration

48. Wakana fee almadeenati tisAAatu rahtin yufsidoona fee al-ardi wala yuslihoona 49. Qaloo taqasamoo biAllahi lanubayyitannahu waahlahu thumma lanaqoolanna liwaliyyihi ma shahidna mahlika ahlihi wa-inna lasadiqoona 50. Wamakaroo makran wamakarna makran wahum la yashAAuroona 51. Faonthur kayfa kana AAaqibatu makrihim anna dammarnahum waqawmahum ajmaAAeena 52. Fatilka buyootuhum

khawiyatan bima thalamoo inna fee thalika laayatan liqawminyaAAlamoona 53. Waanjayna allatheena amanoo wakanoo yattaqoona

Tafsir Ibn Kathir

The Plot of the Mischief-Makers and the End of the People of Thamud

Allah tells us about the evildoers of Thamud and their leaders who used to call their people to misguidance and disbelief, and to deny Salih. Eventually they killed the she-camel and were about to kill Salih too. They plotted to let him sleep with his family at night, then they would assassinate him and tell his relatives that they knew nothing about what happened to him, and that they were telling the truth because none of them had seen anything. Allah says:

(And there were in the city) meaning, in the city of Thamud,

(nine Raht,) meaning, nine people,

(who made mischief in the land, and would not reform.) They forced their opinions on the people of Thamud, because they were the leaders and chiefs. Al-`Awfi reported that Ibn `Abbas said: "These were the people who killed the she-camel," Meaning, that happened upon their instigation, may Allah curse them. Allah says:

(But they called their comrade and he took (a sword) and killed (the she-camel).) (54:29)

(When the most wicked man among them went forth (to kill the she-camel).) (91:12) `Abdur-Razzaq said that Yahya bin Rabi`ah As-San`ani told them, "I heard `Ata' -- i.e. Ibn Abi Rabah -- say:

(And there were in the city nine Raht, who made mischief in the land, and would not reform.) `They used to break silver coins.'" They would break off pieces from them, as if they used to trade with them in terms of numbers (as opposed to weight), as the Arabs used to do. Imam Malik narrated from Yahya bin Sa`id that Sa`id bin Al-Musayyib said: "Cutting gold and silver (coins) is part of spreading corruption on earth." What is meant is that the nature of these evil disbelievers was to spread corruption on earth by every means possible, one of which was that mentioned by these Imams.

(They said: "Swear one to another by Allah that we shall make a secret night attack on him and his household...") They took a mutual oath, pledging that during the night, whoever met Allah's Prophet Salih, peace be upon him, he would assassinate him. But Allah planned against them and caused their plot to backfire. Mujahid said, "They took a mutual oath pledging to kill him, but before they could reach him, they and their people were all destroyed." `Abdur-Rahman bin Abi Hatim said: "When they killed the she-camel, Salih said to them:

("Enjoy yourselves in your homes for three days. This is a promise (i.e., a threat) that will not be belied.") (11:65). They said: `Salih claims that he will finish us in three days, but we will finish him and his family before the three days are over.' Salih had a place of worship in a rocky tract in a valley, where he used to pray. So they set out to go to a cave there one night, and said, `When he comes to pray, we will kill him, then we will return. When we have finished him off, we will go to his family and finish them off too.' Then Allah sent down a rock upon them from the mountains round about; they feared that it would crush them, so they ran into the cave and the rock covered the mouth of the cave while they were inside. Their people did not know where they were or what had happened to them. So Allah punished some of them here, and some of them there, and He saved Salih and the people who were with him. Then he recited:

(So, they plotted a plot, and We planned a plan, while they perceived not. Then see how was the end of their plot! Verily, We destroyed them and their nation, all together. These are their houses in utter ruin,) i.e., deserted."

(for they did wrong. Verily, in this is indeed an Ayah for people who know. And We saved those who believed, and had Taqwa of Allah.)

Surah: 27 Ayah: 54, Ayah: 55 (end of Part 19), Ayah: 56, Ayah: 57 & Ayah: 58 (start of Part 20; used here to give the fullness the following tafsir)

وَلُوطًا إِذْ قَالَ لِقَوْمِهِ أَتَأْتُونَ ٱلْفَٰحِشَةَ وَأَنتُمْ تُبْصِرُونَ ۝

54. And (remember) Lût (Lot)! When he said to his people . Do you commit Al-Fâhishah (evil, great sin, every kind of unlawful sexual intercourse, sodomy) while you see (one another doing evil without any screen)?"

أَئِنَّكُمْ لَتَأْتُونَ ٱلرِّجَالَ شَهْوَةً مِّن دُونِ ٱلنِّسَآءِ بَلْ أَنتُمْ قَوْمٌ تَجْهَلُونَ ۝

55. "Do you practice your lusts on men instead of women? Nay, but you are a people who behave senselessly."

فَمَا كَانَ جَوَابَ قَوْمِهِ إِلَّآ أَن قَالُوٓا۟ أَخْرِجُوٓا۟ ءَالَ لُوطٍ مِّن قَرْيَتِكُمْ إِنَّهُمْ أُنَاسٌ يَتَطَهَّرُونَ ۝

56. There was no other answer given by his people except that they said: "Drive out the family of Lût (Lot) from your city Verily, these are men who want to be clean and pure!"

فَأَنجَيْنَٰهُ وَأَهْلَهُۥٓ إِلَّا ٱمْرَأَتَهُۥ قَدَّرْنَٰهَا مِنَ ٱلْغَٰبِرِينَ ۝

57. So We saved him and his family, except his wife. We destined her to be of those who remained behind.

وَأَمْطَرْنَا عَلَيْهِم مَّطَرًا فَسَآءَ مَطَرُ ٱلْمُنذَرِينَ ۝

58. And We rained down on them a rain (of stones). So evil was the rain of those who were warned.

Transliteration

54. Walootan ith qala liqawmihi ata/toona alfahishata waantum tubsiroona 55. A-innakum lata/toona alrrijala shahwatan min dooni alnnisa-i bal antum qawmun tajhaloona 56. Fama kana jawaba qawmihi illa an qaloo akhrijoo ala lootin min qaryatikuminnahum onasun yatatahharoona 57. Faanjaynahu waahlahu illa imraatahu qaddarnaha mina alghabireena 58. Waamtarna AAalayhim mataran fasaa mataru almunthareena

Tafsir Ibn Kathir

Lut and His People

Allah tells us about His servant and Messenger Lut, peace be upon him, and how he warned his people of Allah's punishment for committing an act of immorality which no human ever committed before them -- intercourse with males instead of females. This is a major sin, whereby men are satisfied with men and women are with women (i.e., homosexuality). Lut said: (Do you commit immoral sins while you see) meaning, `while you see one another, and you practice every kind of evil in your meetings.'

(Do you practice your lusts on men instead of women Nay, but you are a people who behave senselessly.) means, `you do not know anything of what is natural or what is prescribed by Allah.' This is like the Ayah: (Go you in unto the males of mankind, and leave those whom Allah has created for you to be your wives Nay, you are a trespassing people!) (26:165-166)

(There was no other answer given by his people except that they said: "Drive out the family of Lut from your city. Verily, these are men who want to be clean and pure!") means, `they feel embarrassed because of the deeds you are doing, and because you approve of your actions, so expel them from among yourselves, for they are not fit to live among you in your city.' So, the people resolved to do that, and Allah destroyed them, and a similar end awaits the disbelievers.

Allah says: (So, We saved him and his family, except his wife. We destined her to be of those who remained behind.) meaning, she was one of those who were destroyed, with her people, because she was a helper to what they did and she approved of their evil deeds. She told them about the guests of Lut so that they could come to them. She did not do the evil deeds herself, which was because of the honor of Lut and not because of any honor on her part.

(And We rained down on them a rain.) means; stones of Sijjil, in a well-arranged manner one after another. Marked from your Lord; and they are not ever far from the evildoers.

Allah said: (So, evil was the rain of those who were warned.) meaning, those against whom proof was established and whom the warning reached, but they went against the Messenger and denied him, and resolved to drive him out from among them.